Past, Present and Future of Research in the Information Society

Past, Present and Future of Research in the Information Society

edited by

Wesley Shrum
Louisiana State University
USA

Keith R. Benson
University of British Columbia
Canada

Wiebe E. Bijker
Maastricht University
The Netherlands

Klaus Brunnstein
University of Hamburg
Germany

 Springer

Wesley Shrum
Louisiana State University
Sociology Dept.
Baton Rouge, LA 70803
shrum@lsu.edu

Keith R. Benson
Green College
University of British Columbia
Vancouver, BC
V6T 1Z1, CANADA
krbenson@interchange.ubc.ca

Wiebe E. Bijker
Maastricht University
Faculty of Arts and Social Science
6200 MD Maastricht
The Netherlands
W.Bijker@TSS.unimaas.nl

Klaus Brunnstein
University of Hamburg
Faculty for Informatics
D-22527 Hamburg, Germany
brunnstein@informatik.uni-hamburg.de

Past, Present and Future of Research in the Information Society edited by
Wesley Shrum, Keith R. Benson, Wiebe E. Bijker and Klaus Brunnstein

ISBN 978-1-4419-4097-1

e-ISBN-13: 978-0-387-47650-6
e-ISBN-10: 0-387-47650-4

Printed on acid-free paper.

9 8 7 6 5 4 3 2 1

springer.com

Contents

CONTRIBUTORS

Janet Abbate
Virginia Polytechnic Institute and State University, USA

Noha Adley
Bibliotheca Alexandrina, Egypt

Meredith Anderson
Louisiana State University, USA

Subbiah Arunachalam
M S Swaminathan Research Foundation, India

Celso Candido Azambuja
Universidade do Vale do Rio dos Sinos, São Leopoldo-Porto Alegre, Brasil

Emilija Banionyte
Vilnius Pedagogical Library, Lithuania

Martin Belcher
INASP, International Network for the Availability of Scientific Publications, UK

Paul Arthur Berkman
University of California at Santa Barbara and EvREsearch LTD, USA

Jacques Berleur
Facultés Universitaires Notre-Dame de la Paix Namur, Belgium

Wiebe E. Bijker
Maastricht Universiteit, The Netherlands

Paolo Brunello
WITAR, Italy

Klaus Brunnstein
University of Hamburg, Germany

Patricia Campion
Tennessee Technological University, USA

Leslie Chan
University of Toronto, Canada

Kilnam Chon
Korea Advanced Institute of Science and Technology, Korea

Martin Collins
Smithsonian National Air and Space Museum, USA

Bernard Cornu
Université de Formation de Maîtres, France

Paul A. David
Stanford University, USA, and the Oxford Internet Institute, UK

John Dryden
OECD, France

Rick B. Duque
World Science Project, USA

William H. Dutton
Oxford Internet Institute, UK

Anders Ekeland
Center for Innovative Research, Norway

Johan Eksteen
CSIR/Meraka, South Africa

Kirsten A. Foot
University of Washington, USA

Augustin Gaschignard
Scientific and Technical Information System, Ghana

Dmitris Gritzalis
Athens University of Economics and Business, Greece

Qiao Guo
Beijing Institute of Technology, China

Nancy Hafkin
United Nations Economic Commission for Africa, UN

Dina El Halaby
Global Development Network, Egypt

Clifford Harris
Hewlett Packard, UK

Jay Hauben
Columbia University Libraries, USA

Ronda Hauben
Columbia University, USA

Christine Hine
University of Surrey, UK

Qiheng Hu
Internet Society of China, China

Hsin-I Huang
Institute of Information Science, Academia Sinica, Taiwan

Jeremy Hunsinger
Center for Digital Discourse and Culture, USA

Michael Jensen
US National Academies, USA

Mike Jensen
Independent consultant

Wayne Johnson
Hewlett Packard, USA

Russel C. Jones
WFEO Committee on Capacity Building, USA

Dipak Khakhar
IFIP and Lund University, Sweden

P.H. Kurien
IT Secretary Government of Kerala, India

Zhiyong Liu
National Natural Science Foundation of China

Maurice Long
BMJ Publishing Group, UK

Paul Nyaga Mbatia
University of Nairobi, Kenya

B. Paige Miller
Louisiana State University, USA

Alvaro de Miranda
University of East London, UK

Claudia Morrell
Center for Women and Information Technology, USA

Lueny Morell
Hewlett Packard, USA

Karel F. Mulder
Delft University of Technology, The Netherlands

Héla Nafti
Tunisian Alliance of Female Teachers (UNFT), Tunesia

Kai Nan
Chinese Academy of Sciences, China

Iulia Nechifor
UNESCO, UN

Pauline Ngimwa
African Virtual University, Kenya

Margaret Ngwira
University of Malawi, Malawi

Reem Obeidat
Dubai Women's College, United Arab Emirates

George E. Okwach
Kenya Sugar Research Foundation, Kenya

Gary M. Olson
University of Michigan, USA

Antony Palackal
Loyola College of Social Sciences, Kerala, India

Govindan Parayil
University of Oslo, Norway

Dirk-Jan Peet
Delft University of Technology, The Netherlands

Didier Philippe
Hewlett Packard, USA

Werner Pillmann
International Society for Environmental Protection (ISEP), Austria

Zhang Ping
Beijing University of Posts and Telecommunications, China

Enrica Porcari
Consultative Group on International Agricultural Research
(CGIAR), Italy

Carol Priestley
INASP, International Network for the Availability of Scientific
Publications, UK

Chat Garcia Ramilo
Association for Progressive Communications, UK

Thomas F. Ruddy
Society for the Processing and Advancement of Knowledge on the
Environment (SPAKE), Switzerland

Steven Rudgard
FAO, Italy

Margarita Salas
Bellanet LAC, Canada

Daniel Schaffer
Third World Academy of Sciences, Italy

Edit Schlaffer
Women without Borders, Austria

Steven M. Schneider
SUNY Institute of Technology, USA

Raed Sharif
Syracuse University, USA

Wesley Shrum
Louisiana State University, USA

Carthage Smith
International Council for Science (ICSU), France

Diane H. Sonnenwald
Göteborg University and University College of Borås, Sweden

Mikael Snaprud
Agder University College, Norway

R. Sooryamoorthy
University of KwaZulu-Natal, South Africa

Bess Stephens
Hewlett Packard, USA

Aruna Sundararajan
Global E-School, India

Shu-Fen Tseng
Yuan Ze University, Taiwan

Paul F. Uhlir
US National Academies, USA

Barbara Waugh
Hewlett Packard, USA

Jan Wibe
Norwegian University of Science and Technology (NTNU),
Norway

Paul Wouters
The Royal Netherlands Academy of Arts and Sciences, The
Netherlands

Xu Xiaodong
Beijing University of Posts and Telecommunications, China

Tao Xiaofeng
Beijing University of Posts and Telecommunications, China

Baoping Yan
Chinese Academy of Sciences, China

Marcus Antonius Ynalvez
Louisiana State University, USA

Werner Zorn
University of Potsdam, Germany

1. INTRODUCTION: LEARNING FROM THE PAST, PRESENT AND FUTURE

Wesley Shrum, *Louisiana State University*

The event summarized in this volume was one of four official side events that occurred in conjunction with the second phase of the World Summit on the Information Society. Both events were held in Tunisia, near the Mediterranean coast of Tunis, during mid-November 2005. "Past, Present and Future of Research in the Information Society" (PPF) took place over the three days (13-15 November) preceding the main Summit (16-18 November). The chapters in this volume are abbreviated versions of the sessions at the PPF conference. Each author was asked to provide an extended abstract of their presentation and the lead author of each chapter edited these together.[1]

"Past, Present and Future of Research in the Information Society" was a challenge for many reasons. By most accounts, it can be considered a successful meeting—cynics said more successful than the main Summit. But such skepticism depends very much on how such events are judged. First, the World Summit on the Information Society was the only such multilateral event to be planned and implemented in two phases, less than two years apart. Given that the second phase was originally intended to be a follow-up meeting where actions would be reported and evaluated, it is open to debate whether the timing of the phases was ideal—a typical development project takes at least three years after it is funded. Second, not unexpectedly, the WSIS was the first such multilateral event to make use of the full range of modern information and communication technologies from the planning of the event through its final moments. Third, partly owing to the use of these technologies, the WSIS was the first such multilateral event to involve civil society in partnership with governments and the private sector. If the outcomes of international meetings are judged in formal terms of Declarations and Plans of Action, then Geneva (WSIS, phase I) will certainly be judged more successful than Tunis (WSIS, phase II). In my view, such Declarations and Plans are relatively insignificant. But if outcomes are judged in human terms of interactions and meetings, communication and collaborations, then surely Tunis was unequalled.

The title of our event, at various times during its evolution, contained "Science," "Technology," "Engineering," and various combinations of those terms. It eventually became "Research in the Information Society," but it was always "Past, Present, and Future." Any Summit, and any Satellite

Summit must consider where we are, how we got here, and where we are going. Our "road to Tunis" was not an easy one—but in the end it was worth it. I had never planned a meeting before. Neither had Rick Duque—my friend and co-conspirator. If you want to try this yourself, I could recommend getting started with something less complicated than an event during the largest convocation in Tunisian history, especially when you are hit by Hurricane Katrina, the largest disaster in American history, two months earlier.

The idea for a science and technology event in Tunis had little to do with information and communication technology (ICT) and everything to do with sustainable development. I attended the World Summit on Sustainable Development during August of 2002 in Johannesburg, South Africa, as a guest of Bok Marais, one of the key architects of the social scientific review that hammered a nail in the coffin of apartheid. Marvelous as the main Summit might have been, I never entered it—nor did anyone else who was not highly credentialed. What I did, along with most mortals, was to visit the public exhibits in Ubuntu Village. But there were a number of fascinating "side events" or "parallel events" available as well, including one that focused on science for sustainable development. This conference was hosted and funded by the National Research Foundation of South Africa, with its key partners the International Foundation for Science (ICSU), Third World Academy of Sciences (TWAS), and the World Federation of Engineering Organizations (WFEO). What was remarkable about the event, in my mind, was the relative decentralization, the freedom of various groups and organizations to use this opportunity for presentations, launches, and discussions. It was not a political event but a place to air a diversity of viewpoints and experiences—an approach that would become a hallmark of our PPF conference as well. During coffee breaks in the garden of the Wanderer's Club, the idea for a similar event at the WSIS was born, together with officers from ICSU and TWAS.

That fall of 2002, the concept of a Satellite Summit on science and technology in the information society was adopted by Wiebe Bijker, incoming President of the Society for Social Studies of Science. His support, from the initiation of the idea to his editorial work on this volume, was indispensable. After a discussion of the possibilities and opportunities such an event might offer, the Council of the Society endorsed the meeting. This decision, more than any other, paved the way for PPF and introduced science and technology studies into the summit process, as the Society for Social Studies of Science became an accredited civil society entity in a major multilateral enterprise. Subsequently, the science and technology studies component of the conference grew during a meeting of the officers of the

'STS Consortium' (History of Science Society, Society for the History of Technology, Philosophy of Science Association, and Society for Social Studies of Science) in San Diego in May, 2003. In partnership with the Society for the History of Technology, and the History of Science Society, 4S hosted a stream of sessions highlighting science and technology studies in the information society, a contribution that eventually represented a critical component of the PPF meeting. About one third of the presentations were by individuals who could be considered STS (science, technology, and society studies) scholars.

The seed money for the "Past, Present and Future" conference was provided by Louisiana State University's Center for Computation and Technology. Special thanks are owed to Steve Coffee for the web site, launched in January of 2004, and registration interface provided by the 4S. Primary funding for the conference was provided by the Society for Social Studies of Science and Hewlett Packard, with further contributions by the International Federation of Information Processing (IFIP), the Committee on Data for Science and Technology (CODATA), Microsoft Research, and Internet2. However, particular gratitude goes to Wayne Johnson and Barbara Waugh of Hewlett Packard for their personal and financial assistance to the Louisiana organizers in the weeks after Hurricane Katrina. To borrow a phrase from the comic books, they saved the day. Hewlett Packard is also the primary sponsor of this volume.

From August of 2002 through November of 2005, a chain of events culminated in the "Past, Present and Future of Research in the Information Society." These are the lessons I learned in planning and organizing the meeting.

(1) *Organizational decentralization.* While there are two groups that might be considered "lead organizations" for the PPF meeting, they did so only in a restricted fashion. The Society for Social Studies of Science provided funds and organizational legitimacy—not to mention a bank account for wire transfers to Tunisia. Its role was not to dictate a particular program of events for the meeting. The Visions Committee of the 4S, established by former President Sheila Jasanoff in 1998, suggested that a society that has been the major international association of scholars examining issues at the interface of science, technology, and society since 1975 should take a more engaged role in global and policy matters related to its areas of academic concern. The "Past, Present and Future" event was an illustration of this form of engagement, which is not to suggest an outcome, but to make a forum for discussion available.

The second entity is not much of an organization, but a network of collaborators we call the World Science Project.[2] The only thing "world" about it is the name: easily the worst project name in world history. The origin of the name is simple: a graduate student needed a business card and articulated the words that most closely matched the website. Since the web site for the PPF meeting was the simplest available domain name (worldsci), our project became its namesake. World Science Project has three meanings, corresponding to the macro, meso, and micro denotations of science. At its macro level it refers to globalized science, in which all regions of the planet exchange information equally about research and knowledge. At the meso level it is merely our own project—six countries where participants in the research enterprise are followed over time to understand the local and international extent of their communication. It is only at the micro level that we appreciate the name, a small "science project" anywhere in the world—a girl or boy dissecting a bug or taking apart a radio to see how it works. As the Director, this is the only meaning I can accept.

Organizational decentralization was important because a Satellite Summit should not, insofar as possible, be weighted towards any national or regional group. I say "insofar as possible" because individuals from developing areas are much less likely to attend if travel funds are not provided, and this will always lead to a deficit of participation. Since the scientific digital divide was one topic of the meeting, we hoped to have significant representation from sub-Saharan Africa. We knew this representation would be a problem and it is to the credit of the various groups responsible for particular sessions that they attempted to address this issue. The Committee for Data on Science and Technology (CODATA) became a key participant as a result of a recommendation by Paul Uhlir at the U.S. National Research Council, who worked with them on open access issues. Kathleen Cass in the CODATA executive office organized their Berlin meeting in late 2004 and became a key behind-the-scenes person. The International Network for the Availability of Scientific Publications (INASP), especially Carol Priestley and Peter Ballantyne, organized an integrated sequence of sessions addressing key issues involving scientific output and distribution in partnership with the FAO. The International Federation for Information Processing, which organized one of two major science and engineering side events at the Geneva phase of the Summit, became involved through Klaus Brunnstein, one of the editors of this volume. As a result of meeting Chen Huai at the trilateral meeting of U.S., Chinese, and Japanese scientists in December 2003, the National Natural Science Foundation of China sponsored a session. Hewlett Packard, which became one of our key sponsors, and organized two sessions at the PPF, became involved in early 2005, through a nearly random email and follow up call with Wayne Johnson.

What should be emphasized here is the change in organizational participants. The list above is the final group, rather than the group as it existed during any specific point in time during the three year run up to the meeting. In the spring of 2004, to take one example, it would have included Intel, the National Research Foundation of South Africa, the World Federation of Engineering Organizations, the Science and Development Network (SciDev), the International Council for Social Science, and a Microsoft division in the U.S. rather than India. All of these organizations dropped out, for various reasons, sometimes late in the game. But this is to be expected. They were replaced by others that were more interested, as evidenced by their inclusion in the final program. Remember, when you are organizing a Satellite Summit, participants receive an associated benefit no other kind of meeting can provide: they may attend the main summit as well.

In sum, a diverse group of *organizations* were the main driving force behind the meeting. I would strongly recommend this as a model for Satellite Summits or similar events. The main organizers of the event should not have any specific control or right of refusal over the presenters of these subsections of the meeting, so long as their topics fit generally into the themes. The event that results will be less unified than if every session were meticulously planned from the top down. It also yields a rich and diverse sampling of topics, that often surprised and sometimes delighted participants—such as the young academic who said, after a session organized by Hewlett Packard, "you know, these private sector people seem pretty cool." And she soon found out that Barbara Waugh, one of the lead organizers, had once been a bodyguard for Angela Davis.

(2) *Internet-based planning.* The Internet was crucial, and not simply for the development of an online program. Clearly, in the modern era, meeting participants expect and deserve web-based materials, including information about the location, accommodation, and program. But as many have said, email remains the only proven technology for research collaboration, and the same is true of meeting planning. I traveled around the world three times during this period and was in Africa and Asia for about nine months during which much of the meeting organization was done. Internet-based meeting planning, at its most basic, is spending sufficient time in the cyber cafes of Accra, Nairobi, and Trivandrum.

But take careful note of one thing, in view of the organizational decentralization discussed above. In each case, a single person took the lead in putting together sessions for their organizations. So when you are planning a meeting with organizational partners, you must quickly <u>forget</u> that fact, and get to know their people. Call them on the phone if you need to. Visit them if you have a chance. If they are active on email and respond to prompts, you will be fine, regardless of how reliable their organization is.

When they are not—often when you deal with people who are famous (or simply think they are)—the value added will be minimal, and you will regret the name-dropping potential they offer. After organizing the PPF, I doubt that the meek will inherit the earth, but they make it worth living on.

The Internet had another benefit for our Satellite Summit. Since 4S was an official, accredited entity under the Civil Society sector of the WSIS, we had the ability to accredit all of our participants to the main summit as well. To put it another way, even if you thought the "Past, Present and Future" was a waste of time, you could go to the Kram Centre and learn about the global programs and offerings in ICT the following day. Given the state of security in Tunisia last November, this ready ability to "get badged" for the main Summit was a major bonus. The regular emails sent by two or three of the civil society lists for WSIS were invaluable sources, alerting us to deadlines and allowing us to provide information for our participants. Early in 2005, we determined to produce an exhibition for the Kram Centre during the three days following our own meeting. There we could distribute materials for anyone who had contributed to the PPF, including posters for the Society for Social Studies of Science as well as results from our own National Science Foundation project. Meredith Anderson and B. Paige Miller were primarily responsible for this, with artwork provided by Susan Arnold.

(3) *Costs and Control.* One painful and extremely counterintuitive lesson involved a decision made by one organization not to fund the conference. They were initially expected to be our major source of funding and their initial enthusiasm was, truth be told, the source of my own confidence in proceeding. As I recruited participants and organizations, I told them, in all honesty, that the conference would likely be providing travel funds. Given the travel problem for developing area participants, it did not seem possible to plan a meeting without this source of funding. But I was wrong.

In most academic conferences—the annual meeting of 4S, for instance—a single organization implements a periodic event, according to a set of guidelines (or, at least traditions!) used by its planners to meet standard expectations of participants. Travel costs such as airfare and accommodation are paid by participants themselves, together with a registration fee to defray event costs. In the PPF conference—unlike the IDRC conference held in the same hotel during the same period—we followed largely this model after we lost our expected source of funding.

The decision to charge registration and move to a self-funding model was not made all at once, nor was it in the expectation of the funding withdrawal that later occurred. It was made because sometimes there was greater interest in participation than our hotel and organizational capacity allowed. The timeline of the event was such that most of the participating organizations indicated their interest before the main funding source fell through. By the end of 2004, there seemed no turning back. It would be impossible <u>not</u> to have some sort of conference in Tunisia. When, surprisingly, our expected funding source disappeared, the PPF conference was still going to happen. The anticipated consequence was that fewer participants from developing areas would attend, since we could not fund their travel. The unanticipated consequence was that it freed us, the Louisiana organizers, from the significant time and energy associated with implementing the payment of hotel and airfares in accountable ways.

It seems strange to me now, but without the *expectation* of this significant source of funding, the PPF meeting would assuredly never have occurred. I would not have gone forward, others would not have signed on, and the momentum eventually generated would not have been possible. But the funding itself was unnecessary.

(4) *Visits to Sites and Conferences.* In organizing such an event, two kinds of site visits are necessary. It goes without saying that you should not try to manage an event in another country when you have not been there. Wiebe Bijker and I conducted the first site visit in October 2003, and selected what appeared to be an outstanding conference hotel, one that had even hosted an ICANN meeting. However, the meeting staff proved almost impossible to reach over email during the months that followed and we felt this had been all ill-advised choice. This difficulty led Keith Benson and I to revisit the site and change the meeting hotel in May of 2005, which was quite late in the process, given the level of hotel and meetings activity occurring during the Summit high season in Tunis. Human rights issues and security issues led to additional challenges. On one of my two site visits I was detained by the police for taking a photograph of the Kram Centre. After the Jordan bombings, shortly before the Summit, the Tunisian government had tightened security to the point that taxis themselves were unable to approach the Kram within one mile. The Corinthia Khamsa hotel, which proved an outstanding venue for the event,[3] declined to sign a room contract without payment in advance—something we could not offer. We kept the hotel as a meeting site, but shifted course in providing accommodations, since we could no longer guarantee our participants rooms in the meeting hotel. Instead, we created a link to the main Summit accommodation site, and provided feedback to their travel agents on site design.

The second kind of "site visit" was not to Tunisia but to other conferences, in order to observe and learn. Many of us do this without realizing it, but in planning an event it must be explicitly noted. Observe what others do that fits the situation, and see what they do that might work for them, but will not work for you. I have mentioned the importance of the

South African Global Science Forum, the group of science and engineering events held simultaneously with the World Summit on Sustainable Development. Our original idea was to hold the PPF meeting along with the WSIS. But after Rick Duque and I attended the CERN event at the Geneva phase of the WSIS ("Role of Science in the Information Society"), we changed the dates of our PPF event to the three days immediately before the main Summit. Given the new Summit model of greater accessibility and participation by Civil Society, events that are simultaneous with the main Summit simply experience too much competition. We also eliminated the idea of large, formalistic banquets that are wildly expensive and unnecessary when there is an interesting city to explore and participants have spent the entire day at a meeting. The CERN and IFIP events in Geneva taught us much about what, and what not to do.

(5) *Flexibility.* In the summer of 2005, with stress levels increasing owing to the lack of funds and the absence of a room contract for our participants, the hotel rented our meeting rooms to another conference. Hard to believe, but true. After two site visits, a personal guarantee from the sales manager, and apparently good relationships with the staff at an "international standard" conference hotel, the impossible had happened. We had no place to hold the conference. I discovered this, while in the south of India, through an email from Steve Song of the International Development Research Centre (Canada), who remarked that we were both holding conferences in the same place at the same time. Frantic emails, faxes, and phone calls with Khalid Fourati and other excellent folks at the IDRC led to the best of all worlds. Their African Bandwidth Conference, to which they had invited a great number of the Africans that our PPF no longer had money to fund, was going to last a day and a half, and would only involve some minor switching of rooms. Participants at each conference would be free to go to the other, and the benefits would be mutual. So luck keeps coming—whether good or bad, you never know—and crisis turns into opportunity. How do you increase your odds? Check your email every day, don't hesitate to make phone calls when something is unclear, and establish personal relationships in which you yourself are as flexible as you want others to be.

(6) *Hurricanes.* On the 29th of August, 2005, Rick Duque and I sat in front of a computer to begin drafting the final program for the PPF on a computer in Lake Charles. We had evacuated Baton Rouge, Louisiana, the day before, because Hurricane Katrina was coming and no one knew exactly where she would hit. It was an exciting time for us. We had worked towards this day for three years. It was the day we could finally look at our web site with pride, knowing we would soon shepherd a group of interesting people

into a coastal hotel for three days of fascinating presentations on a subject dear to our hearts—science and the Internet in the developing world. As that day wore on, and bled into the next, we lost all interest in Tunisia, in WSIS, in the PPF meeting. Our First World had become Third. Nothing like this had happened—had *ever* happened—before. The levees had failed, and the City of New Orleans had flooded. What we did not know then was that the water would not stop rising for another three days, until the water in the city was level with the lake that now filled it.

Borrowing from Samuel Johnson's comment on the dog that could talk, it was no longer a question of whether the conference would be done well, or poorly. It was a question of whether it would be done *at all*. And we did not care much, in the days that followed, whether there was any "Past, Present and Future" conference. Life—real life—had centered us. The hurricane drew a boundary around our insignificant concerns with meeting rooms, confirmed registrants, and receptions. It revealed our trivial issues in the richness of their triviality. It could not possibly matter whether academics, policy makers, and program managers wandered around a beach hotel, gave a talk, and went off to see the ruins of ancient Carthage. Within the space of a day, I did not care whether the "History of the Internet" or "ICT for Development" was in the El Melia room at 10:30AM. Rick Duque was indifferent to whether merlot or cabernet would work better for the reception on the 13th of November. And it was not over yet. The house where we were working to draft the program was rendered uninhabitable three weeks later by two massive trees through the roof. This was courtesy of Hurricane Rita, which flooded the Lower Ninth Ward of New Orleans for a second time.

The pretentious "world science project" quickly became nothing more than a local hurricane recovery project. Using video ethnographic methods we had developed in Africa and Asia, we tried—though it was beyond anyone's ability—to document the devastation of the Lower Ninth.[4] After the water from the second flood had been pumped out, we received permission to enter and film before residents were allowed to return. On the 13th of November, this moonscape footage of crushed homes and cars in trees provided a visual backdrop for the opening remarks of "Past, Present and Future." We showed it without the soundtrack, because there were few sounds in the ninth ward after the hurricane. We showed it because it represented something we could not have imagined two months earlier, with our attention focused on World Summits. The Lower Ninth Ward became a world where all basic infrastructure—not just the infrastructure of information and communication technologies—had simply disappeared. In the context of a Summit focusing on the Information Society, it was worth seeing.

Looking back, had our Louisiana group stayed home, it is certain that Wiebe Bijker, and R. Sooryamoorthy, and Tony Palackal, and Paul Mbatia, and Dan-Bright Dzorgbo, and many others would have simply taken over and brought the PPF meeting to fruition. This is why you have friends and colleagues. No one and no organization appointed me as the organizer of this event. If you wait for someone to appoint you, you will "just wait"—as they say in Ghana. What happened, in the end, was a momentary consolidation of bodies in physical space, interacting and establishing or maintaining relationships. What kept me going for three years was not just the feeling that it was a worthwhile objective to pursue, but support from many people. They very well know who they are, and do not need to be thanked any more than I do. Which is not at all.

Next time, I hope you will take up the challenge: an adventure is always worthwhile. I will be on the sidelines, to cheer you on.

Notes

1 In many cases PowerPoint versions of the presentations may be found at the conference web site (archived at http://worldsci.net). If you would like to see any of the presentations, email me at shrum@lsu.edu and I will burn you a DVD from the digital video tapes of the three day meeting. A video version of this essay, shown during the exhibition at the main Summit, is also available: "The Making of Past, Present and Future" was produced and edited by Timothy Brown and Rick Duque.

2 Our project has been funded since 2001 by the U.S. National Science Foundation through an Information Technology Research grant. We thank, in particular, Patricia White of the Sociology Program, who has provided enormous support and encouragement throughout this time.

3 Our experience was truly enhanced by Karima Ouertani, who was outstandingly helpful during this entire event.

4 Of the many individuals who went into the field to chronicle the aftermath of the hurricanes, I want to thank in particular Rick Duque, Marcus Ynalvez, Meredith Anderson, and Paige Miller, all of whom were key organizers and presenters at the "Past, Present and Future" event in Tunisia.

2. ICT FOR DEVELOPMENT: ILLUSIONS, PROMISES, CHALLENGES, AND REALIZATIONS

Alvaro de Miranda, *University of East London*[1]
Dirk-Jan Peet , *Delft University of Technology*
Karel F. Mulder, *Delft University of Technology*
Paul Arthur Berkman, *University of California at Santa Barbara and EvREsearch LTD*
Thomas F. Ruddy, *Society for the Processing and Advancement of Knowledge on the Environment (SPAKE)*
Werner Pillmann, *International Society for Environmental Protection (ISEP)*
Marcus Antonius Ynalvez, *Louisiana State University*
Wiebe E. Bijker, *Maastricht Universiteit*

In this chapter we will critically examining some of the illusions, promises, challenges, and realizations of the Information Society. Handed down from the past are specific myths that may create illusions in the present and promises for the future that in effect will hamper the realization of the Information Society in its most promising forms.

In the first section the standard definition of the Information Society and the related issues of digital divide, development, and democracy are scrutinized. We will show that often the usage of these concepts and related policies implicitly draws on technologically determinist assumptions. We identify three myths as constituting this set of assumptions: the myth of technology as *not* human-made, the myth of the technical fix, and the myth of technology's neutrality. When these myths are not adequately deconstructed, the ideological character of the discourses around the Information Society and the digital divide will remain hidden. This would hamper the adequately addressing of the underlying socio-economic dimensions of the digital divide.

The second section follows suit by adding a socio-economic analysis to the socio-cultural and political analysis of the first section. We ask the question how the capacities are currently distributed in this globalized world, and how this distribution is related to hardware and software development. The negative effects of lock-in are identified, and we conclude that a targeted effort to stimulate local socio-technical development would be important to help in bridging the digital divide.

In the third and fourth sections we move to the promises and challenges of the Information Society, especially relating to the large amounts of information that people have to deal with. In the third section a software solution is described that builds on an analysis of the structure of digital information as well as its content and context. In the fourth section a series of conferences is described, aimed at offering a solution for the specific challenge of integrating the huge amounts of environmental data that now exist globally.

In the final section some of the effects of realizing the Information Society are addressed. We wonder what the effects are of foreign graduate education on the Internet use by Philippine researchers. As we will show, such questions can only be answered by analyzing the local context of these researchers. The meaning of 'personal computer', for example, is quite different in the Philippines as compared to countries in the north.

We thus hope to demonstrate in this chapter that the Information Society and the bridging of the Digital Gap can only be realized when supported by a comprehensive research program that includes science, technology, and society (STS) studies. This heterogeneous set of approaches comprises, as we demonstrate in this chapter, a broad range of humanities, social sciences, and engineering disciplines. For bridging the digital divide, a deconstruction of its ideological character is as much needed as a software solution to the information overload; a socio-economic analysis of lock-in processes is as much necessary as a sociological analysis of Internet use in developing countries.

2.1 Technological Determinism and Ideology: Questioning the 'Information Society' and the 'Digital Divide'[3]

The 27 September 2004 issue of *Business Week* featured a cover story entitled 'Tech's Future'. Both the cover and the story were illustrated with pictures of dark skinned women. The one on the cover was of an inhabitant of Recife in the poor North East of Brazil described as a 'prospective PC buyer'. The main story was illustrated by a full page photograph depicting an Indian woman, Neelamma, dressed in a traditional sari decorated with a garland of flowers holding a Hewlett Packard digital camera. The message in the story was driven home by a large font, bolded, subtitle stating: "With affluent markets maturing, tech's next 1 billion customers will be Chinese, Indian, Brazilian, Thai…" This message was illustrated by the case story of Neelamma, a 26 year old village woman from Andhra Pradesh, who, as part of an experiment organized by Hewlett Packard, was charging local villagers "70 cents apiece for photos of newborns, weddings and other proud moments of village life" taken with a digital camera and printed with a portable printer powered by solar charged batteries which had been rented from Hewlett Packard for $9 a month.

Both in the pictorial metaphors and in the textual message Business Week was presenting a particular strategy for bridging what has become known as the 'digital divide'. The poor and those marginalized from the 'Information Society', particularly women and black people, need to be brought into it as potential customers rather than as human beings with needs. This, it is suggested, will simultaneously eradicate poverty and create the conditions whereby basic needs are satisfied.

The strategy promoted by Business Week had been advocated in December 2003 at the 'World Summit on the Information Society' (WSIS) in Geneva. To justify the summit, the WSIS web site cited the existence of the 'digital revolution' which has been "fired by the engines of the of Information and Communications Technologies" and which has "fundamentally changed the way that people think, behave, communicate, work and earn their livelihood... forged new ways to create knowledge, educate people and disseminate information ... provided for the speedy delivery of humanitarian aid and healthcare, and a new vision for environmental protection". Further, "access to information... has the capacity to improve living standards for millions of people around the world" and "better communication between peoples helps resolve conflicts and attain world peace".

But the site also points to the paradox that while the "digital revolution has extended the frontiers of the global village, the vast majority of the world remains unhooked from this unfolding phenomenon" and "the development gap between the rich and the poor among and within countries has also increased". The purpose of the World Summit was therefore to discuss ways to bridge the digital divide and "place the Millennium Development Goals on the ICT-accelerated speedway to achievement".

In its "Declaration of Principles" the WSIS declared that its purpose was: "to harness the potential of information and communication technology to promote the development goals of the Millennium Declaration, namely the eradication of extreme poverty and hunger; achievement of universal primary education; promotion of gender equality and empowerment of women; reduction of child mortality; improvement of maternal health; to combat HIV/AIDS, malaria and other diseases; ensuring environmental sustainability; and development of global partnerships for development for the attainment of a more peaceful, just and prosperous world."

But the general tone for the Summit was set by the UN Secretary-General in his keynote speech: "The future of the IT industry lays not so much in the developed world, where markets are saturated, as in reaching the billions of people in the developing world who remain untouched by the information revolution. E-health, e-school and other applications can offer the new dynamic of growth for which the industry has been looking."

This example is typical of the way the relationship between technology and social change is often portrayed by the media and by policymakers. There are a number of different aspects to this representation. The first is that it ignores the fundamental fact that technology is created by human society. Instead it reifies technology, which in this representation acquires a 'phantom objectivity' as an agent of social change, 'an autonomy that seems so strictly rational and all-embracing as to conceal every trace of its fundamental nature: the relation between people' (Lukacs 1971:83).

The second and inter-related representation involves the myth of the 'technical fix', the implicit assumption that technology provides the best or the only feasible solution to complex social problems. Thus the World Summit on the Information Society, in its Declaration of Principles, implies that information and communication technologies possess quasi-magical powers to provide solutions to the world's greatest social and economic problems such as poverty, disease, illiteracy, race and gender discrimination, and environmental pollution.

The third is the use of myths about technology in order to promote particular policies and help create particular ideologies. The reification of technology, by creating the impression that the technological change is a rational, objective and inevitable quasi-natural process which is driving social change, hides the social forces and social interests behind the change and the fact that there are winners and losers in the process. In this case the new technologies are associated with the neo-liberal 'free-market' ideology and the combination is presented as creating a process in which everybody wins: the transnational corporations find new markets and the poor find new ways to improve their conditions- by making money from other poor people.

De Miranda (2005) traces the way that the concepts of the 'Information Society' in Europe, and of the 'Information Age' in the United States have moved from their origins in academic social science to acquire an important normative role in determining the policies of countries and of international organizations. It shows that these concepts are inherently technologically determinist and argues that their widespread adoption as a normative policy tool is due to their ideological usefulness to the dominant interest groups, which include the ICT corporations. It also demonstrates that the concept of the 'digital divide' plays a similar ideological role. The concept developed during the same period as social and economic inequalities within countries and between countries increased greatly. It reduces the problem of lessening socio-economic inequalities 'bridging the technological divide'. The physical and intellectual development of human beings is thus reduced to the ability to access and use the latest technologies. However some studies have shown that the spread of ICTs have been a contributory factor to increasing these inequalities (cf., *inter alia, Economic Report of the President*: 1994). It is therefore difficult to understand how 'bridging the digital divide' can be seen as the main means to improve socio-economic inequalities. The appeal of this approach to those in power resides in the fact that it enables the creation of new markets for the ICT corporations and justifies like-minded policies and public investments under the guise of 'building the Information Society for all'. The need to accelerate the 'bridging of the digital divide' becomes all the more urgent as IT markets become saturated in the developed countries.

It can be concluded that whilst the 'digital divide' is undoubtedly real and dealing with it is important because access to ICTs can now be considered a basic human need, it can only be 'bridged' within the broader context of tackling the socio-economic divide through effective actions by governments using redistributive policies. But to prepare for such redistributive policies, we need to have insight in the existing distribution of capacities and the possibilities for, and barriers to, their further development. It is to this issues that we turn in the next section.

2.2 Globalization and ICT: Lock-in barriers for capacity building in developing countries?[4]

The last decades ICTs have seen an enormous growth in both homes and businesses especially in industrialized countries. More than any other technology ICTs drive economic and financial globalization as they facilitate rapid transactions and global market transparency. Moreover, the Internet is the means of transport for a rapidly growing service economy. However, globalization and the formation of dominant technologies in the ICT sector pose problems for capacity building, using ICT in developing countries.

Globalization leads to a more rapid spread of products and services than we have ever seen before. Locally a wider variety of products will (has) become available. On a global scale product diversity will decrease as the larger (global) suppliers have a large cost advantage. Understandably this has an effect on local cultures both in the developing world as in industrialized countries.

This applies even stronger for software. Fixed costs of developing software are high, but the marginal costs of selling an additional software package are almost zero. Transport costs are negligible. The current dominant technologies on the hardware market and on the software market of operating systems for home and office computers appear to be in a *lock-in* situation, despite the rapid technology development in the ICT sector. From statistics of several websites, where both the operating system and the browser are detected, we see that about 90 % of the PCs has a *Microsoft Windows* operating system (see for example the website of W3 Schools). With a market share of 90 % it is obvious that there is a lock-in situation in the global software market for operating systems in homes and offices. There is also a dominant technology for the hardware market of PCs. Intel and AMD are the most important players in the market for chips and ICs, with Intel having a market share of about 70 to 80 % for Central Processing Units (CPUs). From the path of technology development of ICT, starting with the separation of software and hardware, the invention of the IC and the use of the chip, via the alliance of IBM and Microsoft's *MS-DOS*, ending with the standards set for communicating between computers via the Internet, it is clear that this sector is locked-in in a regime of hardware and software development (Ceruse, 2003). Lock-ins are formed through a process of positive feedback (Arthur, 1989) and are characterized by a dominant technology as is the case for hardware and software for PCs in homes and offices. The deep entrenchment of a technology makes it virtually impossible to change.

If we consider that ICTs, amongst which PCs in homes, offices, schools and hospitals can give people information to increase their ability to contribute to capacity building in developing countries, we should analyze both the quantity and quality of connected PCs in those countries. Both the number of PCs in different regions in the world, and also the speed with which they are connected with the Internet must be considered.

PCs have become available to a large number of people, first mostly in office locations, but later more and more in homes as well. In 2004 to every 100 people in The Netherlands, there were almost 70 PCs and the situation in most Western countries is not very different, indicating that PCs have seen a tremendous diffusion in the Western world (ITU Yearbook of Statistics, 2005). ICTs and especially PCs with an Internet connection can help to increase development both in Western countries and developing countries, as is the assumption of the World Summit on the Information Society. The amount of PCs in use and sold in developing countries in Asia, Africa and Latin America is a fraction of that, especially in Africa. The number of internet users in Asia is strongly increasing and will probably surpass the number in Europe and North America (eTForecasts, 2005).

Not only the amount of PCs and Internet connections is important to consider, when discussing the potential of ICTs for development, but also their quality (in this case the speed of the connection). From figures of the International Telecommunications Union (ITU) we can see that the countries with the highest penetration of broadband are all European or North American, except for South Korea, Taiwan and Singapore. Those three are among the most modern or industrialized Asian countries (eTForecasts, 2005).

There is not only a difference in the number of PCs in use , number of internet users and connection speed, but also in the number of registered domains per capita of industrialized and developing countries (see for example the website of Zooknic, 2005). This means that the countries with the highest number of country code Top Level Domain (ccTLD) registrations (registrations of domains with TLDs such as .nl, .bj, or .th), also have the most information in the local languages. Those countries are also the countries of which the languages are the ones in which software is available, creating another division. In order for people in developing countries to find information that is useful, there should also be web pages in languages they can read. Connectivity alone should therefore not be a priority, but useful local content in local languages should have the highest priority.

ICT applications can contribute to development and improved education, health care, and governance in developing countries. However, within the current system of hardware and software development this poses some problems. The current lock-in situation and other aspects of globalization in the ICT sector, such as a limited amount of suppliers on the global software and hardware market, form barriers for people to benefit from ICTs. There is little possibility to compete by developing countries because of globalization effects in both the hardware and software market. Next to that there is a large difference in both the quality and the quantity of PCs and internet infrastructure between industrialized and developing countries. A third major issue is the availability of information in local languages. Overriding priority should be given to both developing local content and connectivity in order to prevent frustration and offence by the content of western oriented websites. The number of websites in local languages, but also the languages in which operating systems and software are available form an important, but not unconquerable barrier. These issues should be taken into account when discussing the use of ICTs for capacity building.

Let us now assume, for a moment, that a large part of the world is connected to the Internet and is enjoying the benefits of access to many sources of information. How then to manage the huge information load that is the result? The next two sections address this issue.

2.3   Integrating Digital Information into Knowledge for the 'Information Commons'[5]

Access to digital information has become effectively infinite and instantaneous with nearly 20,000 petabytes of information produced and stored on print, optical and magnetic media each year; microprocessor speeds that have increased 5 orders of magnitude since 1972; existence of the Internet; increasing global capacity to collect and transmit information via satellites; and availability of powerful search engines. The problem is in recognizing that information is more than a commodity with access speed and volume driving global consumption.

The paradigm shift created by digital technologies is the opportunity to utilize the inherent structure of information as well as its content and context. A printed book or record can be managed based on its content and context (as in libraries and archives), but it is not possible to break a printed book or record into smaller units that can be managed dynamically. It is this ability to manipulate the structure of information in an automated manner that distinguishes information management with digital technologies from all of the hardcopy media that have ever been applied in our civilization (Figure 1).

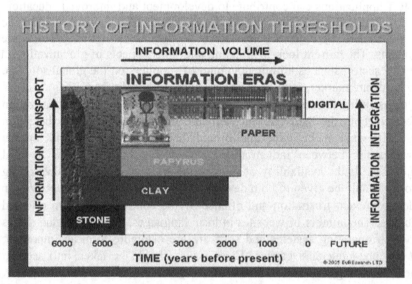

Figure 1: Technology thresholds that have influenced information management in our civilization. Each of the media prior to digital had been used for millennia. Adapted from Berkman et al. 2006.

By utilizing the inherent structure of information as well as its content and context, it becomes possible to comprehensively discover objective relationships within and between digital resources independent of their scale and formats (i.e., "structured" as well as "unstructured" information). An example of the automated granularity technology to leverage the inherent structure of digital information is the patented *Digital Integration System* (DigIn®) from EvREsearch LTD, which has been used to integrate digital collections such as the *Antarctic Treaty Searchable Database* (http://aspire.nvi.net) that is now in its 6th edition (Berkman et al. 2005, 2006).

We have reached the threshold in our 'world Information Society' when access to information is necessary, but not sufficient. The sufficiency comes from generating knowledge. Knowledge (which emerges from understanding information relationships) derives from the process of integration. Such distinctions between the processes of information access and integration underlie the technological solutions for the future when *"knowledge is the common wealth of humanity"* (as expressed by His Excellency Adama Samassekou at the 2004 Committee on Data for Science and Technology, CODATA, meeting in Berlin).

Knowledge is inherently social, in addition to the substantive dimensions than were discussed in this section. In the next section this social dimension is added to the issue of managing the information load that the new Information Society may imply.

2.4 Twenty Years of Conferences Structuring Environmental Knowledge[6]

The debate on sustainable development involves an overwhelming amount of information from various disciplines. In 1986 a group of scientists in German speaking countries collectively built a common intellectual platform combining informatics tools such as databases and information systems with environmental applications. Thus the emerging field of environmental informatics was enriched with some of the first hybrid scientific content involving both fields, and the series of EnviroInfo conferences began.[7]

Data from ever expanding networks of sensors and monitoring activities have since then yielded increasingly detailed environmental information. Informatics brought all this data together, and by the same token it can serve as a tool to manage the flood of information. Indicators derived from this data have provided a structured view of environmental conditions and the dynamics of ecosystems. Products resulting from such structuring with informatics tools show the "State of the Environment" from regional, country-wide and continental perspectives. Global examples of results from such activities are the European Environment Agency's (EEA) "Europe's environment: the third assessment" (2003) and EEA Signals 2004, the Worldwatch Institute's "State of the World" reports, UNEP's GEO Report Series and yearbooks, and the global syntheses prepared during the Millennium Ecosystem Assessment (World Resources Institute 2005).

In recent years EnviroInfo conferences with such themes as "Environmental Communication", "Sustainability in the Information Society" and "The Information Society and Enlargement of the European Union" have promoted network building and the scientific exchange of knowledge and featured unifying visions in their keynote speeches by renowned scientists. One innovative example of a significant EnviroInfo result is the German Environmental Information Network GEIN, which was later showcased at the "Expo" World Fair in 2000. It is a network containing detailed environmental information from nine German "Länder" which takes up over 400,000 Web pages.

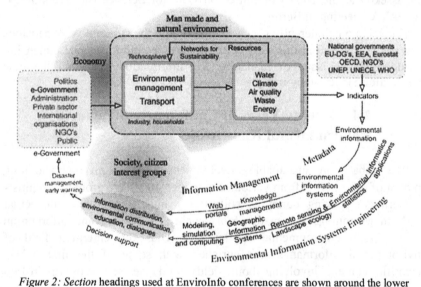

Figure 2: Section headings used at EnviroInfo conferences are shown around the lower part of the figure

Environmental studies are multidisciplinary by nature, and sustainable development is inherently international. Participants at Enviroinfo conferences are given unique opportunities to transcend traditional disciplinary borders. Each session covers at least one environmental application and one informatics tool such as Geographic Information Systems GIS, environmental information systems, Web portals, remote sensing, modeling and simulation.

Figure 2 represents an attempt to describe EnviroInfo topics thought to promote "sustainable development". It is a systems structure in an input/output model representation. The arrows running along the outside represent communication links between the natural and man-made environments (the technosphere), society and the private sector - the economy.

If we move closer to the technosphere/environment part of the model in order to focus on the impacts humans have on the environment, the system structure includes multiple control loops. Environmental goals (e.g. pollution reduction, national environmental action plans, Local Agenda 21, Integrated Product Policy (IPP), the Eco Management and Auditing Scheme (EMAS)) influence politics, government administrations, industry, services and households. Appropriate legislation and political measures such as taxes fostering environmentally friendly technologies along with information, research and environmental communication limit the impact of enterprises, services and citizens on the environment. The combinations of these various fields are topics of Enviroinfo conferences. The information gathering, analysis and communication of environmental information and the embedding of results in decision processes are depicted in the lower part of the figure.

The group of pioneers from 1986 has now grown into an established constituency, and is open to new submissions from qualified participants from all over the world.[8] The conferences have made the transition from being an exchange for environmental information to one for sustainability knowledge, and thus are intended to counteract some of the negative effects of globalization by considering social and economic factors along with the environmental ones.

We now have reviewed the cultural, political, and socio-economic illusions, promises and challenges of the Information Society (in the first two sections), and the resulting promises and challenges of the huge increase of information (in the third and fourth sections). In the next and final section we turn to some of the questions relating to the realization of these promises, especially pertaining to the issue of bridging the digital divide.

2.5   Does Mickey Mouse Matter? International Training, Professional Networks, And Productivity of Philippine Scientists[9]

In the aftermath of the 9/11 attacks, the presence of international students who entered the U.S. for graduate training was highlighted as a matter of policy significance. Recently imposed new requirements, laborious screening procedures, stricter visa restrictions, and budgetary cuts in educational and cultural exchange programs all work to reduce the influx of international students into the U.S. (Ante 2004). If the long-term result is diminished numbers of foreign graduate students trained in the U.S., this could have a significant impact on scientific knowledge production in developing areas.

Few studies have examined the specific consequences on scientific careers as a function of graduate education at the scientific core, even when most scientists in developing areas receive advanced training there. In the Philippine case, scientists are typically trained in Australia, Japan, and the U.S. through sponsored programs (e.g. assistantship, exchange programs, fellowships, grants, and scholarships). Hence, it is reasonable to forward the hypothesis that having been educated and trained at the core influences peripheral scientists' careers and productivity. Partial support for this hypothesis is found in Ynalvez et al. (2005) where they found that receiving graduate training in a developed country enhances self-reported productivity among Ghanaian scientists, but not for Indian and Kenyan scientists. Another support comes from the socio-cultural practice, and the extended translation model of science (Callon 1995). Explicit to these models is the process of enculturation wherein knowledge producers are assumed to be capable of learning so that on-site visit and face-to-face interaction with core scientists enable peripheral scientists not only to learn and understand explicit (or codified) knowledge, but also acquire tacit (or hard-to-transfer) skills. Tacit knowledge or skills is deemed essential to the effective transmission of techniques and practices crucial to knowledge production (MacKenzie and Spinardi 1995).

To date, there is a paucity of studies that have focused on the professional activities of scientists in peripheral areas. Of those who have investigated these activities (Ehikhamenor 2003 a & b), none have ventured into exploring the effects of graduate training at the scientific core on the adoption of technical innovations like the Internet, and the career trajectories of scientists in developing areas. While the effect of level of graduate education has been the subject of much research attention, place of education, which provides a potent mechanism for the acquisition and transmission of tacit knowledge has not yet been systematically studied. Specifically, its role in scientists' adoption of the Internet, their professional network, and productivity has not yet been studied.

In this section, place of graduate education is treated as a causally prior dimension that may determine the configuration of scientists' network characteristics and their productivity patterns and rates. In other words, place of graduate education is taken as independent dimension and then focus is on the population of Filipino agricultural scientists in answering the following questions: First, to what degree has the Philippine research system adopted the Internet? In contrast to Ynalvez et al (2005), here Internet adoption is conceptualized in five dimensions: current use, ready access, extent (years of use), intensity (hours of use in a typical week), and diversity of use. Second, how can disparities in Internet adoption in the Philippine research system be characterized? And third, does place of graduate education play an important role in scientists' professional network and research productivity? In answering these questions, results from face-to-face interviews of 315 agricultural scientists in two knowledge production sectors (state universities and government research institutes) in two Philippine locations are discussed: Los Baños, Laguna (home of the green revolution in rice), and Muñoz, Nueva Ecija (the second largest agricultural research site).

To what degree has the Philippine scientific community adopted the Internet? From the Philippine research locations and sectors that were sampled and studied, it immediately became obvious that the PC (or personal computer) is a far cry from the usual notions of access and use scientists in developed areas have, where they are typically assigned a desktop in their personal offices. In most cases, they will also have laptops. Indeed, for scientists in developed areas the PC, more than fits the definition of a "personal computer" in that it is assigned to a single user and located in the personal office. In contrast, our findings indicate that PCs, as construed in the context of the Philippine research system, rarely translates to personal computers. These technical artifacts are more accurately described as "public computers" which are shared and typically located in communal workstations.

Despite the practice of computer sharing in communal workstations, and with the PC as a prerequisite for connectivity, almost all of our respondents consider themselves current users with ready access. In a way, it can be claimed that Internet adoption in terms of simple access and use is no longer an issue among Filipino knowledge producers. In terms of software-user interaction, those who report current usage use email for a very limited time in terms of intensity of use. Current users may have extensive experience as indicated by years of exposure, but it is also important to take note that extensive exposure is meaningless, especially if intensity of use is extremely low, and even more so if the technical item continually and rapidly evolves. With the low intensities of use that were observed, it is doubtful if Philippine knowledge producers are really able to gain Internet skills and competency that can only result from continuous and intensive practice, and prolonged and extensive exposure. Diversity of use is another important dimension of Internet adoption where Philippine scientists register low. It is indeed doubtful whether Filipino scientists, with minimal experience (both in terms of extent and intensity) on the Internet can master skills that will permit them to do a variety of things with it.

Hence, it was observed that Philippine knowledge producers tend to have achieved high levels of ready access and current usage. But, in more advanced dimensions of Internet adoption like experience and diversity of use, they are obviously registering low. In other words, areas of concern are no longer within the domain of simple access and use, but have already shifted into more advanced areas of extent and intensity of experience, and diversity of use. These new areas of concern seem to have shifted from simple access and user skills to more complex hardware-software-user interaction skills.

How can the disparities in Internet adoption in the Philippine research system be characterized? It is not surprising that location and sector play a role in the "digital divide" observed in the Philippine research system where scientists in Los Baños, and in government research institutes tend to have ready access and extensive experience. With the limited financial and material resources dedicated to knowledge production, it seems practical and efficient for national policy makers and government officials to allocate resources to the premier research community (Los Baños) and to invest on applied rather than on academic research.

With respect to scientists' personal characteristics, the "digital divide" among Philippine knowledge producers predominantly runs across categories of age. Younger scientists are more likely to be extensive and diverse users, a result that is consistent not only with findings in developing, but also in developed areas. However, it is surprising to note, especially in traditional societies like the Philippines where gender is one source of durable inequality that it is only with respect to diversity of use that males dominate. Males and females tend to be on "equal footing" with respect to other aspects of Internet adoption except that of diversity. Because our measure of diversity includes activities pertaining to interaction outside of scientists' immediate work environment, it could be that in Philippine societies, although women have achieved considerable parity with men, women are still only comfortable to interact with men (and women) whom they know through face-to-face interaction or by way of a third party introduction. Hence, there may still be much inertia for women to initiate or start a technology-mediated social interaction, especially if it is a total stranger who is at the other computer terminal.

Callon's (1995) socio-cultural practice model and his extended translation model of science views science actors as capable of learning, and Collins (2001) and MacKenzie and Spinardi (1995) argue that explicit and tacit skills are important in knowledge production. The results reported here support these claims in that it could be observed that scientist education enhances Internet adoption. For simple access and use, explicit knowledge is the main discriminating dimension where higher levels of graduate education translate to current usage and having ready access. Explicit knowledge or the credentials symbolic of explicit knowledge (like having a Ph.D.) are held with deference and prestige in Philippine research systems in a way that scientists who hold credentials and titles symbolic of explicit knowledge tend to be awarded access to resources like PCs and Internet connectivity. As one of our informants in the Philippines mentioned, those who have PCs and connectivity are usually those who have doctorates. For extent and intensity of experience, the place of graduate education is an influential factor. For example, the training culture in Australian scientific communities emphasizes a research practice that demands both extensive and intensive use of the Internet, while the training culture in Japan and in the U.S. emphasizes a research practice that demands extensive use. This result suggests that tacit skills acquired by having Filipino scientists trained abroad seem to result to significant changes in Internet use behavior. It should be noted too that sophisticated and diverse use of the Internet is also influenced by level and place of graduate education, which suggests that advance hardware-software-user skills maybe be greatly enhanced not only by higher levels of graduate education, but also by graduate training at the scientific core.

Does place of graduate education play an important role in Philippine scientists' professional network and productivity? In general, scientist education does not determine network size, but it does matter in configuring network quality. Level and place of graduate education somehow enhances network quality by having a direct positive effect on the proportion of foreign contacts. The effect of graduate education is indeed suggestive of the important role of codified and tacit knowledge in scientific network structure. Codified knowledge provides the necessary credentials fundamental for structuring the interaction among scientists, while tacit knowledge offers the rituals and courtesies necessary for harmonious socialization. Between level and place of graduate education, the latter has a stronger influence on the quality of networks. Among the digital dimensions, diversity of use is an important positive determinant of both size and quality.

In other words, education directly and indirectly affects quality of network mainly through hardware-software-user interaction skills. Meaning the both explicit and tacit knowledge already on its own and can also be enhance through digital use and skills.

Output in domestic journals is influenced by level of graduate education and diversity of use, where doctorates and diverse users are associated with higher productivity. Like for current use, ready access, intensity and extent of use, we significant effect was observed for place of graduate education on domestic output. It can also be seen that traditional bases of social inequality like age, gender, marital status, and number of children do not influence domestic output. Level and place of graduate education, availability of computers in personal offices, extent of experience, and diversity of use mainly influence visibility in foreign outlets. These results suggest that education, privacy, and hardware-software-human interaction skills are crucial for visibility in international science outlets.

While the inequality in foreign output with respect to level of graduate education is straightforward and intuitive in that doctorates have higher productivity than non-doctorates, this is certainly not the case for place of graduate education. Normally one would expect foreign training to be associated with visibility in foreign journals. However, our results show that this is not the case. The inequality is structured in such a way that scientists trained in either Japan or the U.S. tends to have higher levels of output than those trained in either Australia or the Philippines.

Given that Japanese and U.S. training seem to matter compared to other training structures raises the question why this is so. It is still difficult to completely understand this phenomenon, but what can be observed is that Japanese and U.S. training structures somehow influence the careers of Filipino scientists. Maybe the effect of these two training structures can be traced to the larger socio-economic and cultural ties that exist between Japan and U.S. on the one hand, and the Philippines on the other hand. These two core countries, Japan and the U.S., are very similar in the sense that Japan is considered to be the most "Americanized" Asian nation, and that it seems natural for Filipinos to develop high affinity with both Japan and the U.S. given that much of the Philippines' social, economic, and cultural arrangements is influenced by America through previous colonial engagements. Indeed, much of this affinity can be observed among Filipino children who always yearn to meet *Mickey Mouse*, wherever he might be – in Florida, in California, in Tokyo...maybe *Mickey Mouse* does really matter!

2.6 References

Anon. 1994. *Economic Report of the President to the Congress*, 1994, Washington, DC: U.S. Government Printing Office

Ante, Spencer 2004. "Keeping Out the Wrong People." *Business Week*, October 4, 2004, pp. 90-94.

Arnst, Catherine 2003. "How the War on Terror is Damaging the Brain Pool." *Business Week*, May 19, 2003, pp. 72-73.

Arthur, W.B., Competing technologies, increasing returns and lock- in by historical events. *Economic Journal*, 1989. 99: p. 116-131.

Berkman, P.A., Morgan, G.J., Moore, R. and Hamidzadeh, B. 2006. Automated Granularity To Integrate Digital Records: The "Antarctic Treaty Searchable Database" Case Study. CODATA Data Science Journal (in review).

Berkman, P.A., Morgan, G.J., Moore, R., Marciano, R., Suderman, J., Hamidzadeh, B., and Hofman, H. 2005. Antarctic Treaty Searchable Database Case Study. Final Report for the InterPARES 2 Project. International Research on Permanent Authentic Records in Electronic Archives (http://www.interpares.org).

Callon, Michel. 1995. "Four Models for the Dynamics of Science." Pp. 64-79 in *Handbook of Science and Technology Studies*, edited by S. Jasanoff, G. E. Markle, J. C. Petersen, and T. Pinch. Thousand Oaks, CA: Sage Publication.

Ceruzzi, P.E., *A History of Modern Computing*, second edition, 2003, Cambridge, Massachusetts, USA, London, England, The MIT Press

Collins, H. M. 2001. "Tacit Knowledge, Trust and the Q of Sapphire." *Social Studies of Science* 31:71-85.

Davies, Martin. 1989. "Connectionism, Modularity, and Tacit Knowledge." *British Journal for the Philosophy of Science* 40:541-555.

De. Miranda, Alvaro. 2005. "Technological Determinism and Ideology: Questioning the 'Information Society' and the 'Digital Divide'". Manuscript.

Delamont, Sara and Paul Atkinson. 2001. "Doctoring Uncertainty: Mastering Craft Knowledge." *Social Studies of Science* 31:87-107.

Duque, Ricardo, Marcus Ynalvez, R. Sooryamoorthy, Paul Mbatia, and Wesley Shrum. 2005. "Collaboration Paradox: Scientific Productivity, the Internet, and Problems in the Developing World." *Social Studies of Science* 35:755-785.

Ehikhamenor, F.A. 2003a. "Internet Resources and Productivity in Scientific Research in Nigerian Universities." *Journal of Information Science* 29:105-115.

—. 2003b. "Internet Facilities: Use and Non-Use by Nigerian University Scientists." *Journal of Information Science* 29:35-48.

Knorr-Cetina, Karin. 1998. "Citation for H. M. Collins." *Science, Technology, and Human Values* 23:491-493.

Lukacs, Georg. 1971. *History and Class Consciousness*. Translated by R. Livingstone. London: Merlin

MacKenzie, Donald and Graham Spinardi. 1995. "Tacit Knowledge, Weapons Design, and the Uninvention of Nuclear Weapons." *American Journal of Sociology* 101:44-99.

Shrum, Wesley and Patricia Campion. 2004. "Gender and Science in Developing Areas." *Science, Technology, and Human Values* 29:459-485.

Sorensen, Knut H. and Nora Levold. 1992. "Tacit Networks, Heterogeneous Engineers, and Embodied Technology." *Science, Technology, and Human Values* 17:13-35.

Xie, Zhen Zeng and Yu. 2004. "Asian-Americans' Earnings Disadvantage Reexamined: The Role of Place of Education." *American Sociological Review* 109:1075-1108.

Ynalvez, Marcus, Ricardo Duque, and Wesley Shrum. Forthcoming. "Productivity, Collaboration, the Internet, and Reagency in Distant Lands." in *Science of Collaboratories*, edited by G. Olson, N. Bos, and A. Zimmerman.

Ynalvez, Marcus, Ricardo Duque, Paul Mbatia, R. Sooryamoorthy, Antony Palackal, and Wesley Shrum. 2005. "When Do Scientists "Adopt" the Internet? Dimensions of Connectivity in Developing Areas." *Scientometrics* 63:39-67.

eTForecasts, reports on PC world market and Internet users:
http://www.etforecasts.com/products/index.htm, September 2005

ITU statistics:
http://www.itu.int/ITU-D/ict/statistics/at_glance/top20_broad_2004.html, October 2005
http://www.itu.int/ITU-D/ict/statistics/at_glance/Internet04.pdf, October 2005
http://www.itu.int/ITU-D/ict/statistics/at_glance/Internet01.pdf, October 2005
http://www.itu.int/ITU-D/ict/statistics/at_glance/af_ictindicators.html, October 2005
http://www.itu.int/ITU-D/ict/statistics/at_glance/E2_EuropeICTIndicators_2003.pdf, October 2005

W3 Schools, Statistics on web browsers and operating systems:
http://www.w3schools.com/browsers/browsers_stats.asp, October 2005

Zooknic Internet Geography Project, statistics on domains worldwide:
http://www.zooknic.com/Domains/World_Domains.pdf, November 2005
http://www.zooknic.com/Domains/Domains_per_capita.pdf, November 2005

2.7 Notes

1 Authors in order of the section they contributed. The chapter was compiled and edited by Bijker.

3 This section was contributed by De Miranda.

4 This section was contributed by Peet and Mulder

5 This section was contributed by Berkman.

6 This section was contributed by Ruddy and Pillmann.

7 Further details on Enviroinfo conferences can be found in the article by Pillmann, W.; Geiger, W.; Voigt, K.: A Survey of Environmental Informatics in Europe. Environmental Impact Assessment Review, forthcoming in 2006.

8 In 2006 twenty years of EnviroInfo conferences will be celebrated in Graz, Austria; see www.enviroinfo.net

9 This section was contributed by Ynalvez

3. HISTORY OF ICT

Rick Duque, *Louisiana State University[1]*
Martin Collins, *Smithsonian National Air and Space Museum*
Janet Abbate, *Virginia Polytechnic Institute and State University*
Celso Candido Azambuja, *UNISINOS. São Leopoldo-Porto Alegre*
Mikael Snaprud, *Agder University College*

To understand the processes and impacts of a globalizing technology like the Internet, one must account for the historical development of that technology, the process of technology transfer in general, and the local cultural dynamics in unique regions. The Internet will diffuse differently in different regions and among different sectors within those regions. Chile, for historical and cultural factors, should demonstrate a different diffusion and use pattern than India or Kenya. This leads to different definitions of how Internet technologies are constructed within distinct regions and poses challenges for the development of a symmetrical global scientific community fueled by new ICTs. This last statement often weaves itself into the "taken for granted" rhetoric found in multi-lateral conferences like the World Summit on the Information Society (WSIS). It is simplistic to assume that the Internet will resolve inequities in social, political, economic and even scientific terms. It is a noble perspective, but the last 50 years of development failures based on other western technologies and protocols does not provide much optimism. The following session review highlights the complex factors involved in Internet diffusion, post war history, technological culture, case studies in the developing world, and innovations in technology research and development.

The session on History of ICT reflected many of the temporal, transnational and developmental dimensions of research in the information society. American scholars Martin Collins and Janet Abbate retraced the historical contexts of cellular and Internet technology research and development in the post war era. Collins discussed the ways Motorola's transnational Iridium project was constructed by both Cold War political culture and post Cold War market culture notions of the global. Abbate reminded us that "Internet culture" finds its roots in the values of the research community that first conceived and then developed it. Brazilian scholar Celso Candido offered us an overview of the developmental constraints and potentials of Internet technology diffusion in his nation over the last quarter century. Brazil's case mirrors many of the diffusion processes unfolding throughout the developing world. The session concluded with Swedish scholar, Mikael Snaprud's overview of "open-source" platform support for collaboration in ICT training and research.

3.1   One World…One Telephone: The Iridium Satellite Venture and the Global Age[2]

This paper explores the ways in which the boundaries among technology, politics, and concepts of the global were constituted through one of the grand business initiatives of the 1990s—the creation of a global, wireless telephone system via a network of 66 satellites in low-Earth orbit. This venture, initiated by Motorola in the late 1980s and developed through a start-up company called Iridium, represented the largest private capital investment initiative of the last several decades, as well as the largest private venture for a space technology project. The technical system's global scope was mirrored in its investment and business structure, as thirteen non-U.S. corporations and governments (including Cold War adversaries Russia and China) became partners in the project.

The Iridium case bridges two distinct technical and political cultures. Emerging at the end of the Cold War, Iridium had deep roots in that era's government-oriented approach to mega-technical projects—through strategies for managing big technology and through close connections to the US military. But as a privately financed and commercial venture, it exemplified the global market ethos that defined the 1990s. Through the development of a complicated, satellite-based telephony system and through the challenges of organizing an international business Iridium's history opens up the detailed ways in which market notions of the global were created and overlapped with Cold War conceptions of the global.

As a highly visible communications enterprise, Iridium became intimately linked with two ideological themes central to the period: The legitimization of national and transnational policies of deregulation and a belief in global communications technologies as bearers of liberal values and facilitators of individual autonomy. Motorola and Iridium used these technical-political resources to negotiate new sets of relations among their corporate partners, with national and international regulatory bodies, with U.S. agencies, with national governments, and other sites to shape an international framework favorable to their interests. Too, participating non-US investors and partners saw opportunity in Iridium to advance their own national and corporate agendas.

Iridium, thus, provides a telling window on how communications technology, markets, ideology, politics, and US military interests mutually interacted over the 1990s to create particular concepts of the global. Moreover, this case suggests that the global as an intellectual construct and as a short hand for an international economic and political system needs to take into account discrete, purposive efforts to create the "global"—that this construct was not just a natural, 'ramped up' extension of pre-existing capitalism. Stated somewhat differently, the global as a construct is not monolithic, but is the product of multiple, specific undertakings. Viewed from this perspective the global is not (primarily) a problem in definition nor in its phenomenological effects in altering our perception of culture and the world, but a problem in history and politics: How did it happen and why?

The Iridium case focuses on elite rather than on "up from below" actions in constructing the global and highlights several connotations not emphasized in current literature. First, while the transition from Cold War to "post" at the end of the 1980s is an oft cited factor in shaping the global, its import is mischaracterized, giving preeminent emphasis to the erosion of nation state autonomy in face of transnational market forces. Yet Iridium fore grounded the persistence of a Cold War notion of the global, specifically of the US military's interest and actions in creating global technical capabilities—of which Iridium was one. Second, the global signified more than an abstract, amorphous transnational field of action. The global, for actors in the Iridium story, had a literal, concrete, ambitious meaning: creating and exerting control through technological means over the entire planet for military or markets ends. Third, implied in the preceding points, the global had two interconnected expressions, one rooted in military interests (primarily as represented by the US), another market-based, with the latter tending to obscure the former. Lastly, as an elite created instantiation of the global, the business venture fused together in pursuit of its goals a range of distinct instruments: technology, strategies of corporate organization, corporate lobbying (nationally and internationally), neo-liberal ideology, and adoption and use of academic concepts of culture—in short, its tools were heterogeneous and opportunistically applied.

3.2 Scientific Origins and Legacies of the Internet[3]

Though the Internet today is a vehicle for commerce, entertainment, news, and personal communication, its origins lie in scientific endeavor, and it has been fundamentally shaped by scientific practices and values. The Internet was originally created to support scientists, and its technical design reflected the needs and abilities of this group. Many striking aspects of Internet culture, which have been celebrated as "virtual community," grew directly out of the scientific community's ideals of openness, collaboration, and sharing of data and resources. The composition of the early Internet community also mirrored the wider scientific community on which it was based: white, male, and somewhat elite, but also international in scope.

This paper outlines some problems and promises of the Internet's scientific legacy. While the Internet can no longer be managed as a scientific project, the scientific community offers expertise, values, and international networks that can contribute to solving to today's policy dilemmas. At the same time, the experts who develop and promote ICT should be more diverse and inclusive than techno-scientific communities traditionally have been.

Scientific Origins, Design Choices, and Culture

The Internet's predecessor, the ARPANET, was built in the late 1960s by computer scientists funded by a US defense agency. The network had three goals: to save costs by allowing computers to be used more widely; to allow scientists to share resources such as specialized hardware, software, and data; and—most importantly—to strengthen the scientific community by making it easier for scientists to interact and collaborate. In the late 1980s the network was taken over by the civilian National Science Foundation and served scientists in a wide range of fields. While the original Internet was commercialized in the 1990s, next-generation projects such as Internet2 share a similar structure, funded by government (with private sector partners) and run by scientific and educational organizations.

As a scientific project, the Internet was conceived as an object of research as well as a tool for research, and was therefore designed to use cutting-edge experimental techniques and modes of analysis. To help explore the potential of this new technology, its creators made the Internet an open, modular, flexible, system that users could experiment with and modify. Its decentralized design contrasts sharply with most commercial products and systems, which tend to be closed and are designed to be "idiot-proof" rather than inviting users to modify them. The Internet's creators assumed that users would be technically capable, creative, and trustworthy— in other words, scientists like themselves.

These design choices had important consequences. The long-term success of the Internet is largely due to its ability to grow and adapt to new infrastructure, such as Ethernet and wireless, and new applications, such as streaming video and peer-to-peer file sharing. The system's openness to user experimentation encouraged grassroots innovations that became major applications, most notably the World Wide Web and more recently music-sharing, games, and blogs. On the other hand, the Internet's flexibility makes it unpredictable and hard to control. Its openness has made the Internet vulnerable to viruses and other attacks, spam, and fraud. Security measures have had to be retrofitted to reflect the reality that the Internet no longer serves just a community of colleagues but the entire world in all its diversity.

The culture of the Internet was also shaped by the scientific ideals, including openness, collaboration, and decision-making by consensus. This has led to an emphasis on nonproprietary technologies, applications for sharing information and collaborating, horizontal rather than hierarchical lines of communication, and a sense of "virtual community" online. The creators of the Internet also put in place a remarkable consensus process for technical decisions, which is still operative in bodies like the Internet Engineering Task Force. The IETF's bottom-up, consensus-based style has worked remarkably well for developing effective technologies in a timely manner while avoiding control by a single company or country.

While the Internet began in the US, from early days the group that designed it reflected the global nature of the scientific community. Computer scientists from France, England, and Japan were involved in the design of the Internet protocols in the 1970s, and academic computer networks in Europe and Asia connected with the US Internet in the 1980s to provide international email networks well before the Internet itself had become global. Today's next-generation Internet is also an international effort— though uneven levels of participation reflect the reality of unequal resources.

Conflicts and Policy Issues

The Internet's origins as a tool for scientists laid the groundwork for a flexible, expandable, robust system that has successfully served a much larger population. But policy issues arise from the conflicting needs and desires of the Internet's broader user base—including military, business, and ordinary users—and the need to expand and diversify participation.

Scientists' desire to treat the Internet as an open experimental system has repeatedly clashed with the military interest in a stable and secure environment. In 1983, for example, the Defense Department split off the military users from the ARPANET to create a second network called MILNET, so that military users would not be disrupted by scientists' experiments with the network. A more recent dispute has been over the use and export of encryption technology, which the US government has tried to restrict in the name of national security. Computer scientists have argued that such restrictions are futile (since strong encryption is already available outside the US) and have a chilling effect on scientific communication. There is also a gap in the US between the internationalism of the scientific community and the more narrowly nationalist outlook of the government. The US has been at odds with much of the world on issues such as technical standards, export restrictions for encryption, and the move to IPv6, which many countries see as necessary to create a sufficient supply of IP addresses (of which the US currently controls the lion's share.) Computer scientists have in some cases organized to insert the views of scientists into these political debates.

Habits of openness and sharing on the Internet also conflict with the desire of business interests for secrecy, closed proprietary interfaces, and tightly controlled dissemination of intellectual property. The 1970s saw debates over whether technical standards for networking should be proprietary or public, with the eventual triumph of the open TCP/IP standard thanks to US government backing. In the 1980s, tensions over business use of the taxpayer-funded Internet eventually led to its privatization and commercialization. More recent conflicts focus on intellectual property, such as the entertainment industry's push for harsh legal measures to restrict copying. Computer scientists have complained that these laws criminalize normal scholarly research and communication for scientists working in this area.

Finally, because the choice of Internet technology affects so many people, there is a need to make the communities that develop and standardize new Internet technology more diverse and inclusive than techno-scientific communities traditionally have been. The computer scientists who initially operated the network assumed that technical ability would provide the authority to make decisions about the development and administration of the system. This technocratic approach was not necessarily attuned to issues of democracy, justice, or the need to adjudicate between competing interests. To make the design process more democratic requires actively including voices who represent the wider community that will ultimately have to live with the technology. This should include ongoing efforts to get more underrepresented groups involved in science and to support participation by scientists who lack adequate infrastructure. In addition, governance mechanisms should recognize and accommodate political, not just technical, dimensions of design decisions.

Conclusions

One of the themes of the World Summit is that the Internet must be more inclusive. Without public debate on what the nature of the Internet should be, its future may be defined by the strongest actors, defaulting to a militarized, commercialized, and parochially nationalist space. The history of the Internet shows why scientists around the world must be included in the community actively shaping the future of the Info Society. It also suggests that a policy aimed at fostering the global Info Society should include measures to strengthen international scientific communication and to encourage local innovation with information technologies and services.

I suggest three ways in which scientists can positively shape the future of the Internet:

1. Design projects that focus on appropriate technology and include input from local user communities. One possible example is the Simputer, developed by the Indian Institute of Technology and private-sector partners, which provides a low-cost, low-energy Internet device that does not require literacy and can be easily shared by an entire village.

2. Build on existing professional networks. The scientific community has well-established international networks that can be channels for expanding Internet access and stimulating new types of services. Scientific groups have been the spearhead for many Internet projects in the developing world.

3. Participate in public debate on the future of the Internet. Scientists can bring a deeper understanding of the technical issues to public debate and can emphasize the value of open, international, non-commercial communication.

3.3 Brazil in the Information Society[4]

The Information Society is an integrated and complex society. It is revolutionary compared to the industrial society because it brings about crucial changes concerning our ways of social communication and production, our ways of thinking and deciding. Information Society is situated in the post-industrial – maybe we could say post-capitalist - society context.

Brazil is the leader of one of the most important regions in the world. It is a very beautiful, wealthy and promising country, in spite of its enormous and dramatic socio-economical contradictions. Its wealth is based on the great intellectual, musical and physical creativity of the people, on its natural beauty and on the great power of the environment. It is also based on the power of its industry and agriculture, on its accelerated integration in the Information Society, and several other aspects. Because all of this, Brazil will surely play a capital role in the future of the planet.

Brazil occupies a very interesting and complex position in the Information Society. The information business in this county has developed productive forces in different areas, mainly in the industrial sector and in the service sector. In fact, Brazil has made a good jump into Information Society in the last fifteen years, starting free and massive production and commercialization of personal computers from the late 80's and the World Wide Web in 1995.

No doubt, the increasing production and commercialization of PCs is to a great extent due to the expansion of Internet. But Brazil lived under a law of "protected market" for fourteen years, from 1977 to 1991. Nowadays, we can estimate that 30 million computers are installed in Brazil. However a considerable part of this development has happened or is still happening in the black market (about 65%). This digital cannibalism, strange though it seems, has helped the development of the main productive forces of the Information Society in Brazil.

Taxes, for example, are mostly organized via the Internet (about 95%). All large enterprises are being interconnected through the Internet and intra and extranet. The voting process in Brazil is totally computerized. With a population of about 200 million people and about 120 million electors, Brazil uses "voting machines" to define its executive and legislative government and carry out plebiscites. In a recent plebiscite, last October, for example, there were over 300 thousand (exactly 325.458) "electronic ballot boxes".

Scientific research in Brazil is also greatly computerized. All researchers have their electronic Curriculum on the Web, in a database of the National Center of Research (CNPq). All proceedings for budget to research happen on line, too. But, surely, CNPq doesn't have money for all the demands of the academic community. Brazil applied only about 1% of its Gross Domestic Product to research last year. Academic researchers have an online public database for publication and access to doctoral thesis and master dissertations at the Digital Library of Thesis and Dissertations (BDTD) of the Brazilian Institute of Information in Science and Technology (IBICT) that assembles about 30 universities and research institutions.

Remarkably, in January 1996, Brazil had about two hundred thousand people connected to the Internet. In 2000, they were about ten million. Nowadays, Brazil has about thirty million people connected to the Internet. All of the states in the federation are connected through a backbone with a speed that ranges from 4 Mbps to 622 Mbps.

Young people account for an expressive appropriation of the Web in Brazil. About 37% of them are between 18 and 34 years old. This generation has a great participation in virtual communities like Orkut, instant messaging, sent/received e-mail and chat-rooms. They participate intensely in the creation of blogs, web sites, and so on. In June 2005, Brazil was first list of countries when people spend most time on residential navigation (about 17 hours). In the first quarter of 2005, 20% of residential navigation was related to virtual communities; 10% to e-mail use. Nowadays the Internet users have broadband connection. But, publicity investments in the Internet are still very low, corresponding to only about 2% of all publicity in the media in Brazil in April 2005. So, although much of the population is excluded, the most important social sectors are entering or are already in the Information Society.

No doubt, in Brazil the ways we do things are being changed quickly. But, as in other countries, it brings about dramatic and difficult situations of social and cultural marginalization. In Brazil the digital divide is enormous. On the one hand, this is due to our immense social divide: Brazil has high social exclusion and high concentration of wealth. On the other hand, though some political decisions have been made towards favoring "digital inclusion"[5], like "PC connected", "Free Software", "Telecenters", through the "Electronic Government project"[6], they have not been effective in narrowing the digital divide.

Brazil has a good chance to integrate the Information Society and narrow the digital divide. To do this, we need, first of all, a public and private policy of high investment in research and education. But we also need some more general political decisions without which digital inclusion in Brazil is impossible. This is necessary in order to fight unemployment and poverty. We need to fight social misery and marginalization with a serious policy of *minimum income* and so reach a greater social harmony.

Finally, knowledge became the infrastructural base of production, on which the main productive forces of contemporary society are developing. Information Society is very rich, because knowledge is its core commodity and knowledge is a very powerful good. It is a source of wealth that can be shared and is not used up. Thus, research became a strategic "tool" for production and digital knowledge engineering became a crucial question for contemporary society.

Therefore, we need a model for the formal and informal research and for education adapted to the *digital noolithic*, to the new digital economy and new digital culture. We need a global education for creativity, complexity and the essential knowledge focused on the great questions of human life. It means an ethics of social and environmental respect and responsibility. It must be the *ethics of research and digital knowledge engineering*. This is an Ethics to affirm life, justice, and beauty.

3.4 Open Source: Synergies in ICT Education and Research[7]

Open Source Software already has a wide use in ICT education and research. In this paper we outline the current use and further synergies to be drawn from a tight integration of university level ICT courses with scientific research projects based on Open Source software and collaboration with the Open Source community. At Agder University College (AUC), we are not only using Open Source software and methods, we strive to achieve a close integration between our FOSS research and teaching activities - following the so-called research-based-education model.

The FOSS research at AUC is primarily dealing with meta-modeling and with access to Internet content for people with disabilities. Our main research project is the European Internet Accessibility Observatory[8] (EIAO). The project both uses and produces Open Source software to develop machinery for web accessibility benchmarking.

Based on the EIAO project we have defined a course called Web mining and Data Analysis.[9] The course teaches the students basic skills in webmining techniques and Python programming which are used in the course to carry out software development projects. HarvestMan[10] is the Open Source web crawler used in the course. The same webmining techniques, Python programming and crawler are actively used in the EIAO project, which allows us to increase consistency and synergies among our teaching and research activities.

The webmining course illustrates how research activities can be used as a starting point for development of ICT courses. On the other hand, however, teaching activities might also be used as precursors for larger research efforts. A Master level project, recently initiated at AUC by Bruce Perens, on software defined radio based on GNU Radio[11] may be given as a good example. The project attempts to build better user interfaces to the software defined radio components. As such, it develops the basics necessary for the development of more specific research activities concerning how measurement instruments, communication protocols, antennas, etc. may be implemented using Open Source software and Open Source hardware, providing a lower cost and skills threshold to fascinating experiments and research on wireless communications.

The benefits from using Open Source in education seem obvious for ICT courses where the students are allowed to gain a deeper understanding by viewing what is going on under the hood. In several courses we already see that Open Source enables a continuity of student projects and facilitates the collaboration with enterprises and authorities. Still, one semester is often too short to gain the thorough understanding needed to really do useful work in a project.

In our opinion it is important to stimulate involvement of the Open Source community in the research-based-education model. Such involvement may be stimulated by:

- definition of research proposals based on an Open Source policy (e.g., the EIAO project employs the Open Source policy that allows for reuse of code and collaboration with the FOSS community),

- organization of workshops with a clear focus on Open Source (at AUC in the summer of 2006 we will have a conference focusing on Open Source in Education),
- close cooperation with external companies that use Open Source for their business to define student projects (many of the student projects at AUC are carried out as part of collaboration with local SMEs or larger FOSS community projects like Skolelinux[12]),
- improvement of student project- documentation (at AUC we have developed a student report template to improve the quality and consistency of the documentation produced by the students).

It is important to note that the proposed research-based-education approach requires tools that would effectively support distributed collaboration in a similar way like Open Source development. One of our current research activities aims at developing such a tool that would enable effective use of collaborative annotation, a code version server, and trackers to support the development both of code and of teaching content.

To support this development we have already migrated some existing courses to Open Source software such as Plone. We also plan to extend Plone for collaborative development of research projects and Open Content teaching material.

All of the tools and templates used for teaching and for research are included in a continuous development cycle that is increasingly linked with external Open Source projects. The research-based-ed*ucation* approach can potentially release synergies among Open Source projects scientific research and university level ICT education.

We refer the reader to the Open Source research community (http://opensource.mit.edu/), and Open Course Ware, MIT (http://ocw.mit.edu/index.html).
See also Derek Keats' article on "Collaborative development of open content," First Monday, Volume 8, Number 2 (3 February 2003), (http://www.firstmonday.org/issues/issue8_2/keats/) and the interview with Bruce Perens (14.august 2005)
http://madpenguin.org/cms/?m=show&id=4921&page=2.

3.5 Conclusion

The session on History of ICT suggested that ICT histories, case studies of ICT adoption within developing nations, and studies on ICT innovations like "open source" contribute to an organic understanding of the Internet's potential and constraints as a developmental agent. Collin's portrait of the process of control that framed the Iridium project might be applied to the ways the Internet has been constructed as a global agent of power. This may explain why its diffusion has been much more tentative than global cellular penetration. Abbate adds to this the historical conflict in openness between scientific and political cultures. This may also explain the inertial experience of Internet global diffusion. Candido suggests that in unique settings like Brazil, the imperative of creating local capacity in Internet technology is sometimes a process of technological "cannibalism". But successful efforts in reducing digital divides do not always reduce social divides in class-conscience societies like Brazil. Open source initiatives such as those of Snaprud and his colleagues, maintain an optimism that the historical patterns illustrated by earlier speakers may be circumvented. Given access, traditional obstacles may melt as online research communities fulfil the legacy of diversity and inclusion described by Abbate.

3.6 Notes

1 Authors in order of the section they contributed. The chapter was compiled and edited by Olson.

2 This paper was presented by Martin Collins. For an extended version of the argument see Martin Collins, "One World...One Telephone: One Look at the Making of the Global Age, "History and Technology 21 (2005): 301-324.

3 Presented by Janet Abbate.

4 Presented by Celso Candido Azambuja.

5 http://www.idbrasil.gov.br/

6http://www.governoeletronico.gov.br/governoeletronico/publicacao/noticia.wsp?tmp.noticia =212&tmp.area=25&wi.redirect=MBDMQSUYMK

7 This paper was co-authored by Mikael Snaprud, A. Sawicka, A.B. Pillai, N. Olsen, M.G. Olsen, V. Laupsa, and T. Gjøsæter.

8 http://www.eiao.net, partially funded by the European Commission contract number 004526

9 http://www.eiao.net/webmining

10 http://harvestman.freezope.org

11 http://www.gnu.org/software/gnuradio/

12 http://www.skolelinux.org/portal/

4. THE ORIGIN AND EARLY DEVELOPMENT OF THE INTERNET AND OF THE NETIZEN: THEIR IMPACT ON SCIENCE AND SOCIETY

Ronda Hauben, *Columbia University[1]*
Jay Hauben, *Columbia University Libraries*
Werner Zorn, *University of Potsdam*
Kilnam Chon, *Korea Advanced Institute of Science and Technology*
Anders Ekeland, *Center for Innovative Research*

This session focused on the history of the development of computer networks, the linking of these networks via the creation of the Internet, and the emergence of the active participants in these networks, the netizens (i.e., net.citizens). The session included papers about the scientific development of networking technology, and about the impact of the Internet.

The Internet will continue to develop and impact society, but already the Internet has a history, the as yet untold history of its development as a science and a technology. Also, emerging with the Internet has been the netizen. The talks presented in this session considered the historical organizations and threads which brought forth the Internet and the netizen. Papers also explored the vision that gave birth to the contemporary networking developments and the continuing relevance of this vision.

The Internet has made it possible to link diverse networks around the world, and the citizens of these networks, into a global public sphere populated by citizens of the world, by netizens. This development is a product of scientific/technical research, of research in resource sharing, and in interactive communication on both technical and social levels. It is also a product of the activity of the users and of the netizens. The emergence of netizens is one of the spectacular achievements of the creation and development of the Internet, an achievement that as yet has received little attention. The netizens movements in countries like Korea and China are an important component of the international development of netizens. This session explored both the development of the technology and of the online participants in these important technical developments.

The first section documents the need for investigating and analyzing the international contributions to the Internet's origins and the early development and scientific environment in which the Internet was conceived. She described the vision of JCR Licklider, which inspired early computer networking development. Licklider, as other scientists of his era, was especially interested in modeling and the scientific potential of an appropriate model. Licklider was convinced that the creation of a computer network that made collaborative modeling possible would be a great scientific advance. Licklider also considered it important that citizens be involved in scientific and technical policy decisions and that the creation of the Internet would be a way to encourage such citizen involvement. Hauben's talk documented the plastic, collaborative, participatory roots of the origin of the Internet, which provides a foundation for its continuing development. She also documented the research in the early 1990s that discovered the online net.citizen or netizen who had emerged on the net.

The second paper presented Licklider's research on the library of the future and the investigation he did of the human-computer symbiotic relationship which provided a framework for understanding the vision inspiring early networking development and research. Hauben pointed out that Licklider anticipated that the cost of the internet he was predicting would be distributed among the users, the more universal the connectivity, the lower the cost per user. That, in some ways is the secret of today's Internet. The more sharing, the greater the efficiency and the lower the necessary cost to everyone. For Licklider and for society today the basic question is that of access. The great advantage to society of the computer networks will only be achieved if access is a right, that is, if governments insure that no sector of society is being left out and insure that no sector of the online world is blocked. Hauben concluded from his study of Licklider that he positive effect of networking would only be achieved if using the networks was made easy and affordable and interactive.

The third section of this chapter presents one of the important but unknown collaborations to create international networking which are at the basis of the Internet's origins. Zorn described how his research group in Karlsruhe Germany collaborated with Chinese networking researchers to link Chinese computer networks into the CNET networking collaboration. There was a Western embargo on computer equipment to China in the 1980s. World Bank loans funded a project that provided Siemens computers which were not forbidden by the embargo to universities in China. However, creating necessary software and other networking problems had to be solved to connect Chinese networking researchers with the networking development elsewhere. Zorn's talk also described how the details of this collaboration have been ignored when telling the history of how China was connected to the Internet. He also presented an overhead showing the first email message sent from the Chinese computer center to Karlsruhe in Germany and signed by the researchers working on this pioneering connection. The name of the Chinese engineer who is credited with sending this message was not in the list of the names of the researchers sending this initial email message. Also attending the session was the head of the Chinese Internet Society. She was especially interested in Zorn's presentation, welcomed it, and promised that the telling of the history would be corrected in China.

The fourth paper started with the question of how a small country like South Korea could lead the world in Internet usage. He described early computer networking development in South Korea and documented the role of South Korean researchers in helping to bring computer networking to other Asian countries. Chon's presentation showed the early networking connections between South Korea and the Netherlands via UUCP and Usenet. He also described one of the earliest uses of the TCP/IP protocol. The TCP/IP protocol was the basis later for the Internet. Chon, as one of the pioneers of Korean computer networking, provided a framework to understand how South Korea has developed as one of the most advanced providers of broadband access to the Internet for its citizens. Also he presented an account of the embracing of computer networking and online discussion by the Korean population that has resulted in an important set of achievements by Korean netizens. These include the election in 2002 of the President of South Korea by netizens and other pioneering ways that the Internet is having an important impact on society in South Korea.

The final paper challenged the dominant economic paradigm of reliance on the "market," as a form of religion, not as a scientific description of how an economy functions. Ekeland applied his critique especially to the activities of the Internet Corporation for Assigned Names and Numbers (ICANN) created by the US government to manage the international infrastructure of the Internet. Ekeland analyzed how the neoliberal theory behind the creation of ICANN left out the need for government to have a role in infrastructure development and administration and to help to administer the infrastructure toward a public purpose. Ekeland explained how the creation of ICANN falsely depicts the Internet's infrastructure as being able to be regulated by the "market".

All the presentations in this session gave some of the historical basis helpful for understanding the origins and early development of the Internet and for determining what is needed for the Internet's continuing development.

4.1 The International and Scientific Origins of the Internet and the Emergence of the Netizen[2]

The mythology surrounding the origins of the Internet is that it began in 1969 in the United States (US). That is the date marking the origin of the ARPANET, a US packet switching network, but not the birth of the Internet.

The origin of the Internet dates from 1973. The actual goals of the researchers creating the Internet included technical and scientific aspirations. The desire was to create a network of networks; that is, a means for networks from diverse countries to intercommunicate. At the time, there were several national but diverse networks being planned or in development. These included NPI (Great Britain), CYCLADES (France), and ARPANET (US). It was not then technically or politically feasible, however, to interconnect these networks. Instead, a research project including Norwegian, British, and US researchers was created to develop a protocol to make an internetwork possible. This protocol, originally called the Transmission Control Protocol (or TCP), is now known as TCP/IP protocol suite. Along with the research to create the TCP/IP protocol in the 1970s, several other research projects were started to investigate how to link the computer systems of different countries.

By the 1980s, networking research was common in a number of countries and there were conferences where an international group of researchers gathered to share their research results. Though the Internet, as currently known, did not become a reality until the early 1990s, the networking development in the 1970s and 1980s set the foundation for the Internet's rapid spread in the early 1990s.

The mythology attributing the Internet's origin to a military goal is inaccurate. Problematically, it hides an understanding of the importance of the technical and scientific vision that inspired early computer networking development.

J. C. R. Licklider was the scientist who provided leadership for the computer and networking research which later made possible the Internet's development. Licklider's reputation was based on his pioneering research investigating how the cat perceived sound via the localization of sound in its brain.

Licklider's interest in the relationship between the human brain and the computer led him to develop a theory of collaborative modeling. He envisioned how developing computer and human collaboration via computer networking research would make possible an advanced form of collaborative modeling among humans and computers.

The Internet's development offers an important prototype to understand the creation of a multinational, collaborative, and scientific research project. This project depended on and fostered collaboration across the boundaries of diverse administrative structures, political authorities, and technical designs.

Along with the spread of the Internet in the 1990s, was the emergence of the Netizens, the online "net.citizens," who were active participants in helping to spread the Internet and to foster its continued development as an advance in communications that would be available to all.

This paper explores how the Internet developed and spread and how the discovery of the emergence of the netizen occurred. It explores the process by which the role of the netizen in the continued development of the Internet was identified and embraced by many online users around the world. The paper also describes early efforts to recognize the potential impact of the Internet on society. A conceptual framework for the continued investigation of the international and scientific origins of the Internet and the emergence and development of the netizen is proposed in an effort to support the needed continuing research about the origins and social impact of the Internet.

4.2 The Vision of JCR Licklider and the Libraries of the Future[3]

Throughout history, thinkers and scholars have lamented that there is not enough time to read everything of value. The real problem is not the volume of valuable scholarship and recorded thought and reasoning. The historic problem for scientists and scholars has been selecting and gathering the relevant material and processing it in their own brains to yield new knowledge. The goal is to contribute new insights to the body of knowledge and to enhance what we have to draw on and what gets passed on from generation to generation, in addition to biologically inherited genetic information.

Guided by assumptions of how the human brain functions, a grand vision emerged after the Second World War in the United States. New human-machine knowledge management systems would be developed to help researchers consult more of the corpus of all recorded knowledge. Such systems would increase the usefulness of the corpus and accelerate the making of new contributions to it.

One of the fathers of that vision, J. C. R. Licklider, also set the foundation for the development of today's Internet. Licklider combined in his own background and career the fields of psychology and engineering. A thread through his intellectual work is his search to understand and model the human brain. Licklider presented his vision for an intergalactic network, as he called it, especially in two seminal papers, Man-Computer Symbiosis in 1960 and The Computer as a Communications Device in 1968 with Robert Taylor. "The hope is that, in not too many years, human brains and computing machines will be coupled together very tightly, and that the resulting partnership will think as no human brain has ever thought and process data in a new way not approached by the information-handling machines we know today."[4] Less well known but also of significance is Licklider's only book, Libraries of the Future, published in 1965.

For Licklider, the library of the future would be a powerful human-machine-knowledge system. But, it would only come to be if a variety of social and political questions were answered constructively. Among those questions are: Would society set itself the goal of developing intellectual and scholarly resources? Would all the holders of digitized information share their holdings without restriction? Would society resist the commercial pressure to keep knowledge proprietary? Licklider was an eternal optimist, but he thought these obstacles might take a long time to overcome. Also his vision of the library of the future was hollow if it was not available universally. With Robert Taylor, he wrote, "For the society, the impact will be good or bad depending mainly on the question: Will 'to be on line' be a privilege or a right? If only a favored segment of the population gets a chance to enjoy the advantage of 'intelligence amplification,' the network may exaggerate the discontinuity in the spectrum of intellectual opportunity." The basic question Licklider and Taylor raised is that of access. The great advantage to society of the computer networks would only be achieved if access is a right; that is, if governments insure that no sector of society is being left out and, at the same time, also insure that no sector of the online world is blocked. That would indeed produce a more happy world: "What will on-line interactive communities be like? (...) They will be communities not of common location, but of common interest (...) The whole will constitute a labile network of networks -- ever-changing in both content and configuration. (...) The impact of the marked facilitation of the communicative process, will be very great— both on the individual and on society. (...) life will be happier for the on-line individual because the people with whom one interacts most strongly will be selected more by commonality of interests and goals than by accidents of proximity."[5]

This paper looked at Licklider's understanding of the human-computer symbiosis and the computer as a communications device to see the vision and foundation he set for the Internet. It examined his projection of the library of the future. It concluded by looking at whether or not society is getting closer to fulfilling the vision of J. C. R. Licklider.

4.3   German-Chinese Collaboration in the First Stage of Open Networking in China[6]

The German-Chinese Collaboration between Wang Yun Feng (March 15, 1915 to April 29, 1997), Institute for Computer Application (ICA) at the Technical University Beijing and Werner Zorn from the Informatik

Rechnerabteilung (IRA) at the University of Karlsruhe goes back to the year 1983, when the First Joint Conference of Chinese and German Scientific Users of Siemens Computers was held in Beijing. This was the year when TCP/IP replaced the old NCP and gateways came in place to interconnect open email networks like CSNET. It was also the year when Germany launched the DFN program (Deutsches Forschungsnetz - German research network), within which one of the projects under Zorn's supervision started to connect Germany to the international networks by setting up the CSNET relay for Germany. This work was accomplished on August 2, 1984, which initiated many subsequent infrastructural activities including that of trying to connect the friendly related ICA as a Chinese email gateway for the growing number of hosts within the Chinese scientific community.

Despite the existing modern and quite powerful SIEMENS host at ICA, one of nineteen SIEMENS hosts distributed all over China from a World Bank project - none of them with email services - and the normal international telephone network, this project started literally from zero. The presentation relates the milestones and the struggles in between, i.e. raising funds from the government, establishing the first German-Chinese X.25 connection in August, 1986, thus allowing remote dialogue and remote email services, implementing the CSNET/PFMS - software for the BS2000 - operating system, also in 1986, and as the big milestone the first email "'Across the Great Wall" from Beijing on Sep. 20, 1987 to the worldwide network community. This German-Chinese email connection was approved by the NSF as "a natural enlargement of the international telephone and postal services" on Nov. 8, 1987, initializing among other things the development of CANET within China and the registration of the .CN domain on Nov. 28, 1990 as the next big milestone. This allowed China to set up nationally and propagate internationally its own domain addresses. The primary domain name server was run by Zorn's team at the University of Karlsruhe from January 1991 until April 20, 1994, when the CNNIC took over the operation after having set up a direct link between China and the United States, thus opening the usage of the whole suite of Internet services. April 20, 1994 is therefore considered and celebrated as the birthday of the Chinese Internet.

To this day there are timelines on the Internet that incorrectly tell a different story. This following table is offered to try to help accurately set the historical record of the German/Chinese China Connection Project (1983 - 1994).

Date	Event	Actions
1982	Chinese University Development, Project II($ 145 Million) Cities	19 Siemens BS2000, Computers in 11 Major
Sep 83	First WASCO/CASCO Conference in Beijing	"DFN- Deutsches Forschungsnetz" (Werner Zorn)
Aug 84	CSnet Connection Germany <=> US	E-Mail- Gateway for Germany (Michael Finken)
Mar 85	CSnet-Mail/BS2000, Implementation Decision	Starting PMDF- Implementation
Sep 85	Second CASCO Conference in Xi'an	"International Scientific Networks" (Werner Zorn)
Mar 86	Invited Visit	Checking Data Center Facilities
Nov 85	Funding of China Connection by Baden-Württemberg	150,000 DM + 15,000 DM/a for C+C
Aug 86	First X.25 Connection Germany <=> China	DB- Access among others
Sep 87	Third CASCO Conference	"Computer Networks"(Key Note Werner Zorn)
Sep 87	Connecting Beijing and Karlsruhe E2E	PMDF Installation on BS2000
Sep 87	First E-Mail message "Across the Great Wall ..."	2 Teams (Prof. Wang and Prof. Zorn)
Nov 87	NSF approves China Email Connection	Stephen Wolff (NSF), Larry Landweber, Dave Farber
Mar 88	CANET Inauguration and and conference	Minister Yang, Prof. Wang, Dr. C.C.Li
1988	Propagation of CANET- Operation	Prof. Wang, Dr. C.C.Li
Nov 90	Registration of .CN Domain	Application. (Zorn) with technical contact Rotert, administration by Qian TianBai
1991 ff	Operation, Propagation of .CN	Qian TianBai, Dr. Li, Prof. Wang, Rotert, Nipper
Mar 93	Visit W. Zorn	TS- Handover and Strategic Planning
Apr 93	Plan to migrate to full internet Services	Leased Line Proposal to SNI (W Zorn)
Jun 93	End of further Activities	Denial by SNI (MoB H.- D. Wendorff)
May 94	Operating Primary DNS in Karlsruhe	CNNIC takes over DNS after direct US link

4.4 Brief History of the Internet in Korea and Asia[7]

The TCP/IP network in South Korea started on May 15, 1982, one of the earliest Internet deployments in the world. The initial TCP/IP network, called SDN (System Development Network), consisted of two nodes with 1200 bps bandwidth. In January 1983, a third computer at KAIST (Korea Advanced Institute of Science and Technology) was connected to the SDN, which resulted in a system that could be described as a network of computers.

SDN served the research and education community of South Korea with a primary focus on network research, although it had international links with UUCP initially. The international links covered several countries. From 1983, SDN was connected to various sites in Asia in addition to North America (hplabs and seismo in USA, CDNNET in Canada), and Europe (mcvax in the Netherlands). The network linking Asian countries was called AsiaNet, and included Australia, Indonesia, Japan, Korea, and Singapore.

In parallel with the TCP/IP development, communications on personal computers using bulletin boards and other means also proliferated. These two network developments along with the availability of WWW contributed to the explosive Internet growth in the 1990s. Online communication using PC communications operated as a separate service independent from the Internet until 1995, when regular PC network users were able to connect to the Internet using commercial networks. The most notable significance of the PC communications is that it contributed to the development of the concept of online communities. These developments resulted in South Korea being the leading broadband country with various applications used widely by the population. In 2005 the number of home users with broadband Internet access exceeded 12 million, a figure that includes over 80% of the households in Korea.

It was in the early 1990s that individuals of the general public were able to express their diverse political and social opinions through the Internet. Various people and groups started to set up websites.

The Red Devils support club for the national soccer team played a very active role mobilizing massive cheering crowds in the 2002 World Cup Games.

When two middle school girls were killed by a U.S. armored tank in June 2002, on-the-street candle light vigils by netizens and online memorials spread throughout the country. In addition, during the December 2002 presidential election, there were many active online and offline campaigns organized and played out by many netizen groups such as People Who Love No Moo Hyun(Nosamo). These netizen groups did not spring up suddenly with the introduction of the Internet. Rather, they are extensions of online communities that were formed through the PC communications in the early 1990s, using the Internet as their newer communication medium.

The Internet is becoming part of the social infrastructure in Korea lately with many aspects of daily life done through the Internet including social and political activities. Convergence of the Internet with telecommunications and broadcasting is taking place now.

Figure 3. SDN Network Configuration (as of May 1985)

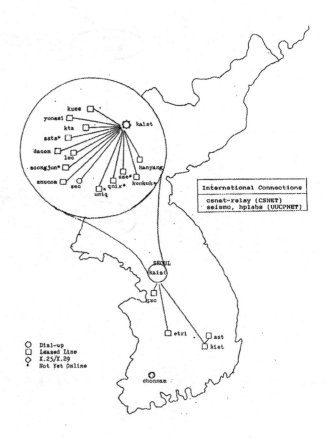

Figure 4. AsiaNet – UUCP and USENET (source: PCCS, Oct 1985)

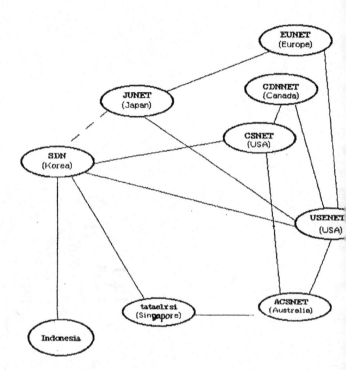

4.5 Netizens and Protecting the Public Interest in the Development and Management of the Internet: An Economist's Perspective[8]

This paper discusses various aspects of Internet governance with a focus on the role that "economic theory" plays in this discussion. The fundamental questions are, of course, what is the most important aspect of the Internet and what is meant by the free exchange of information and opinions. These are both a common good and a public good. The commercial use of the Internet is of secondary importance from an Internet governance point of view.

This is not the dominant point of view, however, among economists. There is no such thing as an "economic theory" or one and only one way that economists view the Internet. Instead, there are several variants including neo-classical, evolutionary, institutional, and post-Keynesian theories, just to mention a few. Each is a broad church containing important and distinctive currents with characteristic and individual points of view. None of these theories, and in particular the policies they recommend, are neutral, objective, or purely scientific. Indeed, no social-science theory can be value-free. This paper takes as its starting point the policy recommendations made from "main-stream" economists regarding Internet governance.

"Main-stream" economic theory is defined as that which uses perfect competition as a static equilibrium for its benchmark to determine the optimal, "first best" state of markets. In equilibrium and at the reference state, everything is taken as given ("initial endowments", prices, technology) and there is no role for government/institutions in the basic model. The need for regulation stems from "market failure." The paper argues that "main-stream" economics is too narrow in its analysis of Internet governance. First of all, it does not discuss the justice, the legitimacy of the "initial endowments," the initial distribution of power, and/or property rights. There was international research cooperation from the beginning, but today the ultimate control over root servers and the DNS is with the US government.

Economists writing on Internet governance do not treat this question; it is taken as a given and left to the lawyers. The legal specialists have been mostly concerned with the controversial status of ICANN as a private institution making public policy. Secondly when it comes to the actual governance of the Internet, the DNS system, trademark issues, etc., "main-stream" economists believe in using only the markets. This raises several important questions, not the least is the fact that markets measure success only in monetary terms. So, where does this leave those who have legitimate needs not backed by money.

But even on the condition that we shall leave certain parts of Internet governance to markets, do markets actually function roughly as the model that perfect markets predict? If not, how do we regulate the role of markets-- and the markets themselves--in order to serve the public interest? Is the Internet a natural monopoly or should "we" encourage more competition among different "Internets," different DNS systems? What is the dynamic of such competition and who will this competition benefit?

Thus, it is important to ask, what is the role of "economic theory" in the discussion about Internet development and governance? To reiterate, there is no "economic theory" in the singular. There are different paradigms in economics and different schools of thought inside each paradigm, As mentioned previously, there are "main-stream" neo-classical, evolutionary, post-Keynesian, Marxian, and radical institutionalist theories. But it is the neo-classical theory that is most important for this discussion, including its unique theoretical foundations. It is static, ahistorical, and has a special theory of human rationality. This is the fundamental reason why "economics" and "economists" are in perpetual conflict with the other social sciences, if they have not succeeded in imposing the Gary Becker world view on the topic (crime, suicide, marriage). The fact that one paradigm, the neo-classical theory, often poses as the "economic theory," is in itself a phenomenon that needs critical analysis.

Since neo-classical theory is so extremely dominant—that is, it has a profound influence on policy formulation including Internet governance--we need to understand it to develop a theoretical and empirical critique. Most people, including most economists, do not realize the extreme static nature of this theory. They think that it is the result of a dynamic process where prices change, firms compete, and then an equilibrium is reached. This is not the case. When there is "asymmetric information," there is no reason why the government or the research community should not know better than "markets." The internet is, of course, a prime example of such "asymmetric information." By habit, neo-classical theory takes the "initial endowments," that is the distribution of wealth, as a given. "We study efficiency, politicians handle distribution," is an apt description. But this is only possible in a completely static framework. At the same time, it is important for the self-image of "objectivity" and "rigorousness" that economists often use as a contrast to other social science disciplines.

The economic tension dates from the privatization of the internet pushed by the Clinton-Gore administration. In July 1997, Clinton directed the Secretary of Commerce to privatize the Domain Name System. The Federal

Regulation became known as the "Green Paper," complete with its implicit assumption that there should be democratic and representative control over the Internet. The goal was to prevent control by a single government or a private institution. Thus, the internet was shaped by two social groups, the researchers who created it and the initial enthusiastic and competent users. Both groups are fortunately still with us. As a result, the question of "by whom" the internet was created cannot be seen in isolation from "for whom" it was created and "for what purpose."

Other international governing bodies, for example the UN, the ITU, and the ICANN, all have their own "imperfections." None are completely representative of their constituents. The basic solution to this characteristic is to strengthen the internet-based discussion, thus consciously empowering the participants who are currently in structurally unfavorable positions. In these cases, neither "markets" nor "bureaucracy" represent the solution.

In summary, of the several and diverse economic theories, the neo-classical is clearly the most ideological of them. With its weak scientific foundation, there is need for very strong policy in the form of normative conclusions. Clearly, markets work, but they must be made to work for the purposes of serving humankind. Thus, a dynamic and realistic understanding of markets is crucial. After all, the fundamental law of markets is that competition creates monopoly; only innovation counteracts that tendency. One must grasp the fundamental contradiction within a democratic system featuring market economic structures. That is:

One man = One vote

versus

One dollar = One vote

Only truly democratic systems can address this contradiction to ensure the equitable development of society, including the internet. Thus, fundamental criterion for a real and balanced economic theory is that it is democratic. That is, society is paramount in the theoretical framework and markets occupy a secondary role.

4.6　Notes

1 Authors in order of the section they contributed. The chapter was compiled and edited by Ronda Hauben.
2 This paper was presented by Ronda Hauben.
3 This paper was presented by Jay Hauben.
4 JCR Licklider, Man-Computer Symbiosis, 1960
5 J.C.R. Licklider and Robert Taylor, The Computer as a Communication Device, 1968
6 This paper was presented by Werner Zorn.
7 This paper was presented by Kilnam Chon.
8 This paper was presented by Anders Ekeland.

5. ICT AND DEVELOPMENT

Dipak Khakhar, *IFIP[1]*
Bernard Cornu, *Universitee de Formation de Maitres*
Jan Wibe, *PLU-NTNU*
Paolo Brunello, *WITAR*

5.1 The IFIP World Information Technology Forum (WITFOR) process: From Vilnius (2003) to Gaborona (2005) and Addis Ababa (2007)[2]

The WITFOR process

In World Summits on Information Society in Geneva (WSIS 2003) as well as in Tunesia (WSIS-2005), roles of Information and Communication Technologies (ICTs) for and in Developing Countries played an important role. This had been argued since the 1990s but only the United Nations' Millennium Plan forced economists, politicians and the public to analyse the situation and problems of many regions in "the South" more careful.

In the International Federation for Information Processing (IFIP), problems and opportunities of ICTs for Developing Countries have been discussed since the 1980s. Several Technical Committees (esp. those addressing Education, Networking and Social Implications of IT) have devoted much work and many conferences, many of which in Southern regions, to related themes. Moreover, a special committee (Developing Countries Support Committee) assisted experts and students from related regions to attend events on advanced technologies and methods in Northern regions.

Based on this experience, IFIP developed (in mid 1990s) a concept of a conference series in which experts from (technically) developed countries should discuss how to adapt ICTs to the needs of DCs, and how to apply such ICTs in special projects to demonstrate their opportunities and to shape them to avoid or overcome potential deficiencies. These conference are planned in close cooperation with a national government, UN organisations such as ITU, FAO, UNESCO, World Bank and others, with the active support of experts both from ICT and application areas – such as medicine, agriculture, education, law etc.

The first event of this kind was organised by the government of Lithuania together with IFIP,

in September 2003 in Vilnius. The result of WITFOR 2003 – the Vilnius Protocol - was presented both to UNESCO General Conference 2003 (October 2003, Paris) and to the World Summit on Information Society 2003 (Geneva, November 2003) by the then Ambassador of Lithuania, HE Adamkus (now president of Lithuania). This very successful event was followed by the 2nd WITFOR conference, held in August 2005 in Gaborone, Botswana. The result of WITFOR 2005 – the Gaborone Protocol – was presented to WSIS-2005 by the government of Botswana.

As this report is written, the 3rd WITFOR is being prepared to be held in the UN Center in Addis Ababa, Ethiopia, in August 2007, under the guidance of the government of Ethiopia and IFIP, and again with strong support of different UN organisations, esp. including UNESCO, ITU and World Bank.

Results from WITFOR 2005 in Gaborone:

The World Information Technology Forum (WITFOR), which is an initiative of the International Federation of Information Processing and which was launched in Lithuania in 2003, is developing into an instrument to take WSIS a step forward, i.e. from policy to action. Thus, WITFOR 2005, which was held in Gaborone Botswana, was designed to help developing countries overcome financial and skills obstacles through the use of innovative practices, partnerships and shared resources in the use of ICT.

The outcome of WITFOR 2005 is "Gaborone Declaration" and, attached to it, "Proposed Projects and Actions". Refer to enclosure and also to the WITFOR 2005 website, www.witfor.org . The projects listed are best practice case studies from around the world, as well as new ones, which countries can copy and adapt to their needs.

Following WITFOR 2005 in Gaborone, the Gaborone Declaration was presented at the 33 General Conference of UNESCO in Paris in October 2005 and the Gaborone Declaration was unanimously adopted by the Conference.

The theme for WITFOR 2005 was "ICT for Accelerated Development", and the specific objectives were:

- to find ways of utilising ICT for accelerated development in line with the UN Millennium Development Goals and the WSIS Plan of Action;

- to pay special attention to the needs of developing countries and to assist them in accelerating development through the applications of ICT;

Some 800 delegates, representing 66 countries and all continents of the world met in Gaborone Botswana from 1 August to 2 September 2005 to address the above theme and objectives under eight separate sub-themes or Commissions. These were:

- Building the Infrastructure
- Economic Opportunity
- Empowerment and Participation
- Health
- Education
- Environment
- Agriculture
- Social, Ethical and Legal Aspects

Each Commission, which were chaired by a team of international experts, were tasked to present a best practice case study from anywhere in the world, propose a project that can be implemented as a partnership projects between countries (N-S or S-S), ideally with a research component, and with the potential to bridge the digital divide.

The Forum was opened by His Excellency the President of Botswana and the participants included the Prime Minister of Namibia, about 20 Ministers and another 10 VIPs. Other delegates were senior government officials, CEO s from the Private Sector, academics and some NGOs. The participation was greatly enhanced through the financial support from the EU-African/Carebean/Pacific Group, which offered support for one delegate from each ACP country, SPIDER (Sweden), UNESCO, and the European Commission. Presentations were of high professional quality, the case-studies attracted much interest, and the Gaborone Declaration was adopted. The Commission co-chairs all delivered their assignments as expected and all to a very high professional standard. Although there as no formal evaluation of the Forum, all verbal reports indicate that delegates were very happy with the delivery of the sessions and the outcome.

The project proposals emanating from WITFOR are presented as an annex to the Gaborone Declaration as Proposed Projects and Actions. Some projects were already launched at WITFOR. For example, a SADC Education project that will provide a virtual resource centre for teachers, and a Europe-SADC Health project that aims to develop a health information system using open-source software. The European Commission's 6th Framework Programme's Information Society Technologies (IST) program has already provided seed funding for the health project, referred to as the BEANISH project (Building Europe Africa collaborative Network for applying IST in the Health Care Sector), to be implemented as a partnership project between two European countries and six African countries.

The Forum successes included adequate funding, the wide range and level of participants, the involvement of the private sector and NGOs, the private-public sector partnership, the sharing of best-practice socio-economic ICT projects from around the world, the initiation of new projects, and the adoption of the Gaborone Declaration. The Forum was also well publicised and many could watch the proceedings from their homes. The Forum was broadcasted throughout Sub-Saharan Africa by satellite television and throughout the world through web casting. High-profile sponsors were able to exhibit and showcase state-of-the-art technology. These included large ICT multinationals as well as the European Commission, UNESCO and many others. The local community, in particular the local telecommunications regulator and telecommunications providers, including many other local ICT private sector companies, also took a very active part in WITFOR, both as organisers or sponsors.

The WITFOR event and all documentation can be found on the website, www.witfor.org. The plan is that the ideas for projects should grow and that the website develops into a valuable resource for developing countries around the world. WITFOR 2007, which will he held in Ethiopia, will be an opportunity to take stock of successes.

5.2   The Stellenbosch Declaration: ICT In Education: Make It Work[3]

The participants of the IFIP 8th WCCE (World Conference on Computers in Education), held in Stellenbosch, South Africa, July 2005, address to all stakeholders in ICT in Education: teachers, practitioners, researchers, academics, managers, decision-makers and policy-makers, the "Stellenbosch Declaration", in order to improve the integration of ICT in Education as a resource for better teaching and learning and as a preparation of citizens for the Knowledge Society.

This Declaration has been produced from the ideas provided by speakers and participants in the WCCE 2005. It will be widely disseminated all around the World, and particularly in the next international major events, such as the WSIS (World Summit on the Information Society), Tunis, November 2005. All IFIP members are invited to contribute in disseminating this important contribution of IFIP to the development of ICT in Education.

Abstract of the Declaration[4]

As educators, we want not only an Information Society, but a Knowledge Society, enabling all children and all people to access Knowledge and to benefit from being educated. Education is a key issue in the Knowledge Society, and Educators have a major mission. Particularly, it is the responsibility of all educators and decision-makers around the world to help developing countries take part in the developments of ICT in Education.

Six major areas will shape a beneficial use of ICT in Education:

Digital Solidarity
In the field of Education, ICT should help develop "Digital Solidarity". This requires strong and joint actions of all stakeholders to guarantee the right of participation in the digital society for all students in the world. We recommend a Digital Solidarity Action, that will define as the most important aim for the next five years, that every child in the world has access to a digital information and communication infrastructure.

Learners And Lifelong Learning
In the Knowledge Society, every learner is a lifelong learner. The content and the methods of initial education must take into account preparation for lifelong learning. ICT is a key tool for developing lifelong learning. The development of lifelong learning needs an integration of education into the real world - ICT should be used for this purpose. Lifelong learning must be encouraged in all countries, as a tool for reducing the Digital Divide.

Decision-Making Strategies
In order to help decision-makers and to make decisions meet the real needs, bridging research, practice, experimentation, innovation with decision-making is essential. Decision-makers should make better use of the experience of Practitioners and the findings of Researchers. In turn, Practitioners and Researchers should make their findings and results more visible and usable for the Decision-makers. Educators and researchers should help in elaborating a vision and making it explicit.

Networking
The Knowledge Society is networked. Networks in Education offer many ways to access knowledge, offer many possibilities for networking people and developing collaborative work and enhancing the "collective intelligence". There is a need to develop networks and to involve all countries, particularly developing countries, in the education networks. Help

in making real this sentence of an African child: "I am a child of Africa and a citizen of the world".

Research

The development of ICT-based education and training processes is a growing reality. There is therefore a need to continue research work on the development of these technologies and their applications. A certain realignment of research priorities is necessary: Bridging the gap between technology and pedagogy; development of solid theoretical frameworks; development of an understanding of the use and the effects of ICT in Education; finding an appropriate balance between fundamental, applied, and development research as well as between public research and research made by the private sector. The output of research should be made widely available, as open source, for improving practice, decision-making, and resources development.

Teachers

Being a teacher in the Knowledge Society requires new specific competencies: a teacher has to deal with new knowledge, new ways for accessing knowledge; with a networked world and with new types of co-operation and collaboration; with a society in which knowledge plays a crucial role; with lifelong learning. Teachers are the key agents in the education system. It is our common responsibility to help all countries to train and recruit teachers, and to involve all teachers in international networks. ICT changes teaching and learning, but technology is not the main issue. "Technology matters, but good teachers and good teaching, matter more".

5.3   The Burundi: Sewing the Digital Divide through Education[5]

What happens when you put 5 Italian teachers videoconferencing with 5 Burundian colleagues for the first time? Well, you might observe a slight excitement on both sides, a genuine emotion face to this "miracle" of seeing each other and talking while being 6000km faraway from each other. It might occur that all the technical worries about video and audio quality will be swept away by the substantial difficulty of using English as a common language. It might also happen that breaking this intercontinental barrier to reach a real person on the other side will light up the motivation to learn English better. For sure, nobody is left untouched and you can feel some "human energy" flowing back and forth. This is what happened on October the 11th 2005, between 2 technical high schools: the Istituto Tecnico Alessandro Rossi (ITAR) in Vicenza, in northern Italy and the Lycée Technique Alessandro Rossi (LTAR) in Ngozi, in northern Burundi.

WITAR (World Istituto Tecnico Alessandro Rossi – www.witar.org) is an Italian non-profit association born within the ITAR alumni association. The ITAR is the oldest Italian technical institute, founded in 1878 by Alessandro Rossi, an illuminated textile entrepreneur. In this institute 5 generations of technicians have been formed and trained, thus significantly contributing to the industrial development of the Venetian region. This industrial model, constituted by a multitude of small, reactive and highly performing companies, led the Veneto from absolute poverty in the 50s to be one of the wealthiest regions in Europe.

WITAR action is based on the belief that promoting that technical culture and craftsmanship in the developing countries might be an effective way to fight poverty and improve life quality in those countries.

As its first project, WITAR decided to support a then nameless Burundian technical institute, now renown nationwide as Lycée Technique Alessandro Rossi de Ngozi (www.ltarngozi.org). From 2003 through 2005 WITAR raised and invested about 300.000US$ in this project, mainly coming from private institutions or companies led by ITAR alumni.

The most innovative component of this project is the e-learning program that WITAR started in early 2005. This has been made possible by a VSAT antenna which provides the Burundian school with a broadband satellite connection, both donated by Eutelsat. Unlimited access to the Internet means access to the vast variety of online training resources and enables the people in the two schools to communicate and collaborate together.

The Burundi Project e-learning program

This program has 2 main goals:
➢ To allow an online cultural exchange between teachers and students of the 2 schools.
➢ To support teaching taking advantage of the Internet.

To attain the first goal we built 5 couples of teachers, one Italian and on Burundian, teaching the same technical subject:
- mechanics,
- electronics,
- electrotechnics,
- informatics.

A couple of English teachers were also involved in order to support communication amongst the other couple, since English has been chose as the common language. In fact both Burundians and Italians study English as their main foreign language, and English is undoubtedly The worldwide language for everything technical.

These are the couples who were finally videoconferencing, after exchanging a few preliminary emails.

The underlying idea is to first enable the teachers to familiarize with this new way of collaborating so that thereafter students could be involved in the shared online activities. In fact, 4 homologous classes were chosen on both sides creating 4 "twin pairs".

This first ice-breaking phase turned out to be quite long, since English mastery was pretty poor on both sides and the use of email not that familiar (typing skills are still to be developed). In the beginning the correspondents were simply asked to introduce themselves, so that a personal relationship could be established before focusing on school issues.

This correspondence is not just an ice-breaking activity, but serves a medium and a long term objectives. On the medium term we believe that a growing knowledge of "The Other" inevitably "drips" onto the closest entourage, increasing their awareness of the different life conditions "on the other side". On the long run, we hope that some correspondences will survive beyond the time bonds of this specific project and become real strong friendships, so that new autonomous partnerships between the two territories will develop.

The second main goal of this project – supporting teaching – has been conceived on three levels:

1. Methodological training on online searching:
    - developing effective search strategies,
    - browsers and search engines advanced use,
    - web forum participation,
    - exploiting learning objects repositories.
2. French online courses availability and participation:
    - Virtual universities (courses, video-lessons, web casting, pod casting)
    - Self-teaching websites (tutorial and manual repositories)
3. Videoconferencing and online collaboration on the web, through a shared web space:
    - using Moodle[6] as Learning Management System,
    - using Wiki to write documents collaboratively,
    - using web-based groupware to coordinate the work,
    - managing mailing lists,
    - collaborative conception and design of LTAR's website, trough the use of a Content Management System.

With regards to this last level, we are experimenting Moodle as a support for both traditional teaching and distance learning.

Besides e-learning, WITAR sends regularly some Italian volunteers as trainers for specific intensive courses (i.e. computer maintenance, soldering, etc.) which might last up to a month.

How is it going?

The designing phase of the project within the two schools (choosing teachers and classes, explaining the underlying logic) and the technical setup (equipping the computer lab, installing the VSAT antenna, testing videoconference software) required one and a half school years (fall 2004 until spring 2006).

These first months are the most difficult: on both sides the teachers must make a remarkable effort in order to write in English and use the PC. Plus, they have to find some time for it outside their regular working hours, on a voluntary basis. Undoubtedly we encounter some resistance to explore new ways of teaching. On the Burundian side, frequent black outs are a major hurdle to overcome to ensure coordination. Surprisingly enough, on the Italian side the policy on the access to the Internet by ITAR's students was much more restrictive than on the Burundian school, due to the stricter security rules on local network use.

In order to prevent creeping into a prejudicial superiority complex on the Italian side and a reciprocal inferiority complex on the Burundian side, we decided to focus the first communication activities between students on cross-cutting skills, such as problem solving, internet searching mastery, creativity, which are less likely to reveal a knowledge gap that certainly exists on the technical subjects.

In the following phase, once the groups will feel at ease with both the communication and the technical infrastructure, teachers will step up designing shared activities more directly focused on school subjects, based on the "intersection" between Italian and Burundian education plans.

Meanwhile some ITAR's professors spontaneously prepared a first experimental video-lesson (on metal mechanical properties) that has been made possible by the sophisticated heavy machinery owned only by the Italian school. This video has been sent and shown to the Burundian teacher first and then to his students. Right after both the professor and the students had the chance to ask some questions to the author of the video-lesson via videoconference.

"Be a lively hub on the Net!": this is, at its core, our encouragement to the Burundians and the Italians as well, meaning that no matter where you are, being on the Internet is being part of a network of networks, connecting

people who share similar problems and solutions. Attaining this awareness and knowing how to take advantage of it can be an effective way to switch from self-helplessness to emancipation.

5.4 Notes

1 Authors in order of the section they contributed. The chapter was compiled and edited by Olson.
2 This section was contributed by Prof. Dipak Khakhar, Department for Informatics, University of Lund, Sweden, dipak.khakhar@ics.lu.se
3 This section was written by Prof. Bernard Cornu, Université de Formation de Maitres Grenoble, France, and Chairman of the Declaration Committee: bernard.cornu@inrp.fr; and Prof. Jan Wibe, PLU-NTNU Trondheim, Norway, and IFIP TC3 Chairman: jan.wibe@plu.ntnu.no.
4 The full text is available on the IFIP website and includes recommendations and suggestion for possible actions.
5 Paolo Brunello, WITAR representative in Burundi, head of the e-learning program: paolo.brunello@witar.org
6 http://www.ltarngozi.org/moodle/

6. ROLES OF ICT IN THE INFORMATION SOCIETY

Dmitris Gritzalis, *Athens University of Economics and Business*[1]
Klaus Brunnstein, *University of Hamburg*
Jacques Berleur, *Facultés Universitaires Notre-Dame de la Paix, Namur*

6.1 Information Society and the Research on ICT Security in the Developing World[2]

The strategy of the European Union is to establish Europe as "the largets knowledge base economy" by 2010 (Lisbon Strategy). This is supported by several programs, esp. also addressing developments of Information and Communication Technologies with some emphasis on security.

About the developments of "security"

In the 1960s, in the phase of "Primitive Computing", security was not of major interest. With the development of "Mainframe Computing" in the 1970s, began to be important though for only very few areas and for few users. In the 1980s, with the advent of "Personal Computing", with basically insecure operating systems, security was regarded as "add-on" service and function. Only in the 1990s, with the advent of "Networked Computing", "built-in security" became an important requirement. Presently, in the 2000s with its "Ubiquitous Computing" concept, security becomes a primary concern, in the sense as "security-to-start-with".

Development for Wireless Computing

Wireless Computing is the essential technology to support global access for business and individual users:

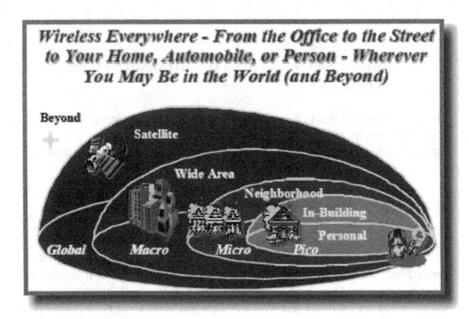

Figure 5: Wireless Computing

Security requirements for wireless computing developed in steps, from initially "poor security" to presently rather "robust" systems:

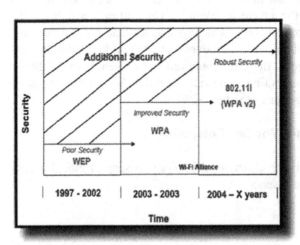

Figure 6: Subsequent security protocols

Relationship of consumption and production:

In the development of global, ICT supported economy, several trends can be observed:
1) Concerning consumption:
   - Increasing inequality between countries
   - Polarization
   - Complex evolution of poverty
2) Concerning production:
   - Growing individualization of labor
   - Over-exploitation of resources
   - Social exclusion
   - Perverse integration

Survey: Protection of Critical Infrastructures:

With the integration of ICTs into business and enterprises (as well as governments and relations to individuals), essential infrastructures such as telecommunication, energy production and distribution, transport of critical goods and special monitoring systems become critically dependent upon the availability and safe working of embedded ICTs. Several projects in various regions address related problems and solutions (see Table 1).

	Initiatives	Regulations	Organisations	PPP
Canada	Strategic Infrastr.Init. (SII), National CIP Program (NCIPP)	Emergencies Prepared Act, Emergencies Act	Office of CIP and Emerg. Prep (OCIPEP), National CIO Subcom. on Info. Prot. (NCSIP)	Information Sharing and Analysis Centres
U.S.A.	Presid. Comm. on CIP (PCCIP) National Security	CFAA, PATRIOT	Dept. of National Security	Info. Shar. and Analysis Centre (ISAC), Nat. CyberSec. All. (NCSA)
Australia	Interdept Comm.. on Protect. of the NII (IDC), E-Sec. National Agenda	Electronic Trans. Act 1999, Cybercrime Bill 2001	E-Sec. Coord. Grp (ESCG), CIP Group (CIPG), NOIE; ASIO	Business-Government Task Force on Critical Infrastructure
Sweden	Commission on Vulnerability and Security	Govemm.Bills 2001 (Society's Sec. and Prepar.; Continued Renew. of Total Defense	Swedish Emergency Mgmt Ag.(SEMA);	Private Sector Partnership Advisory Council

Table 1: some infrastructural projects with key characteristics

To conclude this section, we summarize:
  ➢ ICT must support the integration of social development and economic growth for all, with a fair focus on the non favored countries.
  ➢ ICT security research results should support civic disobedience movements, in order to fight authoritarian regimes.
  ➢ ICT security research results must be also utilized for the benefit of the citizens, against the interests of authoritarian regimes.

6.2 Requirements for Security in the Information and Knowledge Society[3]

Introduction: From Industrial to Information Societies

In the history of mankind, several technologies have contributed to change economic and individual conditions and perspectives. While most technical inventions – such as horse-driven cars, windmills and ships – developed rather slowly concerning technology as well as regarding their impact on society, James Watt´s invention (1761) of the vapor-pressure driven "machine" changed economic conditions and in their wake the world order at significantly higher pace than any technology before. In their first – stationary – form, production of industrial goods was operated by heavy machines with relatively small power (though large compared to human "manufacturing") but it was the start to essentially change the production of related goods. This change gained more speed and had more effects when Watt´s machines became sufficiently light and more powerful as to drive wagons on iron rails ("locomotion") to support faster transport of material resources to the fabrication sites and of products to consumers. Both the stationary and the mobile machine supported developments of the "Industrial Society" which gained more momentum with other technical inventions and developments such as electrical energy, telephony and the energy production from resources such as oil and uranium.

When comparing economies and state organisation, law, education and the role of individuals between the advent of Watt´s engine and 1960 when computers began to significantly spread into (then large) business and universities, then economic and societal changes are evident, at least in the so called (technically) "developed countries". And changes affected many areas: from hierarchical to democratic organizations, legal systems supporting individual rights, opportunities for education and medical support for all, etc. But over the span of about 200 years of industrial history (1762-1960), the speed of change was rather slow.

As basis of predicting future developments of ICTs, an analysis of similarities and differences in developments of industrial technologies may help. Concerning economic effects on political economies, economical theories (Schumpeter, Kondratieff et al) have observed cyclic behaviors in Industrial economies where new technologies stimulated economic growth. When concentrating on essential ("lead") technologies, industrial developments can be classified into essentially 4 cycles, each with about 40-50 years of duration (~45 years)

Faster than industrial technologies before, Information and Communication technologies (ICTs) continue to change economies and societies in ways affecting many aspects of human lives. "Traditional" communication – telephony using terrestrial cables, satellite and mobile cell-based communication – has enlarged human communication space even in its previously analogous, now also digitalized forms. Cables are still the major basis of digital networks but in some areas, flexible mobile communication is a major factor of information exchange in enterprises and daily life.

Concerning "lead technologies", it is interesting that phase 1 of the Information Economies depended upon initially large, heavy and difficult to handle "engines" (mainframes and their software) operated by specialists in "computer centers" – similar to factories in the Industrial economies - which developed into smaller and more powerful machines (Mini, Micro and Personal Computers). With their advent, transport of digital results between remote sites became important and networks developed both within enterprises (Intranets, Local Area Networks) and globally. The development of The Internet – designed and intended for scientific and military communication – became the major "lead" technology for the 2nd phase, similar to the development of railway transport in the 2nd phase of the Industrial Age.

In the Industrial age, railways enabled faster transport of resources and products as well as they also supported human transport on broad scales. Thus, railways changed economic and human relations as they enabled to progress from local to regional and finally global activities. In similar ways, Information and Communication technologies have started to rapidly and deeply affect many relations established within the Industrial societies.

From Local-Area Networks (LANs) to the Internet as a cooperation of many Wide-Area Networks (WANs), digital communication based on the uniform Internet communication Protocol (IP) is changing many relations (surveyed in figure 1) in and between enterprises (Business to Employee, B2E; Business to Business, B2B), but also between business and customers (business to customer, B2C) and governments (B2G). In the same sense, though with lower speed of development, individual relations as patient (Health to Patient, H2P), student (School to Student, S2S, Student to University, S2U) and citizen (Citizen to Government, C2G) use technical features of digital communication combined with storage and processing of information. Essential processes of the Information and Communication Societies will be based upon production of digital values such as Information Search (e.g. Data Mining, I-Search): Changes in education such as distant and e-Learning as well as in democratic processes, e.g. e-voting are underway.[4]

Admittedly, speed and impact of these developments vary grossly over the planet. As in the Industrial Age, several countries (better: regions within nations) advance technical developments rapidly and benefit from their advantages esp. including the transfer of related products and methods into other parts of the world. The uneven distribution of development between regions and nations also implies that e-relations develop rather differently over the planet. With respect to the opportunities of modern technologies, the "digital gap" hinders less "developed areas" to participate in this global process for the best of their people. On the other side, this "digital gap" protects less-developed areas to be affected by unwished side-effects and serious (e.g. security) problems of these technologies which affect enterprises, governments, organisations and individuals growingly with undesired effects.

Vulnerabilities of Information and Communication technologies

After short times of usage of these technologies, organisations and individuals have become so dependant upon proper functioning of these highly complex and hardly understandable systems that any deviation from "normal" behavior may have adversary if not damaging effects. It belongs to the daily experiences of "users" of Information and Communication Technologies that computerized systems fail rather often for reasons which a "normal user" can hardly analyze or understand. Failures range from unforeseen crashes, infections with malicious software esp. imported from Intranet or Internet communication to loss of data and programs and to a complete loss of any digital function and of connectivity.

A Risk Analysis of contemporary ICTs reveals a variety of reasons why such systems fail to work properly or to work at all. Following the "life cycle" of ICT concepts and products, risks can be graded into "vulnerability classes" which range from paradigms dominating their design – paradigmatic risks – over risks from deficiencies in the quality of production and products – implementation risks – to risks in ways how systems are used – usage risks. In addition, ICTs may be deliberately misused for criminal purpose.

Paradigmatic risks (Vulnerability Class 1):

Risks in this class are deeply inherent in assumptions made in the design process, and in the methods applied in the production (and implementation) of hardware, systems and application software. Assumptions range from the concept that complex problems can be solved by cutting them into parts ("modules") which can be produced independently and subsequently combined to yield systems of high complexity. Apart from problems of adequate "cutting" of the modules and of their adequate interoperation, contemporary systems have become so complex that even experts can hardly understand their effects. In order to achieve more functionality and interoperability, complex systems are combined with others to produce even higher grades of complexity. When systems from different origins with no common "interface" are combined, instruments are needed to "glue" such systems together; such "glueware" – "script" programming languages such as Java or Virtual BASIC – must be powerful to achieve many different adaptations which also provides easy means of exploitation even by less qualified "script kiddies". Indeed, the plentitude of malicious software (computer viruses and network worms, Trojan horses, trapdoors, backdoors, spyware etc) is essentially based on script languages used e.g. in office systems (Visual Basic for Applications etc). In summary, concepts and tools used in the design process very deeply influence both functions and risks of these digital technologies.

Risks from inadequate implementation (Vulnerability Class 2):

The production of digital technologies, esp. system and application software (and to a lesser degree also of hardware and their "drivers") has many weaknesses, the most evident of which are inadequate qualification of programmers, inadequate testing and production under heavy time pressure. Undesirable results of conceptual and programming faults materialize mostly at user sites where such software behaves in unpredictable manners including destruction of achieved work and broken connections. Numbers of experienced "computer emergencies" are rapidly growing, with sometimes millions of servers and even more local computers being affected by software weaknesses and "infected" by network "worms".

Software weaknesses are inherent in all kinds of contemporary software but the predominant effects materialize on systems of the most dominant system and software producers. Here, Microsoft leads both the markets of sold software and the world of software flaws as well as of malicious software living upon Microsoft's insecure software design and imperfect software implementation. The following table (1) lists programming faults, detected within last year. Although there are also many problems with non-MS systems (e.g. Linux), Microsoft systems dominate the scene of those incidents where in some cases many millions computer systems were affected.

Risks from usage (Vulnerability Class 3):

Not surprisingly, usage of unsafely designed and insecurely implemented software presents additional risks. After distributed software reaches user sites, installation and administration of system and application software when improperly performed may adversely affect performance and proper functioning of such software. Due to the complexity as well as due to inadequate documentation of these systems, users hardly understand effects of their attempts to "properly" use such systems. Consequently, users apply "trial and error" methods in learning to work with new features, rather than trying methodologically to understand which functions may have which effects, and which precautions should be taken to avoid unwished side-effects. This somewhat "explorative" way to use systems rather often leads to a risk-prone attitude with potentially hazardous effects, e.g. by clicking on unknown attachments without due care.

Software manufacturers often argue that failure of software is mainly caused by improper actions of users. But in many – if not most – cases, the human-computer interface (e.g. the display of functions and operations on the screen, or the handling of input devices such as mouse and keyboard) are inadequately designed and users are not properly supported by help functions (which when existing in many cases are so complex that users are further mislead). While users are primarily interested to do their work, one must admit that they rather often tend to forget about any precaution and even sometimes bypass security measures when thinking that their work performance is reduced.

Risks from deliberate misuse (Vulnerability Class 4):
Digital Information and Communication technologies provide many opportunities for deliberate misuse including criminal purposes. Though only few cases of criminal misuse have been reported and prosecuted, some of which were broadly covered in media although few of which produced major damage (such as the SoBig worm affecting some 100 millions of emails and several 10.000 enterprise servers), deliberate misuse for criminal purposes has not yet reached a significant impact on business and government use. Consequently, both legal provisions and the ability of prosecution agencies is less developed than in other areas of criminal law. But there is no doubt, that further development of ICTs will be associated with growing misuse, esp. as long as Class 1 and Class 2 vulnerabilities are so dominant in contemporary ICTs.

Impact of Vulnerabilities on Information and Knowledge Societies

As industrial technologies in the industrial age, Information and Communication Technologies will unavoidably affect many (though not all) parts of human organizations, economies, government and individual lives. As in the industrial society, these technologies are driven by supply-side concepts, and an analysis of any impact upon customers is (too) rarely in the scope of ICT developers. Consequently, such impact comes over the users – which have rarely any choice of avoiding ICT applications - without any possibility for them to understand or contain unwished effects.

Some of these changes have materialized in the first phase of the Information Society (based upon stationary operation), such as dependability from complex systems: as nobody can control whether results are correct in any detail, a consciousness of blind reliance among users has developed:

"this must be true because this was produced by a computer". This pattern of over-reliance and risk acceptance are even now, at the beginning of the 2nd phase (network-based operation) dominant. Comparable to those animals (lemmings) which blindly follow their forerunners, users tend to accept risks of PCs and The Internet as they feel unable to avoid them. In some sense, the more technologically a society advances, the more risks are blindly accepted. This seems to be a general pattern in contemporary societies as sociologists and philosophers observe and even label them as "risk societies" (Beck).

Besides general impact such as acceptance of risk, impact on individual attitude and behavior can also be observed. While email as tool of direct and fast communication supports personal and business needs very well, at the same time it enforces an adaptation in user behavior. At best, email enforces fast reaction and thus tends to dominate the time management of users: if you await fast reaction, you must also react quickly, independent whatever else you are doing. Replying to email resets any other priority. This becomes esp. critical when unwished email seems to require reaction, such as malicious software requesting sanitary actions or floods of unwished email (spamming).

In general, usage of time changes significantly with contemporary communication systems. Similar to workers in industrial factories, users in connected ICT systems behave as *slaves of engines* which they can hardly understand and control. It remains a major task of education in the Information Age to unable *users to master these engines rather than becoming controlled by them*.

Actions for Reducing Risks of Contemporary ICTs

In general, risks many be reduced in several ways:

- ➢ With *"risk avoidance"*, Information and Knowledge systems must be structured in such a way that a class of given risks cannot materialize. Example: this strategy implies that a system is designed and constructed so that it cannot fail.
- ➢ With *"risk reduction"*, methods and mechanisms must be realized which reduce unintended effects when some risk materializes, hopefully with lower probability. Example: this strategy implies that a system may fail but that there are curative mechanisms which reduce the damage when the system fails.
- ➢ With *"risk acceptance"*, nothing preventive or curative is done ("don't care" strategy). Example: although one knows about the vulnerability of a system, one simply hopes that nothing will happen and so one does nothing to prevent or reduce the risk.

While risk acceptance is what the vast majority of users practice, risk reduction is the strategy which many enterprises and governments presently apply: in order to reduce impacts of crashing systems and programs, "computer viruses" and "worms", hacker attacks, mass distribution of unwished email etc, special forms of security software (antivirus software, firewalls, intrusion detection systems etc) are deployed to reduce threats.

Risk acceptance may be regarded as acceptable strategy as long as large damage can be avoided. This strategy will be no longer acceptable when large damage cannot be avoided with minor protection methods. At the end of the 2nd cycle of the Information Society, interdependability will have reached a degree that many small failures combine to blackouts similar to (though more serious than) recent power outages in USA and Europe.

In order to avoid that networks become so strongly interconnected that any failure becomes "critical" for large parts of societies and economies, the only solution in the next decennium is to redesign basic technologies as to become inherently safe and secure. Regrettably, mankind will only learn – as in the Industrial Ages – by severe accidents how urgent the need for safe and secure system designs even today is.

6.3 Governance in the Information Society - Social and Ethical Aspects[5]

The *Declaration of Principles* of the first phase of the World Summit on the Information Society – WSIS (Geneva, December 2003) – insisted on the fact that "the governance of the Internet should constitute a core issue of the Information Society agenda", and having been unable to reach a consensus before the Summit of 2003, "the Secretary-General of the United Nations was asked to set up a working group on Internet governance, in an open and inclusive process that ensures a mechanism for the full and active participation of governments, the private sector and civil society from both developing and developed countries, involving relevant intergovernmental and international organizations and forums, to investigate and make proposals for action, as appropriate, on the governance of Internet by 2005." WSIS, 2003 The same *Declaration of Principles* asked for ethical insistence. The *Tunis Agenda for the Information Society* gave birth to the Internet Governance Forum (IGF), as a Forum for multi-stakeholder policy dialogue on Internet Governance WSIS, 2005.

We can no longer say today – if ever we could – that we lack regulation because notably the Internet escapes the territorial sovereignty. There is, without doubt, a calling into question of the traditional regulatory framework, but its exact impact remains to be seen. Some stress the prevalence of technical regulation and self-regulation over traditional public regulation. Our intention is to analyse these three sources of regulation – or of governance - and to propose a critical reading of the case for each one to be the only source of regulation of the Internet.

The question of Internet regulation and governance is without any doubt, technical, political and ethical.

This paper is just an extended abstract, as required by the editors. The writing will be sometimes schematic.

Governance

A proposal of a 'workable definition', requested by the WSIS WSIS, 2003, Plan of Action, §13, has been proposed by the Working Group on the Internet Governance: *"Internet governance is the development and application by Governments, the private sector and civil society, in their respective roles, of shared principles, norms, rules, decision-making procedures, and programmes that shape the evolution and use of the Internet."* WGIG, 2005, p. 4 That definition implies a 'multi-stakeholder' approach.

Technical Governance

Three organizations
It is more and more recognized that the technical regulation of the Internet is assured by 3 specific organisations: the Internet Engineering Task Force (IETF), the World Wide Web Consortium (W3C), and the Internet Corporation For Assigned Names and Numbers (ICANN) Simonelis, 2005. Nobody will contest that we are facing a 'nebula of actors'. Ricou, 2005 But in reality the real actors are a few: we cannot surely say that they favour a 'multi-stakeholder' approach!

The IETF is considered as 'the protocol engineering and development arm of the Internet'. It comprises 133 Working groups in 8 areas (+/- 2000 volunteers) and produces RfC (Requests for Comments, i.e. technical norms; since April 1969 until June 2006: 4562 RfC) (www.ietf.org). It has functioned until now along a consensus method under the auspices of 'benevolent dictators' (*The Economist*, June 10, 2000).

The W3C is an 'open' organisation without juridical status, hosted alternatively by INRIA (Fr) - on January 1st, 2003, it has been replaced by ERCIM, European Research Consortium for Informatics and Mathematics -, MIT (USA) or KEIO University (Japan). When saying 'open', we cannot forget that the annual full membership is US$ 50000! (www.w3c.org)

ICANN is an international private and non-profit organization created

(1998) by the USA Department of Commerce (www.icann.org). It has the responsibility for Internet Protocol (IP) address space allocation, protocol identifier assignment, generic (gTLD) and country code (ccTLD) Top-Level Domain name system management, and the root server system management functions. It also designates the organisations retaining control of registry (ex. ISOC for .org, VeriSign for .net...). Its structure is under discussion since the beginning. The Governments, for instance are just represented by an advisory Committee (GAC), and the 'At Large Committee' is not really functioning. There is a real concern about unilateralism by the US Government in its control of the DNS root and its supervision of ICANN. The perception is that ICANN's governance model does not properly balance the interests of developed and developing countries and suppliers and users, etc. IGP, 2005

Social and Ethical Issues of the Technical regulation

Among the main critical questions related to the technical governance, it is sure that many authors focus on the fact that the technical regulators encroach beyond their limits. The Internet Governance Project has shown that, among the issues that can be linked to Internet Governance, ICANN is covering all the issues in terms of policy development, rules, and recommendations, whilst the UN organizations are strictly limited to their domain of competence Mathiason et al, 2004, Table 1, p. 14 (Table 1).

Issues areas	Issue
Human rights	Privacy
	Content Regulation and Freedom of Expression
Intellectual Property Rights	Copyright
	Trademark
	Other IPR Issues
International Economic	Trade and eCommerce
Relations	Consumer Protection
	Competition Policy
	Taxation
Enforcement of Order	Network and IS Security
	Crime
	Authentication and Identity
	Cyber-terrorism
	Spam
Operational Policies for the	Global Resource Management
Internet	Interconnection

Table 2. Issue areas and issues in the Internet Governance Process

Let us mention schematically some of the social and ethical issues that we have collected along our different discussions and reflections:

- An Internet's root server system of 13 main routers in the world: 10 in the USA, 2 in Europe, 1 in Asia (ICANN coordination): is it acceptable?
- Which are the rules for attributing '.org' to Public Interest Registry (PIR) by ICANN to ISOC, and other TLD?
- Issues at stake with IPv6, for example. 3,4 1038 addresses (340 trillions of trillions of trillions of trillions): to do what? For which kind of society? To the advantage and benefit of whom? We must also assess the resistance: again migration costs from IPv4 to IPv6 (Computer, IEEE-CS, August 2001)
- Does Internet technical regulation reinforce 'public resource' / 'common good' aspects?
- There are many public policy concerns: competition, consumers' protection, IPR, privacy, freedom of access... In the hands of whom?
- DNS issues: they are identifiers for social identity, commerce...
- Respect of the countries diversity, regarding its own Internet (legislative) policy; GAC in ICANN is an 'advisory committee';
- Is it normal that private organizations take important decisions shaping the future of society and our ways of living without a clear mechanism of participation. This is a major issue in our modern world where democracy and ethics are merging.
- ICANN: how to resolve disputes of the vested interests as represented in the organization?
- Where are the developing countries in ICANN, in GAC? (see Digital Freedom Network: "ICANN through its actions and inactions has succeeded in sidelining the interests of developing countries", May 19, 2003, http://dfn.org)
- Where are developing countries, and also China, in this negotiation of standards?
- The possible architectures of Cyberspace are many, "the values that these architectures embed are different, and one type of difference is 'regulability' – a difference in the ability to control behavior within a particular cyberspace. Some architectures make behavior more prone to bit regulated; other architectures less so. These architectures are displacing architectures of liberty." Lessig, 2000
- Limits and validity of technical norms?
- How should the 4600 technical norms (RfC) decided by 2000 people and few organizations without recognized status become universal norms?

Self-regulation

Instruments for self-regulation

We have known in the '90s a proliferation of self-regulation instruments such as codes, guidelines, charters: 'The Ten Commandments of Computer Ethics' (Computer Ethics Institute, 1992), 'One planet, One Net: Principles for the Internet Era (CPSR, 1997), the 'User Guidelines and Netiquette' (Arlene H. Rinaldi, 1999), the 'Wartburg Online Magna Charta - Charta of Freedom for Information and Communication' (1997), the EuroISPA Codes/Guidelines of Conduct (EuroISPA, 1997-1999), the Internet Society of New Zealand, Internet 'Twelve Commandments' - Principles for use of the Internet (June 1999)... IFIP-SIG9.2.2 has analysed 40 such documents covering informatics and computing in general, as well as the Internet in particular. In this last domain, it has examined instruments of self-regulation for virtual communities, for service providers, for governmental and private actors, for specific sectors and services such as health, publishing, eCommerce, software publishers... IFIP-SIG9.2.2, 1999.

A short look at the Table of Contents of the Code of Practice of the ISPA-UK shows immediately the sensitive domains: general requirements (legality, decency, honesty, fair trading, customer contracts), promotion (scope, pricing information), data protection and privacy, Internet Watch Foundation, transfer of domain names, best practice, complaints procedures and sanctions (complaints, ISPA complaints procedures, refusal to adjudicate/referral to third party, sanctions), changes to the code ISPA-UK, 2002. More generally, the European Internet Service Providers Associations (ISPA) identify several domains to be self-regulated: concern about 'illegal material' (child pornography, racism propaganda,...), youth protection; commitment to cooperate with hotlines...; data protection, confidentiality and e-mail secrecy; need for decency: no violence, no hatred, no cruelty, no incitement to commit crimes; fair trading, acting decently with the customers, giving them clear information, including about pricing, etc. In other domains, such as in sectoral codes, the focus is more and more on contractual clauses, and on practices in accordance with professional standards, the best commercial practices... Deserving attention are the recommendations, in the domain of eCommerce, of the Global Business Dialogue on eCommerce GBDe, 2001-2005. There are other organizations pushing their own list of issues, according to their own interests! Most of the time, we drafted the conclusion that those instruments were eventually more self-protecting than self-regulating!

Social and Ethical Issues of self-regulation

Here again, let us mention some of the main social and ethical issues as they appear to a careful scrutiny:

- Self-regulation: what is its place in the normative order?
- Content: who decides what is to be considered as a policy or a social or ethical issue?
- How should private actors have a normative role for all?
- What is the role of the regulators to protect citizen and customers?
- The signs of real participation of the actors are rare: where is democracy?
- Is self-regulation making the economic actors more responsible?
- The titles and preambles of the self-regulating instruments should make explicit the status of those documents, and they should all be negotiated in a participatory manner.
- Those documents are more self-protecting than self-regulating, which is the opposite of giving the public the capacity of knowing and evaluating our behavior in society. Do they protect all the parties, or aren't they protecting only their authors ?

IFIP-SIG9.2.2 has suggested some minimum requirements, and 'Criteria and Procedures for Developing Codes of Ethics or of Conduct'IFIP-SIG9.2.2, 2004. It has made suggestions about the orientations regarding the title, questions to be examined in terms of content, the process in writing a code, and its evaluation and validation. It has recommended:

- More professionalism from professional bodies, i.e. clearer statements on issues in specialized fields where they develop their competence;
- To anticipate threats and dangers;
- To increase international exchange between professional societies and institutional groups, respecting the cultural, social, and legal differences;
- To reflect on the "shift from deontology for informaticians to a deontology of informatics under the control of the law" (Herbert Maisl);
- To question self-regulation in terms of improvement of commitment and responsibility of organizations. Is it not too minimalist?
- To increase self-regulation legitimacy by promoting large participation of all the concerned parties;
- To refrain from slogans such as: 'The least State possible is the best', 'Let us avoid a greater degree of statutory regulation', 'Let business self-regulate the Net': these slogans belong to the "knee-jerk antigovernment rhetoric of our past", and cannot persist without

damage for a democratic society Lessig, 2000. They are surely not favoring the cooperation between private and public.
- To clarify the relationship between deontology, self-regulation, the law, and ethics.

Legal Regulations

Main Objections, and Legislative Work

Usual objections to the law in Cyberspace are the territoriality of the law under the state sovereignty, - although we see progressively new 'juridical spaces' emerging: the European Union, the World Intellectual Property Organization (WIPO), the OECD, the WTO, ...; the more or less rigid character of the law, its low flexibility; the delay in its elaboration; the restricted expertise of the legal world; the rapid development of the technical evolution, etc. But there is an intense legislative work.

The European Regulatory Framework for electronic communications infrastructure and associated services count no less than 8 Directives, covering the following fields : Promoting Competition, Universal Service, Consumer Protection, Privacy Protection, Digital Broadcasting, Market Access, Interconnection and Interoperability, and Numbers, Spectrum & Rights of Way European Union, 2006.

The USA are not left behind with their Digital Millennium Copyright Act of 1998, the Children's Online Protection Act of 1998 (COPA, Commission on Online Child Protection), the Children's Online Privacy Protection Act of 1998 (COPPA), the USA-UE Safe Harbor Principles, the USA Patriot Act 2001, the new US Draft of Internet and Broadband Legislation Proposal (November 2005)...

We must also mention the Convention n° 185 on Cyber crime of the Council of Europe, signed on November 2001, and which includes the agreement of USA, Canada, Japan, South Africa. That Convention rules the following issues: illegal access, illegal interception, data interference, system interference, misuse of devices, computer-related forgery, computer-related fraud, offences related to child pornography, offences related to infringements of copyrights and related rights, and attempt and aiding or abetting.

Social & Ethical Issues in the Regulation of the Internet and of the Information Society

We may say that:
- The process of regulation is everywhere.
- At each level – technical, self-regulatory, and legal – it is difficult to really identify the actors. There is a nebula of actors. Who is finally

regulating? Lack of transparency. Predominance of vested interests – not always the same.

- The question 'Who is regulating?' is an ethical question and a democratic question.
- At a political level, there is a need to fix the agenda and the action plan (see WSIS, phase Geneva December 2003 and Tunis November 2005).
- At a research agenda level: we have to decide what is needed, e.g. to prepare the parties to the Internet Governance Forum decided by the WSIS in Tunis IGF, 2006.
- In a way, our analyses show that, at the self-regulation and legal levels, the trend is to have minimum regulation. But, there is no real democratic process and no real ethical concern.
- Or, in other words, ethics and democracy are 'under control'. But who is controlling? There are lobbies.

In our view, we must try to have criteria to distinguish issues at stake and issues with a more ethical content, such as "As soon as the interests of the majority are at stake and that people concerned risk to be made more fragile and vulnerable by self-regulation, the public authority must interfere and ensure that the 'horizon of universality,' in terms of access, control and participation, remains open." Berleur, 1999 Or following the traditional *Golden Rule,* "Treat others only in ways you are willing to be treated in the same situation" Gensler, 1994 This criterion is inspired by the 'Categorical Imperative' of Immanuel Kant: "I ought never to act except in such a way that I can also will my maxim should become a universal law."

Along that criterion we think that:

- The role of ethics is to keep open an horizon of universality;
- We have to avoid the appropriation by anybody; above all if there are vested interests which do not respect the balance through appropriate levels of democratic discussion.
- The regulation is multidimensional and must find its coherence and consistence. A 'multi-stakeholder' approach is an imperative.
- But today, it is still a 'battlefield'.

6.4   References

Berleur, 1999, Jacques Berleur, Self-Regulation and Democracy: Choice and Limits?, in: *User Identification & Privacy Protection, Applications in Public Administration & Electronic Commerce,* Simone Fischer-Hübner, Gerald Quirchmayr & Louise Yngström, Eds., Proceedings of the joint IFIP-WG8.5 and WG9.6 Working Conference, Stockholm 1999, DSV - Dept of Computer and Systems Sciences, Stockholm University/Royal

Institute of Technology - on behalf of IFIP, Report Series 99-007, ISBN 91-7153-909-3, pp. 1-19.

European Union, 2006, European Union, New Regulatory Framework for electronic communications infrastructure and associated services, http://europa.eu.int/information_society/policy/ecomm/index_en.htm

GBDe, 2001-2005, Global Business Dialogue on Electronic Commerce (GBDe), Recommendations: Tokyo 2001, Brussels 2002, New York 2003, Kuala Lumpur 2004 & Brussels 2005, http://www.gbde.org/recommendations.html The recommendations are about consumer confidence, Internet payments, convergence, cybersecurity, digital bridges, eGovernment, new business models, IPR, SPAM, taxation, and Trade/WTO.

Gensler, 1994, Harry J. Gensler, *Formal Ethics and the Golden Rule*, Loyola University Chicago, Fall 1994, *ad instar manuscr.*, pp. 101-125.)

IFIP-SIG9.2.2, 1999, *Ethics and the Governance of the Internet*, Jacques Berleur, Penny Duquenoy and Diane Whitehouse, Eds., IFIP Press, 1999, ISBN 3-901882-03-0 http://www.info.fundp.ac.be/~jbl/IFIP/Ethics_and_Internet_Governance.pdf

IFIP-SIG9.2.2, 2004, *Criteria and Procedures for Developing Codes of Ethics or of Conduct*, To Promote Discussion Inside the IFIP National Societies, Jacques Berleur, Penny Duquenoy, Jan Holvast, Matt Jones, Kai Kimppa, Richard Sizer, and Diane Whitehouse, Eds., IFIP Press, Laxenburg - Austria ISBN 3-901882-19-7, http://www.info.fundp.ac.be/~jbl/IFIP/Criteria_and_procedures.pdf

IGF, 2006, Internet Governance Forum, at http://www.intgovforum.org

IGP, 2005, The Internet Governance Project, What to do about ICANN ? A proposal for Structural Reform, April 5, 2005, http://www.internetgovernance.org/

ISPA-UK, 2002, Internet Service Providers Association – UK, Code of Practice, http://www.ispa.org.uk/

Klein, 2002, Hans Klein, ICANN and Internet Governance: Leveraging Technical Coordination to Realize Global Public Policy, *The Information Society – An International Journal* (Taylor and Francis, ed.), vol. 18, n°3, 2002, pp.193-207.

Klein, 2005, Hans Klein, ICANN Reform: Establishing the Rule of Law, (November 2005). *Internet Governance Project.* Paper IGP05-010. Available at http://internetgovernance.org/pdf/ICANN-Reform-Establishing-the-Rule-of-Law.pdf

Lessig, 2000, Lawrence Lessig, *Code and other laws of Cyberspace*, Basic Books, 2000

Mathiason et al, 2004, John Mathiason, Milton Mueller, Hans Klein, Marc Holitscher and Lee McKnight, Internet Governance: the State of Play, (September 9, 2004). *Internet Governance Project.* Paper IGP04-001. Available at http://internetgovernance.org/pdf/igsop-final.pdf

Ricou, 2005, Olivier Ricou, Internet, commerce et politique, Version 1.4 du 8 avril 2005, (see in particular the chapter 3 'Le gouvernement de l'Internet' and its Figure 3.2) http://www.ricou.eu.org/commerce-e/commerce-e/index.html

Simonelis, 2005, Alex Simonelis, Technical Regulations, A Concise Guide to the Major Internet Bodies, Dawson College, Montreal, in *Ubiquity, Views* - Issue 5 (February 16-22, 2005), http://www.acm.org/ubiquity/views/v6i5_simoneli.html

WSIS, 2003, *Declaration of Principles, Building the Information Society: a global challenge in the new Millennium,* Document WSIS-03/GENEVA/DOC/4-E, and *Plan of Action,* Document WSIS-03/GENEVA/DOC/5-E, http://www.itu.int/wsis/

WSIS, 2005, Second Phase of the WSIS (16-18 November 2005, Tunis), *Tunis Agenda for the Information Society,* WSIS-05/TUNIS/DOC/6 (rev. 1)

WGIG, 2005, Report of the Working Group on the Internet Governance, Château de Bossey, June 2005, http://www.wgig.org

6.5 Notes

1 Authors in order of the section they contributed. The chapter was compiled and edited by Brunnstein.

2 This section was written by Dimitris A. Gritzalis (dgrit@aueb.gr), Information Security and Critical Infrastructure Protection Research Group, Dept. of Informatics, Athens University of Economics & Business, Greece.

3 Klaus Brunnstein, Faculty for Informatics, University of Hamburg, Germany: brunnstein@informatik.uni-hamburg.de and http://agn-www.informatik.uni-hamburg.de .

4 Following contemporary implementation, such processes are labeled "e-" for "electronic", thus indicating the implementation using electromagnetic media and processes. As future technologies will likely use photonic and quantum technologies, it seems advisable to label such relations as "d-relations" thus addressing their digital nature.

5 This section was written by Jacques Berleur, member of IFIP-TC9 (Computers and Society) and IFIP-SIG9.2.2 (Ethics of Computing), Facultés Universitaires Notre-Dame de la Paix, Namur, Belgique: jberleur@info.fundp.ac.be , http://www.info.fundp.ac.be/~jbl .

7. INTERNATIONAL COLLABORATIONS THROUGH THE INTERNET

Gary M. Olson, *University of Michigan[1]*
Paul A. David, *Stanford University and the Oxford Internet Institute*
Johan Eksteen, *CSIR/Meraka*
Diane H. Sonnenwald, *Göteborg University and University College of Borås*
Paul F. Uhlir, *National Academies*
Shu-Fen Tseng, *Yuan Ze University*
Hsin-I Huang, *Institute of Information Science, Academia Sinica*

The past decade has seen remarkable advances in the availability of tools to support scientific collaboration at a distance. This is especially good news for international collaborations, where in the past constraints on collocation and travel have made such collaborations a major challenge. The emergence of advanced cyberinfrastructure and associated tools is changing the landscape for international collaborations. However, as the papers in this session show, there is much more than good engineering involved. There is a complex interplay of social, organizational, legal, and technical issues. Just because something is possible does not mean it will happen. Many forces involving incentives to work together through emerging technologies and policies that govern how such work might proceed serve as inhibitors to success. The papers in the session that led to this chapter explore a number of these issues.

The Science of Collaboratories (SOC) project at the University of Michigan seeks to understand these kinds of issues. The goal of the project is to review as many science collaboratories as we can find, and determine what factors differentiate success from failure. We define a collaboratory as: "... an organizational entity that spans distance, supports rich and recurring human interaction oriented to a common research area, and provides access to data sources, artefacts and tools required to accomplish research tasks."

We have identified more than 240 projects that satisfy at least parts of this definition. In looking at the patterns of success and failure of these projects, we find a series of factors that serve to differentiate these outcomes:

- The nature of the work. Work that is easily divisible is more readily carried out at a distance than work that is more integrated.
- Common ground. It's critical that the participants in long-distance collaboration have common concepts and vocabulary.

- Collaboration readiness. Participants in such projects must both be willing to collaborate (often such projects are put together for exogenous reasons, such as funding opportunities) and possess the requisite skills for collaboration.
- Management, planning, and decision making. Geographically distributed collaborations require special care be taken for how they are managed, how decisions are made.
- Technology readiness. Both the individuals involved and their supporting social and technical infrastructure must be capable of using effectively the many collaborative technologies that are now available.

These factors are discussed in much more detail elsewhere (e.g. Olson, 2004; Olson et al, 2004). The following sections in this chapter discuss related issues as well. They represent a broad perspective on the issues that help us think about the international dimensions of scientific collaboration.

7.1   Toward a Cyberinfrastructure for Enhanced Scientific Collaboration: the Institutional Foundations are the Really Hard Part[2]

A new generation of information and communication infrastructures, including advanced Internet computing and Grid technologies, promises to enable more direct and shared access to more widely distributed computing resources than was previously possible. Scientific and technological collaboration, consequently, is more and more coming to be seen as critically dependent upon effective access to, and sharing of digital research data, and of the information tools that facilitate data being structured for efficient storage, search, retrieval, display and higher level analysis. The February 2003 report of the Atkins Committee to the U.S. NSF Directorate of Computer and Information System Engineering urged that funding be provided for a major enhancement of computer and network technologies, thereby creating a cyberinfrastructure whose facilities would support and transform the conduct of scientific and engineering research. The articulation of this programmatic vision, now embraced by NSF, reflects a widely shared expectation that tackling the technical engineering problems associated with the advanced hardware and software systems of the cyberinfrastructure will lead to revolutionary payoffs by empowering individual researchers and increasing the scale, scope and flexibility of collective research enterprises. Animated by much the same vision, the e-Science Core Programme in the U.K. has been developing an array of open standards middleware platforms, intended to support Grid enabled science and engineering research – under the banner the e-Science is about 'global collaboration.'' .

But engineering breakthroughs alone will not be enough to achieve the outcomes envisaged for these undertakings. Success in realizing the potential of e-Science – and other global collaborative activities supported by the "cyberinfrastructure," if it is to be achieved, more likely will be the resultant of a nexus of interrelated social, legal and technical transformations. The socio-institutional elements of a new infrastructure supporting research collaborations – that is to say, its supposedly "softer" (non-engineeringl) parts -- are every bit as complicated as the hardware and computer software, and, indeed, may prove much harder to devise and implement. The roots of this latter class of challenges facing "e-Science" lie in the micro- and meso-level incentive structures created by the existing legal and administrative regimes. Although a number of these same conditions and circumstances appear to be equally significant obstacles to commercial provision of Grid services in inter-organizational contexts, the domain of publicly supported scientific collaboration will provide a more hospitable environment in which to experiment with a variety of new approaches to solving these problems.

Towards that end, several institutional "solution modalities" can be proposed that feature a modular contractual approach to the flexible design of research collaboration agreements in the public research sector. Appropriate mechanisms for the organization of e-science cannot simply be legislated or put in place by administrative fiat, even if the policy climate was more receptive to the notion that this is an important matter to which political leaders should attend. Similarly, the problems created by the international nature of collaborative e-Science cannot be left to be solved by the international harmonization of formal legal rules. Legislation and the harmonization of legal rules have a potentially stultifying effect on the development of new and more appropriate institutional mechanisms. When legislation is enacted and international conventions are agreed, they tend to have the effect of petrifying the norms regulating a given area of behavior. In any case, the international harmonization of legal rules is a slow and frustrating process; harmonization would be a particularly daunting task given the range of legal issues that might impact upon the conduct of collaborative on-line research. Further, the harmonization of legal norms is only even partially effective in assuring that disputes determined under the same norms will find the same result in different courts. To establish norms that can facilitate collaborative e-Science, we must therefore look elsewhere than to formal law reforms and legal harmonization.

The core of many of the difficulties arising in the contractual organization of scientific collaboration is that the actual work is to be done by individuals in laboratories, but the agreements that underpin collaborations are usually made by the institutions which employ them. It is appropriate that scientists should be relieved of the burdens of negotiating contract details. Yet, taking the contracting process out of their hands presents a number of dangers. One likely difficulty is that the process of setting the terms of inter-institutional collaborations might be affected by the conflicting interests of the university or other host institution. This problem often is very real and may be exacerbated by the structures for obtaining legal advice that operate in most universities: legal counsel have the responsibility to protect the institution from the hazards of entering into collaborations, "hazards" that include emerging from a collaborative undertaking with a visibly smaller share of the gains than other parties have enjoyed. Yet, the typical public research institution will be entering into agreements about matters (such privacy of personal data) on which their powers to assure delivery are highly uncertain, and which can expose them to considerable risks. Reasonable nervousness on the part of responsible administrators and their respective legal counsels consequently may adversely affect the traditional structure of the institutional relationships under which academics work. The effect of each party to an inter-organizational collaboration seeking to protect itself at the expense of the others tends to raise the costs of the entire undertaking. In the calculus of "due diligence" the lawyers are predisposed to protect the immediate and palpable interests of their client, the university, whereas the researchers are left, less comfortably, having to decide whether to argue for their own career interests or for the more transcendent and speculative benefits that society at large might derive from the proposed project. Additional problems arise from the fact that in a collaboration in which the participating institutions are contributing components that are complementary, there is an understandable temptation for each of the parties to try to extract as large a part of the anticipated fruits as they can. This is likely to result in reducing the efficiency of the project design, as well as in a protracted and costly bargaining process. Inter-institutional conflicts over research credits and intellectual property rights can only be become more difficult if the parties try to anticipate the consequences of the increasingly mobile pattern of employment among academic researchers in the sciences.

The challenge in designing appropriate legal arrangements for collaborative e-Science is, therefore, to construct agreements that are adequately clear and determinative without damaging the trust and informal norms essential to the day-to-day conduct of collaborative research within and among the institutions involved; and to provide processes for constructing those agreements that involve the scientists without unduly burdening them with negotiations over legal complexities. Some adverse consequences of the introduction of formal, contractual norms may not be avoidable, since these may displace the efforts that the parties might otherwise devote to resolving conflicts informally. But, the goal must be to avoid the worst outcomes. Acknowledging these realities, David and Spence (2003) recently have argued for a more "bottom up" approach to constructing appropriate institutional infrastructures for e-Science, one that calls for the creation of a coordinating and facilitating mechanism in the shape of a novel public agency. They envisage the establishment of a new independent body -- to be called the Advisory Board on Collaboration Agreements (ABCA). Its remit would be to guide, oversee and disseminate the work of producing, maintaining, evaluating and updating standard contractual clauses, those being the constituent elements from which formal agreements may be more readily fashioned by the parties undertaking particular 'Grid-enabled' collaborations in science and engineering research. This advisory body would, of necessity, play a leading role in enunciating a set of fundamental principles to guide the formulation of those contractual clauses, and thereby ensure that the effects of the agreements into which they are introduced will not be inconsistent with the intent underlying those principles.

In other words, what is proposed is the establishment of a new "public actor", an independent entity with on-going powers to initiate, co-ordinate and provide resources required to support and, above all, articulate principles for developing an array of model contractual clauses, each of which that would treat some specific problem (among the myriad legal issues that have been seen to arise from the formation of research collaborations). Included among these specific problems would be such questions as those concerning appropriate forms of licensing for middleware and higher level software applications; and terms of the private contracts that holders of copyrights might utilize in so-called "dual licensing" of GNU General Public License software in order to permit third party commercial exploitation of publicly funded software systems. Much of this detailed work could be entrusted to specialized task force-like "study committees" comprising individuals with diverse expertise: scientists and engineers familiar with the organization and conduct of collaborative projects, legal scholars and practitioners, social scientists with expertise regarding the workings of academic research institutions, and others with detailed knowledge of the policies and administrative rules of pertinent funding agencies in particular national jurisdictions.

7.2   Reasons, Reality and Recipes: a Developing Country Perspective[3]

There is a growing recognition of the positive correlation between growth of activities in science, research and development (R&D) and the developmental agenda of improving the quality of life and stimulating economic growth in the developing world. At the same time, however, there is a growing concern of the widening gap in scientific endeavor and ability to engage in these endeavors between the developed and developing world. Considering indicators of technology related achievements and its impact on society, such as Science and Technology Capacity Index (STCI) (Wagner et al., 2003), Technology Achievement Index (TAI) (Wagner et al., 2001), Technological Capabilities Index (ArCo Index) (Archibugi & Coco, 2004), this widening gap is not only illustrated clearly, but allow for analysis to find recipes to address this gap.

With less than 1% of global scientific output being ascribed to Sub-Saharan Africa and the fact that the number of researchers per 1000 of the workforce generally lower than two in developing countries compared to the four and higher in most developed countries, the potential for scientific collaboration to access the growing global body of knowledge and mitigate against the lack of own research capacity seems obvious.

The ability of scientific collaboration, enhanced in most cases, through the use of information and communication technologies (ICTs) to impact positively on challenges faced by the developing world cannot be overstated. Progress is being made and a number of examples where successful collaboration activities are ongoing exist and is growing. The lack of a greater number of success stories in this regard from a developing world experience indicates a number of barriers that might need to be addressed before the full impact of "e-collaboration" is realised. This paper identifies a few of these challenges and provides broad suggestions on the way forward given these constraints based on the rationale for and some experiences and trends in "e-collaboration" in science and technology from a South African and broader African perspective.

Large-scale scientific experiments and initiatives such the Large Hadron Collider experiment at CERN, the e-VLBI and Square Kilometer Array astronomy experiments and a number of e-science related experiments are often drives the development, used to motivate for and illustrate the benefit of ICT-enabled "e-collaboration". Even though supported, these often do not form the rationale for developing countries to get involved in e-collaboration activities. The recognition of the positive correlation between science, R&D

and development and the necessity to access the global knowledge pool to impact positively on the local challenges is becoming the major driver.

To benefit from the opportunities that e-collaboration promise, one needs to take the local context into consideration. Wagner et al (2001), for instance, point out that one needs to reach a certain level of scientific absorptive capacity before collaboration has positive effects on the scientific productivity of a nation. Besides the absorptive capacity a number of other considerations need to be noted in terms of developing world scientific systems and collaboration potential including:

- Lack of infrastructure (support, communication, research) often hampering activities;
- Scientific output is relatively low creating questions about the culture of scientific excellence;
- A lack of understanding and awareness on decision making level of the differences between research infrastructure and, for example, commodity internet connectivity;
- Cultural challenges e.g gender representivity; and
- Scientific activities often based largely on local need factors e.g. communicable diseases (HIV), with little external research interest that can lead to collaboration.

These same factors also provide a number of unique opportunities such as:

- Offering unique natural resources (for example Southern Oceans, Southern Skies) for researchers across the globe to do collaborative research on; and
- The need for developing countries to pro-actively manage brain drain and diaspora ("Suitcase science" often lead to "brain drain"), strengthening the need for collaboration.

A number of successful and active collaborations exist. These range from individual contacts between researchers through to virtual cooperation in the astronomy area (e.g. e-VLBI, South African Large Telescope, the High Energy Stereoscopic System).

These collaborations are assisted by the recent connection of South Africa the GéANT research network and establishment of the Centre for High Performance Computing in Cape Town. Several collaborative research efforts in the HIV/AIDS domain illustrate the effectiveness of e-collaboration in areas of critical importance in the developing world.

Key success measures to consider and quantify for initiatives
- Human Capital Development
- Absorptive Capacity Growth
- Infrastructure development
- Network growth
- Growth in research output
- Impact of research

In looking at the opportunities, the challenges and
analyzing the success and failures of existing activities, a few key areas that
need to be considered in e-collaboration for developing countries emerge:

- Context matters – consider culture, infrastructure and absorptive
  capacity;
- Reasons matter – link the e-collaboration activities to clear measures
  of success in existing and emerging strategies on institutional or
  national or even regional level.;
- One size does not fit all – design a holistic portfolio response to the
  various e-collaboration activities that fit into existing or emerging
  strategies and exploit current systems of support before
  contemplating new strategies or resources.
- Ensure that partnerships are actively pursued between all the actors
  involved (Government, Research and Technology Organisations and
  Academia)

e-Collaboration provides huge promise to address challenges within the
developing world. The success of e-collaboration activities is highly
dependent on a number of contextual issues such as absorptive capacity,
cultural differences and infrastructure capacity. Taking these into account,
through appropriate linkages to existing strategies and through appropriate
local partnerships between the relevant actors, the e-collaboration promises
can indeed be turned into positive impact in the developing world.

7.3 Scientific Collaboration across Diverse Institutions and Disciplines[4]

Scientific collaboration is human behavior that facilitates the sharing of
meaning and completion of tasks with respect to a mutually-shared scientific
goal. This human behavior takes place in different contexts, including
institutional and scientific contexts which can vary across different types of
institutions, geographic and economic regions, and disciplines. These
differences enrich the scientific process and introduce new challenges
throughout the collaboration process. By examining and illuminating these
challenges, we can develop strategies to enhance scientific collaboration (see
table 3).

Table 3. Factors that impact the scientific collaboration process

Stages of Scientific Collaboration			
Foundation	*Formulation*	*Sustainment*	*Conclusion*
Scientific goals	Research vision, goals & tasks	Emergent challenges	Definitions of success
Local, national & international politics	Leadership & organizational structure	Learning	Dissemination of results
Socio-economic considerations	Information & communications technology	Communication	
Resource accessibility	Intellectual property & other legal issues		
Social networks & personal factors			

Scientific collaboration typically consists of four stages: foundation, formulation, sustainment and conclusion (Sonnenwald, 2007). The foundation stage includes policies, relationships and knowledge that exist before a collaboration is formed. There are a number of factors in this stage that are required for scientific collaborations to be considered (and subsequently initiated) or that can prohibit collaborations from ever being considered and initiated. These factors are: scientific goals; local, national and international politics; socio-economic considerations; resource accessibility; and social networks and personal factors Sonnenwald (2007).

The characteristics of these factors vary across different types of institutions and disciplines. For example, not all scientists have the same type and quantity of resources available to them. In a study on collaboration between historical black universities (HBUs) and research intensive (RI) universities in the U.S. (Adessa & Sonnenwald, 2003), it was observed that faculty at the HBUs had three times the teaching load as their collaborators at RI universities, no postdoctoral fellows and few Ph.D. students to draw on when conducting research, and no research support services available to them. As one HBU scientist explained, 'They my colleagues at the RI university just don't know what it's like here.' These differences are typically not discussed and yet can have a large impact on collaborations.

During the formulation stage, scientists initiate and plan collaborative research projects. When collaborative research involves multiple scientists from different disciplinary backgrounds and institutions, additional planning and additional time for planning are required for success. Research suggests that: research vision, goals and tasks; leadership and organizational structure; use of information and communications technology (ICT); and intellectual property and other legal issues need to be considered in greater detail than in single investigator research. For example, when collaborating across different types of institutions and countries, it can be important to recognize that not all partners may have the same access to ICT. This may be influenced by local politics in addition to local resource allocations. Scientists from prestigious universities, working with local scientists, can often help influence local politics and resource allocations.

After a collaboration is formulated and work begins, each collaboration needs to be sustained over some period of time in order for the collaboration to achieve its goals. Even with the best foundation and formulation, numerous challenges can emerge during the sustainment stage. Challenges can be identified and addressed through an ongoing process of evaluation in which organizational structure and tasks, communication and learning are examined and evolve. When communication is infrequent or irregular in this stage, goals and tasks may become disconnected, and stronger partners may take over aspects of the project. As one scientist at an HBU explained: "My colleagues at the RI university decide they can do our part faster, so they do it without giving us a chance." In comparison, his colleague at the RI university reported: "They at the HBU are not tuned into our research focus." (Adessa & Sonnenwald, 2003).

In the conclusion stage, results from a collaboration ideally emerge. There can be different types of successful results and dissemination of results. For example, one result from a collaboration between a HBU and RI university was knowledge transfer regarding use of ICT to HBU students' family members. Dissemination of results is an important component of all scientific work. Reaching consensus regarding authorship inclusion and order may be challenging, and these difficulties increase as competition increases (Atkinson, et al, 1998). What constitutes a significant contribution meriting co-authorship versus inclusion in the acknowledgments section of a paper? Where and when should papers be published? When evaluating results, local tenure and promotion committees, as well as colleagues, may not take into account different values and expectations with respect to publication forums and authorship order.

Recognition of differences between institutions and disciplines, and alignment of these differences during the formulation and sustainment stages are linked to success (Adessa & Sonnenwald, 2003). Equal funding across institutions and disciplines is not necessarily the best solution. Rather equitable funding and allocation of resources that take into account differences and provide each scientist with resources, including time, necessary to contribute and meet goals in a realistic way are key.

7.4   Global Information Commons for Science Initiative[5]

Global digital networks have the potential to increase access to and use of data and information from publicly-funded research dramatically, but only if access to the information is unimpeded by artificially imposed economic, legal, and technological barriers. Open availability in the online environment creates an unobstructed, instantaneous, global, and potentially comprehensive database. It greatly enhances and facilitates: scientific inquiry, diversity of analysis and opinion, new types of research and methods of analysis, and prevents duplicative work and research inefficiencies generally. It eliminates the cost barriers on the transfer of information to researchers and students who are unable to afford high subscription prices, or the costs and delays of interlibrary loans. Overall, the different forms of open access online promote interdisciplinary and international research, particularly in integrating scientists in the developing world more into the global research system, and accelerate scientific progress and innovation by making diverse information resources much more easily available. Indeed, many new models of open availability of publicly-funded scientific information have already have been developed within the international research community, as summarized below. Examples of open data and information production activities include:

- Open-source software movement (e.g., Linux and thousands of other programs worldwide, some of which originated in academia);
- Distributed Grid computing (e.g., SETI@Home, LHC@home);
- Community-based open peer review (e.g., Journal of Atmospheric Chemistry and Physics);
- Collaborative research Web sites and portals (e.g., NASA Clickworkers, Wikipedia, Project Gutenberg).

The following are examples of open data and information dissemination and permanent retention:

- Open data centers and archives (e.g., GenBank, the Protein Data Bank, SNP Consortium, Digital Sky Survey);
- Federated open data networks (e.g., World Data Centers, Global Biodiversity Information Facility; NASA Distributed Active Archive Centers);
- Virtual observatories (e.g., the International Virtual Observatory for astronomy, Digital Earth);
- Open access journals (e.g., BioMed Central, Public Library of Science, + > 1800 scholarly journals);

- Open access hybrids, based primarily on a subscription model, but including a mix of restricted subscription-based and open author-pays articles (e.g., PNAS, Springer Open Choice)
- Delayed open availability, following some restrictive period that varies from one or more months to one or more years (e.g., PNAS or Science, which make their subscription based articles available after six months and one year, respectively);
- Open institutional repositories for that institution's scholarly works (e.g., the Indian Institute for Science, + > 400 globally);
- Open institutional repositories for publications in a specific subject area (e.g., PubMedCentral, the physics arXiv);
- Free university curricula online (e.g., the MIT OpenCourseWare); and
- Emerging discipline-based commons (e.g., the Conservation Commons).

The common elements of all these different types of initiatives are that the information is made openly and freely available digitally and online. In many cases, the material is either made available under reduced proprietary terms and conditions through permissive licenses (e.g., the GNU license for open source software, or Creative Commons licenses for open access journals or for some works in open repositories), or it is in the public domain. In other cases, such as delayed open availability by STM publishers to their journal articles, the works remain protected under full copyright, but are made freely and openly accessible.

These various examples now provide valid proofs of concept for all information types, in most disciplines, in many countries, and across all institutional categories—whether government agencies, universities, not-for-profit organizations, or even for-profit firms. Taken together, these activities are part of the emerging broader movement in support of both formal and informal peer production and dissemination of publicly funded scientific (and other) information in a globally distributed, volunteer, and open networked environment. They are based on principles that reflect the cooperative ethos that traditionally has imbued much of academic and government research agencies. Their norms and governance mechanisms may be characterized as those of "open science information commons" rather than of a market system based upon proprietary data and information.

There exists a solid economic and legal basis for the practical development of a "contractually constructed commons" approach to counteracting the deleterious effects of encroachments made upon the public domain by intellectual property rights. At the core of the new approach which the Global Information Commons for Science Initiative (GICSI) would encourage is the voluntary use of the rights held by intellectual property owners, allowing them to construct by means of licensing contracts those conditions of "common-use" that emulate the key features of the public domain which have proved so beneficial for collaborative research in all its forms. Thus, essential ownership rights can be preserved and utilized in a way that contributes to maximizing the social benefits and returns on the public's investments in research. Creating legal coalitions or "clubs" for the cooperative use of scientific data, information, materials and research tools that are not in the public domain, offers a practical, "bottom up" way to reduce if not completely remove the adverse effects that patent thickets, copyright royalty stacking, and similar impediments can have upon the conduct of fundamental, exploratory research programs. The resultant pooling of data and information for in a specific research domain is properly described as "creating an information common for science" -- inasmuch as a "common" is a collectively held and managed bundle of resources to which access by cooperating parties is rendered open (though perhaps limited as to extent or use) under minimal transactions cost conditions. Furthermore, and somewhat paradoxically, cooperative licensing arrangements of the kind envisaged by the Initiative will enjoy the full legal protections afforded the participants by the intellectual property regime itself. Common-use licensing to promote broad access and reuse of intellectual property rather than restricting it, is being widely used by free and open-source software development communities, and others applications of this legal strategy currently are being developed by the Science Commons (under the auspices of Creative Commons: http://science.creativecommons.org).

The Global Information Commons for Science Initiative is proposed by the ICSU family of data and information organizations, under the leadership of the Committee on Data for Science and Technology (CODATA), to study, promote, and help coordinate these many different "information commons" activities internationally. The GICSI is a multi-stakeholder initiative arising from the second phase of the World Summit on the Information Society in Tunis in November 2005. Within ICSU, the organizations that are participating in this Initiative in addition to CODATA are the International Council for Scientific and Technical Information (ICSTI), the International Network for the Availability of Scientific Publications (INASP), and the World Data Centers (WDC). Collaboration on this Initiative already has been established with the InterAcademy Panel on International Issues (IAP), the Academies of Science in Developing Countries (TWAS), the Organisation for Economic Co-operation and Development (OECD), the United Nations Economic, Scientific, and Cultural Organization (UNESCO), and the Science Commons (a subsidiary of the Creative Commons). The Initiative has the following goals:

(1) Improving understanding and increased awareness of the societal and economic benefits of easy access to and use of scientific data and information, particularly those resulting from publicly funded research activities;

(2) Promoting the broad adoption of successful methods and models for providing open availability on a sustainable basis and facilitating reuse of publicly-funded scientific data and information;

(3) Encouraging and coordinating the efforts of the many stakeholders in the world's diverse scientific community who are engaged in efforts to devise and implement effective means to achieve these objectives, with particular attention to developing countries.

All three goals will be promoted through the construction of an online "open access knowledge environment", as well as specifically targeted projects carried out within the Initiative and in collaboration with its participating stakeholders, which are expected to be expanded substantially. The Initiative will be developed more fully and is expected to be funded later in 2006.

7.5   Reexamining Academic-Industrial Collaboration: The Impacts of Information Communication Technologies on Knowledge Sharing and Innovation[6]

The widespread adoption of computer-mediated-communication (CMC) has facilitated the increase of team-based collaboration. As Koku and Wellman (2000) suggested, email has allowed spatially disperse, intellectually kindred scholars to communicate and collaborate. To more extent, CMC has the probability to enhance the social ties in the collaborative network and then stimulus the productivity (Walsh and Bayma, 1996; 2000). Interestingly, there are debates on the impact of email use in scholarly collaboration networks: do CMC connect a denser network (Coleman, 1988) or a looser network with many structural holes (Granovetter, 1973; Burt, 1992) and the debate on the relative advantages of strong tie versus weak tie.

Some argue that weak ties are most important for information exchange and for bridging the distinct social worlds and information spaces (Granovetter, 1973; Burt, 1992). Burt (2004) particularly pointed that people in the "bridge" position could be more possible to receive and transit the "good idea" which connotes more innovative or more professional information. Others suggest that although weak ties are helpful for information search for simple knowledge, it is the strong tie facilitates information search for complex knowledge (Murray and Poolman, 1982; Hensen, 1999). Instead of the dichotomy of effect, Uzzi (1996) found a curvilinear relation that firms were most successful if they had a mix network, consisting a few strong ties and many weak ties. Uzzi revealed that important information flow across strong ties, yet a network with too many strong ties becomes inbred. This discrepant discussion of strong ties and weak ties and the successful factors concerning in the collaboration project prompted our current study.

To begin with, we explored a government-lead, technical steering committee—the IPv6 research collaboration team, its collaborative pattern of research alliances and the role of ICTs plays in the collaboration. Two questions were asked: does the use of CMC enhance collaboration, transform team network structure, and thus facilitate academic productivity? Whether the bonding of dense network and strong tie enhances information exchanges and increase productivity, or it is structural hole and weak tie that bridges the network and enrich individual performance? Moreover, under what kinds of network structure and ties can the routine, professional, and

Regression Predicting Scientific Collaboration

Variables	Network Holes	Publications a
Age	.762**	-.145
Time of Computer use	.723**	-.098
Phone Contact	-.527*	-.089
Email Contact	.322△	.849**
F2F Contact	.184	.133
Network holes	-	.659
Routine information	-	.159
Professional information	-	.988*
Adj R square	.319	.507

$\triangle p<0.1$ *p<0.05, **p<.001
a. Amount of IPv6 related publications during 2004-2005.

Table 4. Regression analysis of computer use

private information be exchanged among team members? A web-based, ego-centric network survey is conducted among 42 IPv6 collaboration team members. The descriptive statistics and regression models are used to test the relationship of email usage, network structure, strength of ties, information sharing and academic productivity (see table 4). A citation analysis and Ucinet software is employed to delineate the network of co-author publication among the IPv6 team members.

Ninety-five percent of participants are male and most of them employed in the public university (74%). We observed that the use of CMC does not increase heterogeneous collaboration across institutions, members in each sub-project team are generally from the same university or research institute. The regression (see table 1) analyses probed that email and CMC facilitates communication among team members, it enhances weak ties and has positive effect on publication productivity. Unlike the weak ties assumption, the formal interaction (face to face) was found to promote discussing new idea and updating research progress, whereas, it is negatively related to share information on private life and individual's other work.

Strong ties play very significant roles in facilitating all routine, professional, and private life information exchanges within the network. Only team members who come from the same institution and with strong ties will we find higher level of exchanging information regarding to their professional works beyond or outside the Ipv6 project. Those who exchange information heavily show a high academic productivity. The regressions indicate impact of strong tie on academic productivity is through members' active interaction and heavy information exchanges. Based on the results, in contrast to Burt's theory, the advantages were found within strong ties rather than in weak ties. The findings support the dense network and strong tie hypotheses, furthermore, the mechanisms of network bonding effect on high academic productivity are clarified. Compared with Uzzi's successful "less strong ties and more weak ties" network, we discovered this may be a unique academia milieu of "more strong ties but less weak ties" pattern in Taiwan. If so, the continuing effect and the implication of knowledge sharing and innovation creating in this dense networks should be further discussed.

7.6 References

Adessa, C., & Sonnenwald, D.H. 2003. „Exploring collaboration among historically black universities and doctoral/research universities in the USA". UNESCO Conference on Teaching and Learning for Intercultural Understanding. Human Rights and a Culture of Peace. Jyväskylä, Finland.

Archibugi, D., & Coco, A. 2004 "A new indicator of technological capabilities for developed and developing countries (ArCo)". *World Development*, 32: 629-654.

Atkinson, P., Batchleor, C., & Parsons, E. 1998. "Trajectories of collaboration and competition in medical discovery". *Science, Technology, & Human Values*, 23: 259-284.

Burt, R. S. 1992. *Structural holes*. Cambridge, Mass: Harvard University Press.

Burt, R. S. 2004. "Structural holes and good ideas". *American Journal of Sociology*. 110: 349-399.

Coleman, J. S. 1988. "Social capital in the creation of human capital," *American Journal of Sociology*, 94: S95-S120.

Granovetter, M. 1973. "The strength of weak ties," *American Journal of Sociology*, 78: 1360-1380.

Granovetter, M. 1982. "The strength of weak ties: A network theory revisited", In Peter V. Marsden and N. Lin (Eds.), *Social structure and network analysis* Sage.

Hansen, M. T. 1999. "The search-transfer problem," *Administrative Science Quarterly*, 44:82-111.

Koku, E., Nazer, N., & Wellman, B. 2001. "Netting scholars: Online and offline," *American Behavioral Scientist*, 44: 1750-72.

Murray, S. O., and Robert C. P. 1982 "Strong ties and scientific literature. *Social Networks*, 4:225-232.

Olson, G.M. 2004. Collaboratories. In W.S. Bainbridge (Ed.), *Encyclopedia of Human-Computer Interaction*. Great Barrington, MA: Berkshire Publishing..

Olson, G.M., Olson, J.S., Bos, N., & the SOC Data Team 2004 International collaborative science on the net (pp. 65-77). In W. Blanpied (Ed.), Proceedings of the Trilateral Seminar on Science, Society and the Internet. Arlington, VA: George Mason University

Sonnenwald, D.H. 2007. Scientific collaboration: A synthesis of challenges and strategies. In B. Cronin (Ed), *Annual Review of Information Science & Technology*. Medford, NJ: Information Today.

Sproull, L., and Kiesler, S. 1991. *Connections: new ways of working in the networked organization*. Cambridge: MIT Press.

Wagner, C.S., Brahmakulam, I., Jackson, B., Wong, A., & Yoda, T.,2001 "Science and technology collaboration: building capacity in developing countries?", MR-1357.0-WB,March 2001

Wagner, C.S. Horlings, E. & Dutta, A. 2003 "Can science and technology capacity be measured?", RAND Corporation.

Walsh, J. P., and Bayma, T. 1996. "The virtual college: Computer-mediated communication and scientific work," *The Information Society*, 12:343-363.

Walsh, J. P., Kucker, S., and Maloney, N. G. 2000. "Connecting minds: Computer-mediated communication and scientific work," *Journal of the American Society for Information Science*, 51: 1295-1305.

7.7 Notes

1 Authors in order of the section they contributed. The chapter was compiled and edited by Olson.
2 This section was written by Paul A. David, Stanford University and the Oxford Internet Institute
3 This section was written by Johan Eksteen, CSIR/Meraka, South Africa
4 This section was written by Diane H. Sonnenwald, Göteborg University and University College of Borås, Sweden
5 This section was written by Paul A. David, Stanford University and the Oxford Internet Institute, and by Paul F. Uhlir, National Academies
6 This section was written by Shu-Fen Tseng, Yuan Ze University, and Hsin-I Huang, Institute of Information Science, Academia Sinica

8. UNIVERSITY RELATIONS FOR CAPACITY BUILDING—HIGHLIGHTS OF HP'S PROGRAM

Barbara Waugh, *Hewlett Packard*[1]
Russel C. Jones, *WFEO Committee on Capacity Building*
Lueny Morell, *Hewlett Packard*
Bess Stephens, *Hewlett Packard*
Didier Philippe, *Hewlett Packard*
Iulia Nechifor, *UNESCO*
Edit Schlaffer, *Women without Borders*
Clifford Harris, *Hewlett Packard*

The purpose of this panel was to give visibility to some of the efforts of a large global company to build capacity in the world.[2] A few in the audience confirmed afterwards that their preconceptions of corporations had changed – they could now tentatively allow that maybe corporations could do good as well as do well, and in fact, that maybe some companies understand that they will do better by doing good. Several other attendees proposed projects for collaboration, and indeed collaboration has ensued.

Russ Jones, Chair of the Capacity Building committee of the World Federation of Engineering Organizations and a consultant to HP, opened the panel with a definition of capacity building, desired outcomes of such efforts, and an overview of initiatives underway through UNESCO and the World Federation of Engineering Organizations, often in collaboration with large companies, including HP. Lueny Morell, a director in HP University Relations, then went into greater depth on one of the projects mentioned by Russ – Engineering for the Americas. Begun as a grassroots effort to build capacity in Latin America, it has now developed into an OAS-sponsored initiative involving government, universities and industry in the region, focused on quality assurance to ensure cross-border movement, retain and develop capacity in the region, and reverses the brain drain.

Bess Stephens, VP of HP Philanthropy, laid out the objectives and 2006 programs of HP Philanthropy. Didier Philippe, Director in HP Corporate Affairs, then described an innovative HP pilot funded out of Bess's program, to support microenterprise development. This pilot has now scaled to 58 training centers in 13 countries and has evolved into an ecosystem for mutual support, open to new partners for further proliferation and sustainability.

Iulia Nechifor, UNESCO program officer, then went into depth on one of the UNESCO and HP UR and Philanthropy projects: the South Eastern Europe 'Alleviate the Brain Drain' initiative, that has connected students and faculty in that region's universities with their counterparts in the Diaspora, including joint research, exchange visits and participation in larger worldwide HP sponsored university consortia. Edit Schlaffer, director of Women without Borders, discussed her organization's ambitious web-based project to connect women and youth around the world, enabling them to 'show their faces,' and connect for worldwide empowerment; she mentioned support for Women without Borders from corporations, including from HP. Cliff Harris, director of Education and Healthcare for HP Europe, Middle East and Africa discussed a breakthrough managed learning environment that is now country-wide in Northern Ireland, a proof-point for technology enabled education that leapfrogs many current 'developed world' environments, and has been adopted by other countries in the region.

8.1   Technical Capacity Building in Developing Countries[3]

In the pursuit of a more secure, stable and sustainable world, developing countries seek to enhance their human, institutional and infrastructure capacity. To do so they need a solid base of technologically prepared people to effectively improve their economies and quality of life. Such a base will facilitate the infusion of foreign capital through attraction of multinational companies to invest in the developing country, assist in making the most of foreign aid funds, and provide a basis for business development by local entrepreneurs. In a coordinated approach, UNESCO and WFEO are mounting major efforts at technical capacity building in developing countries.

What outcomes are desired?

The following outcomes are desired from current technical capacity building efforts:
- Technical capability is needed for developing countries to engage effectively in the global economy.
- Indigenous science and technology capacity is needed to insure that international aid funds are utilized effectively and efficiently – for initial project implementation, for long-term operation and maintenance, and for the development of capacity to do future projects.

- In order to stimulate job formation, a technical workforce pool is needed, made up of people who are specifically educated and prepared to engage in entrepreneurial startup efforts that meet local needs

Two complementary approaches are being pursued in parallel to achieve these desired outcomes:

- UNESCO "Cross-sectoral activities in technical capacity-building" decision, to enhance engineering programs within that organization
- WFEO Committee on Capacity Building, to provide an action oriented program for forward motion

UNESCO plans for capacity building

In 2003, the United States of America rejoined UNESCO after an absence of 18 years. The US government indicated to UNESCO that it wanted a significant portion of the increased funds that it would provide to its budget to be allocated to enhancing its programs in engineering and engineering education. A major proposal on how to mount an enhanced program, entitled "Cross-sectoral activities in technical capacity-building", was developed and submitted to UNESCO for consideration. This effort, to be housed in the science sector and reporting directly to the Assistant Director General for Science, will focus broadly on building personal and institutional capabilities in developing countries to address poverty reduction, economic development, and related issues. Presented by the US Ambassador to UNESCO at the April 2005 meeting of the UNESCO Executive Board, this approach has been adopted and referred to the UNESCO Director General for implementation.

WFEO Standing Committee on Capacity Building

Motivated by a renewed interest in engineering and engineering education at UNESCO, at least partially driven by the decision of the United States of America to rejoin UNESCO after an 18 year absence, the Word Federation of Engineering Organizations (WFEO) Moved in October 2003 to establish a new Standing Committee on Capacity Building, with the United States as the host of the international organization.

Following is a list of the activities being pursued by the WFEO Committee on Capacity Building:

- Engineering for the Americas
- African initiative
- Virtual exhibit, e-conferences
- Entrepreneurial conference
- Black Sea University Network workshop

- Gender issues
- South-south interactions
- Engineers without borders
- FIDIC collaboration
- UNESCO/WFEO Expert Conference

Conclusion

State-of-the-art science and technology capacity must be built in developing countries if they are to be able to compete effectively in the global economy. A well-educated technical workforce must be in place in a developing country before technology-based multinational companies will be attracted to make investments there in production facilities and other areas. The day is past when such companies would simply introduce expatriates from developed countries to attempt such operations. Current political and economic realities require that a well-educated and trained indigenous workforce is needed to sustain technically based industrial operations in developing countries. Recent offshoring of operations to countries like India and China by companies in well developed countries illustrate this point.

A technical workforce is also needed to fuel entrepreneurial startup efforts that meet local needs. Well-educated engineers and scientists in developing countries will find appropriate ways to extend R&D results to marketable products and services responsive to local needs – to their personal economic benefits as well as to the economic benefit of their countries. Further development of such entrepreneurial startups can lead to products and services that profitably extend to regional markets, and eventually to global markets.

Indigenous science and technology capacity is also needed in developing countries to assure that international aid funds sent there are utilized effectively and efficiently – both for initial project implementation and for long term operation and maintenance. Too often in the past, major projects in developing countries have failed to meet desired and designed objectives because there is not a local base of technically qualified people to assist in implementation in ways that are compatible with the local culture and environment.

Thus it is clear that developing countries need their own indigenous technological expertise. They cannot afford to buy it from developed countries, and even when technical expertise from developed countries is provided by external funding it is often ineffective in appropriately responding to local needs and constraints. Capacity building of technical expertise in developing countries is thus key to enhancing their ability to become economically self- sufficient.

8.2 Engineering for the Americas[4]

Stimulated by the globalization of the engineering profession and the industries that it supports, and by increased interest in trade between countries and regions in the American hemisphere, a grass-roots movement to enhance engineering and technology education in the hemisphere has been gathering momentum through discussions at conferences over the past four years. The movement has been dubbed "Engineering for the Americas", and it has involved educators, industry representatives, government officials, and professional groups as it has evolved. The basic concept calls for engineers educated in high quality institutions in each country in the hemisphere, with quality assurance systems in place to guarantee consistently high caliber graduates. Mutual recognition of such engineering graduates across national boundaries, combined with cross-border trade agreements, will facilitate the flow of work and human resources throughout the hemisphere to optimal locations – for distributed economic development. This open mobility will then form the basis for a knowledge-based, hemisphere-wide economy, which is competitive in the overall global economy. Each country in the hemisphere, as well as the sum of all countries in the hemisphere, should benefit.

Recognizing the importance of this movement, the Office of Science and Technology of the Organization of American States has worked with the previously ad-hoc group to formalize the "Engineering for the Americas" concept and program. A hemispheric initiative with this title was developed in meetings convened by the OAS in mid-2004, and incorporated in the Declaration of Lima and the Plan of Action of Lima, which were adopted by the meeting of Ministers and High Authorities of Science and Technology in November 2004. The initiative calls for enhancement of engineering education, development of quality assurance mechanisms, harmonization of degree patterns, fostering of innovation, and government commitment to providing necessary upgrading to engineering and technology education. It has been also endorsed by the Presidents in the Fourth Summit of the Americas in Mar del Plata, Argentina in November 2005.

With the support and leadership of organizations like OAS, USTDA, the InterAmerican Development Bank, companies like Hewlett-Packard, Microsoft, National Instruments, CEMEX, NYCE and Neoris, and thought leaders in engineering education and accreditation from the Americas, a major workshop was held in Lima, Perú early December 2005 to address how to effectively implement the Ministerial proposed actions. Around 300 attendees met to discuss the definition of the productive sector's needs, understand needs and opportunities in enhancement and quality assurance for engineering education, and plan for appropriate processes in each country to finance needed enhancements. A plan for sustainability of the Engineering for the Americas movement was also discussed.

The Engineering for the Americas movement continues to grow and expand, and plans are being developed by the multi-stakeholder group to facilitate and finance regional and country plans to enhance engineering education and quality assurance mechanisms that will improve the Americas competitive edge.

8.3 HP's 2006 Philanthropy Strategy and Road Map[5]

HP Corporate Affairs Strategy 2006

Philanthropy is a key component to HP fulfilling its Global Citizenship Objective, one of the company's seven Corporate Objectives, and reflects our long-standing commitment to making a positive contribution to the global community. HP's leadership in Global Citizenship is a competitive differentiator for the company. In addition to philanthropy, other important focus areas of our Global Citizenship work include the Environment, Ethics and Privacy. Objectives of the Global Citizenship work include the following: HP's employees demonstrate citizenship beliefs; HP's brand reputation is protected and improved; and access to information technology is increased.

HP Philanthropy Strategy 2006

Three key strategies are tied to HP Philanthropy Programs in 2006: transform teaching and learning through the use of technology and training; address community needs through access to technology, resources and knowledge; and drive awareness, education and advocacy of HP's global citizenship objective, beliefs and programs with employees.

HP Philanthropy Program Offerings 2006

HP believes that community organizations are vital to improving the quality of life for all residents. Investing in these organizations strengthens those communities and supports HP's reputation as a good citizen in the community.

The 2006 programs focus on giving equipment to proliferate the HP brand in local communities and take work out of the system; there will be an increased emphasis on partnering, building communities of practice, and serving those in greatest need in HP communities.

HP strives to build the right balance between strategic philanthropy and reactive philanthropy. Strategic philanthropy is aligned with business objectives, differentiating brand in a competitive environment, attracting and retaining employees, earning license to operate, and deepening relationships with core stakeholders. In the past, local and country philanthropy was largely reactive to ad hoc local conditions. In 2006 HP is creating a base for local and country giving that is strategically managed in part by Corporate. The corporate components will be structured in such a way that they can localized. Targets will be non-profits and educational institutions near major HP sites and areas of market interest.

HP's 2006 Philanthropy Program Offerings include the following:

- The Technology for Teaching Higher Education Program. This program provides grants of technology and cash to colleges and universities. Outside the U.S. higher education institutions will participate by invitation. The grants will recognize work by faculty to redesign courses, and integrate mobile technology into teaching to improve student success. Grant recipients participate in an annual worldwide conference of recipients hosted by HP.
- The Advanced Technology Grid Initiative. This program is also targeted to colleges and universities. The technology awarded includes Itanium servers. Participation is by invitation.
- The HP Technology for Teaching K-12 Program (primary and secondary schools). These mobile technology grants are open to K-12 public schools. Recipient teacher teams integrate HP technology into their teaching in a variety of subject areas, with an emphasis on math and science education. There is an emphasis on including schools that serve low-income students. Teachers who are part of recipient teams also participate in technology education professional development and an on-line community of recipients.
- The HP Technology for Community Program. This program offers technology grants to non-profit organizations. Areas of focus will vary from country to country but grants will be given to community organizations providing support and services in areas such as health and human services, workforce development, environment, community and economic development, and arts and technology.
- HP's Employee Giving Program. These programs are available to HP employees in various countries around the world. Many of these

programs include cash and product matching opportunities. There is an emphasis on product giving to maximize investment.[6]

8.4   Micro Enterprise Acceleration Program: intent, model and achievement[7]

I will describe the creation, business model and results of an innovative WW Digital Ecosystem, the Micro Enterprise Acceleration Program (MAP). The program intends to enhance and leverage local/regional resources and capabilities to grow local business and make them more sustainable. It achieved results by balancing local and global resources, expertise and strengths through creation and use of multiple stakeholder networks of NGO's, Public and Private organizations interfaced through on-line services, blended e-learning models and face-to-face localized delivery of open-sourced curriculum. Growing out of a pilot HP initiative on Micro Enterprise development in the US, the digital ecosystem found value in its organic development and shared management approach. Delivering results (and demonstrating impact) and expansion (and diversification) of the funding base are the key drivers for sustainability.

The project goes beyond the basic ITC infrastructure program and builds upon ITC components to deliver comprehensive support to Business Development Service (BDS) providers and to equip Micro business owners with ITC hands-on business skills.

Digital Eco system: Project description

The small business sector plays a critical role in stimulating economic development through job creation and innovation8. ICT can help small businesses improve their competitiveness and reach new customers.

25-30% of the world's labor force is unemployed or underemployed. Globally, micro enterprises represent the biggest source of new jobs. However their growth is constrained by lack of competitiveness, low productivity, low owner and worker skills.

The Digital Ecosystem grew out of the HP Microenterprise Development Program in the United States, which supported nonprofit microenterprise development agencies in communities to promote economic growth through training, technical assistance and small loans.

The Digital Ecosystem has now developed in the US and EMEA, based on an innovative network of diverse stakeholders using a two tier model to reach the community-based BDS (business development services) organizations. First, global partners establish the vision, develop worldwide open-source curriculum, train the Master trainers, and set up services. Then, a set of partners at the country level manage the country selection of BDS providers, country localization, training of trainers, and connection with the public sector.

The shared objective was to provide a comprehensive set of benefits surrounding basic ICT and to establish a trans-national eco system to help micro enterprise growth.

Digital Eco system: spread and partners

The set of features include: class room ICT equipment, hands-on curriculum, training of trainers, and an on-line sharing platform.

In 2004/05, 26 education pilot centers were established in the US and 32 in Europe, Middle East and Africa in 12 countries including Egypt, France, Finland, Germany, Ireland, Israel, Italy, Malta, Nigeria, Portugal, Russia . Each education pilot center is operated by a local BDS provider. Each initially received a set of education ITC equipment through the HP Philanthropy program.

Worldwide partners include HP, Making Cents, IESC, and Media Sparc. A global advisory board of leading economic development NGOs was also set to guide the development.

Regional/country partners include: the Business and Innovation European Network, University of Lagos, Fondation de France, Chambers of Commerce from Italy and Germany, Russia ITC foundation for SME development, International Trade center from the UN, to name a few.

The BDS centers were local training organizations already delivering business services to several thousand micro business owners. By December 2006, the project intends to show the full utilization of the ITC components, measurement and evidence of impact of the Digital ecosystem. Innovation lies in the creation of a specific hands-on curriculum to teach micro business owners how to grow their business with ICT, and in the learning community which is generating much needed social capital for these small business owners.

8.5 Piloting Solutions for Alleviating Brain Drain in South East Europe[9]

The UNESCO-HP Partnership for Alleviating Brain drain in South East Europe (SEE) was born in 2003 as an attempt to respond to the severe shortage of educated human potential in the region as a result of the devastating war and break-up of former Yugoslavia. Indeed, in the 1990s the countries of South Eastern European (SEE) suffered loss of lives on a massive scale, upheaval of social structures and disintegration of many social institutions – all of which has been widely reported during and after the conflicts.

What is less widely reported is the serious loss of intellectual capacity in the region. Under the prevailing economic conditions, careers in research have simply become 'unattractive'. This has led not only to 'external brain' drain but also to a massive 'internal brain drain' towards less prestigious but better paid professions. Despite this unfavorable trend in most SEE countries these countries have strong research potential and large resources of well-educated people. .

The project for Alleviating Brain drain in South East Europe (SEE) was developed by the UNESCO Education Sector, following a request by Member States in the region. In partnership with Hewlett Packard (HP) University Relations Programme, the UNESCO Venice Office is implementing the project that provides resources to universities in SEE, including technological and financial resources so that young scientists from the region can co-operate with each other and with the Diaspora.

HP provided state of the art equipment that allows the use of grid computing technology for the sharing of computer power and data storage capacity over the internet. The equipment was given to the Universities of Belgrade and Podgorica in Serbia and Montenegro, to the Universities of Sarajevo and of Serb Sarajevo in Bosnia and Herzegovina, to the University of Split in Croatia and recently to the Polytechnic University in Albania and the Ss. Cyril and Methodius University in Former Yugoslav Republic (FYR) of Macedonia. In addition, financial support allowed young researchers to undertake short term visits abroad and establish research partnership with co-nationals.

The apparent small scale of the project is deceptive when considering the global connections and network that it is generating across the world. The type of work carried out means that the scale and potential of the project is very significant in the world-wide scientific and academic community.

Indeed, the project has already had an important impact in the scientific and research communities not just in the SEE region, but also with the participating scientific institutions across the world.

After two years of operation, all participating universities have succeeded in creating teams of young scientists who found their own scientific interest within the project. The devotion and energy of their mentors was essential for the active involvement of an important number of young scientists, as well as for the success of the research projects.

Individuals as well as institutions have benefited from the approach project, with many of the participating academics realizing personal advantages. One professor in Split has established contacts with many Croatian researchers and officials as well as foreign scientists and discussed possibilities for research collaborations. Based on his experiences and analysis this physicist has written a novel, looking at the sociological aspects of Croatian scientists in South America.

At local and national levels there is a new cooperation among inter-faculties, and between scientists and decision-makers (University Rectors and relevant Ministries involved in education and science.

At regional levels the initiative has had an important political impact and has contributed to overcoming boundaries and enhancing dialogue between people in a region that has recently known mistrust and unrest. Contact has been made among the previously opposing communities of the former Yugoslavia. Project get-together meetings in Dubrovnik (Croatia) and Ohrid (FYR of Macedonia) brought together specialist communities from five countries involved in the 1990's conflicts and universities from the bordering countries that were directly or indirectly affected.

The project has created global communities of interest by providing the unique opportunity for young researchers from Balkan countries to benefit from latest IT technology and enabling them to join world class research teams. The University of Sarajevo (Bosnia and Herzegovina) and the University of Split (Croatia) have joined the Gelato Federation, a global research community dedicated to advancing the Linux Itanium platform through collaborative relationships, which includes more than 40 Universities around the world.

The programme has also enabled a significant number (40) of exchange visits for scientists. Young professors and students from the beneficiary universities have been able to visit major laboratories abroad, including the United States, Canada, France, Switzerland, Chile, Argentina and the Russian Federation. They have established research partnerships, gaining access to international networks and sharing the latest scientific knowledge. Moreover, a significant number of scientists from the Diaspora now have the option of returning for short stays to give lectures on new research topics to their compatriots – something that benefits them individually, the students, and the institution. This has also led to the elaboration of an important number of joint research projects which have been submitted for funding to various donor sources or which are currently seeking funding. The University of Montenegro has succeeded in obtaining additional resources, including software, from Mentor Graphics, USA. Additional sources of funding have been identified for the continuation of activities, including a 3 year grant for exchange visits for Montenegrin physicists in Hamburg, Germany.

The active role and advice of HP representatives in the overall implementation of the project was very important, paving the way for the University of Sarajevo and of the University of Split into the Gelato Federation. This type of interactions and exchange of experience between industry and university has a very positive effect and should be strongly encouraged.

Recent events as the EGGE Grid Summer School (Budapest, July 2005) and the UNESCO-CERN event sponsored by HP 'Grid: the key to Scientific Cooperation' (CERN, September 2005) allowed the scientist participants in the project to actively joint the European Grid Community.

Further information about the Piloting Solutions for Alleviating Brain Drain in South East Europe can be obtained from: www.unesco.org/venice or i.nechifor@unesco.org

The Partners:

UNESCO Office in Venice (www.unesco.org/venice)

The overall mission of the UNESCO-ROSTE in Venice is to foster cooperation, to contribute to capacity building and to provide specialized expertise in the fields of natural sciences and culture within the Central and Eastern European region – in particular the countries of South Eastern Europe. Its programmes seek to build human and institutional capacities in the basic and engineering sciences, foster collaborative research in the field of the environment, especially in ecological and water sciences, contribute to the protection of cultural heritage, and promote cultural diversity and intercultural dialogue. Within its broad remit, UNESCO ROSTE is implementing the project Piloting Solutions for Alleviating Brain Drain in South East Europe alongside other projects and initiatives within the region that compliment its application.

Hewlett Packard (www.hpl.hp.com/research/ur/)

The UNESCO-ROSTE partner in the project is Hewlett Packard, which signed an agreement in April 2003 to support the project with technical equipment and funds. It has played an active part in facilitating all aspects of the project and supplementary presentations and support initiatives.

The Beneficiaries:

Seven universities are participating in the project:
- The Polytechnic University of Tirana (Albania), Department of Physics (http://www.upt.al) promoted joint research and combined PhD

programmes, such as free access to ICTP laboratories and libraries in Trieste, Italy, using grid computing facilities.

- University of East Sarajevo (Bosnia and Herzegovina), Faculty of Electrical Engineering (http://www.unsa.ba/eng/pmf.php) has organized exchange visits, as well as provided courses in the field of database development, networking and Internet technologies and data acquisition systems. Together with partner institutions from abroad, the faculty expanded a joint research project.

- University of Sarajevo (Bosnia and Herzegovina), Faculty of Natural Sciences and Mathematics (http://www.unssa.rs.ba). Through distance learning supported by the grid computing technology, the University of Sarajevo, Faculties of Natural Sciences has been able to create a database and website on the Bosnian scientific Diaspora. Both universities in Sarajevo have developed new e-learning programs that have been introduced into the curricula.

- University of Split in Croatia, Faculty of Natural Sciences (www.okolis07.pmfst.hr/cpaw) actively participates in European projects and use EU funds to develop and expand as an institution. HP resources helped the university use new high tech equipment in dissemination and research, creating the right combination to help and encourage the university to start a number of new activities and projects. In addition to other activities, a database and an interactive website of Croatian physicists around the world were developed enabling those in SEE to share information with educational and research institutions abroad.

- University of Skopje (FYR of Macedonia), Faculty of Sciences and Mathematics, Department of Computer Science and Faculty of Electrical Engineering (www.ukim.edu.mk/index.php?lan=en&pon) established partnerships with leading European institutions that have technical expertise in grid computing and created an interoperable research and educational grid cluster in Macedonia.

- University of Montenegro (Serbia and Montenegro), Faculty of Natural Sciences and Mathematics (www.ucg.cg.ac.yu/), Department of Physics & Faculty of Electrical Engineering. In Montenegro, the University's Electrical Engineering and IT departments have improved communication with experts from abroad through the installation of a new server and computer classroom. Additionally, the creation of a website including relevant information about project activities has allowed the university to conduct joint work in the field of power electronics with Atomic Energy Canada Ltd.

- University of Belgrade (Serbia and Montenegro), Faculty of Electrical Engineering (www.bg.ac.yu and http://automatika.etf.bg.ac.yu)

developed 'Piloting Distance eLab Experiments', in particular a system for remote training of a deaf person.

8.6   Bridging the Gap — Empowerment Strategies for the New Female Arab Leadership[10]

Include – Involve – Invest

Women without Borders is an international research-based advocacy and PR organisation for women in politics and civil society, based in Austria. We support women all over the world as they strive towards the participation in all levels of decision-making. Through global dialogue, targeted information, with model projects and the creation of alliances with international partner organisations, Women without Borders empowers women towards positive change. We call on all decision makers to include women, on women to involve themselves and on communities to invest in women.

Presenting the Middle East Women

An educated, effective and connected female talent pool is emerging as the acceptable face of Arab modernisation. Women must show their face in the new knowledge based societies – they must make their presence known.

Women need to share in the creation, distribution, management and use of information.

The West, in particular, should reach out and connect with this extraordinary movement.

The "Bridging the Gap" Project is a major new research project which poses the question, who are the women of the Arab modernisation? How can they maintain the momentum and help to empower the next generation of young women to bridge the gap between their education and becoming future political and economic leaders for their societies? From graduate to post graduate and beyond, this project promotes real access to women's empowerment.

Bridging the Digital Gender Divide

Women who struggle with cultural expectations and lack the competence and confidence to be connected, fall into a gender gap. Issues that are of interest and concern to women have to be in the arena of the knowledge society. Women from the Middle East have the capacity to invent and promote a new digital space for women on a global level. This new media empowerment will be an open, interactive, participatory web-platform on women's issues: the women-information.net

Women without Borders is introducing a new internet vision: www.women-information.net

- to provide a daily news service, with local and global perspectives
- to enable women to engage in the Information Society
- to overcome the digital gender divide
- to raise awareness for the "hidden culture of women"
- to provide on-line web classes for future female leadership training
- to promote the creation and use of national and international networks
- to offer creative and participatory training in on-line formats

Bee what you want to be!

Targeting girls and boys is crucial to the success of any effort to empower societies. Youth in particular tend to be more open minded, less restricted and ready to embrace alternative solutions. Under the umbrella programme of Girls Fit for Leadership! The women-information.net will run innovative model programs that offer youth attractive forums to develop the competence and confidence for a positive healthy life based on human rights and democratic values. With the chance to simply log in and learn, young girls can join the on-line training everywhere!

This program encourages self-awareness and develops personal capacity for a new generation of strong girls. Under the logo of a smart bee the on-line course introduces themes of individual exercises and tuition such as self-identity, gender awareness, communication and synergy. The course enables girls to discover their own personal force and zones of impact so they can achieve their aspirations in the future.

Women without Borders tries to bridge the gap through research-based activities making the female potential in the Arab region visible and aim to overcome the digital gender divide by providing access to information and ensuring freedom of expression for the development of a more socially balanced and prosperous world.

Let's work together for a gender-just future!

8.7 ICT for Education: the Northern Ireland example[11]

Born in 1960 I grew up in Northern Ireland during the time of "The Troubles.' My school bus was stoned at least once a week sometimes more for the 7 years of my Secondary schooling, and was firebombed 3 times. I lost two friends before their 21st birthdays to the troubles in the streets. I never met a student from the other religion (only in fights, I was a young teenager and knew nothing else) until I went to Senior College – even though they lived only a few miles away in another neighborhood.

Emerging from "The Troubles," Northern Ireland was literally shell-shocked. Our infrastructure was poorer than other regions of the UK and our best academics were leaving the country in large numbers. However, being an optimistic race we had a few visionary leaders who imagined our province as thought-leading, beginning with its educational system. Beginning in 1990 planning began, which eventually blossomed into Northern Ireland's Classroom 2000 (C2K) program. C2K has become a world-leading initiative that demonstrates best practice for the use of Information and Communications Technology (ICT) in schools.

Far more than merely providing schools with a few PCs and an Internet connection, the C2K program is the most extensive of its kind in the world, providing children throughout the province with PCs in the classroom, as opposed to a specialized computer laboratory.

So successful has it been that one of the key partners in the program, the leading IT products and services provider HP, is establishing a centre of excellence called the Education Innovation & Competence Centre (EICC) at its premises in Belfast. This will have a dual role: to showcase the benefits of C2K to interested visitors from other countries; and to carry out research, along with education authorities, as to how to make best use of ICT in schools in the future.

School children throughout Northern Ireland have access to a secure learning environment over the Internet, from which they can make use of educational software in a safe and controlled manner. Each child can also communicate electronically with other children throughout the province using a secure form of e-mail which restricts access only to children and teachers participating in the C2K program.

The program, run by the Western Education and Library Board, involves 900 primary and 450 post primary schools throughout the province and serves some 350,0000 students and teachers. It comprises between 70 and 80,000 PCs distributed across Northern Ireland. According to Jimmy Stewart, director of the C2K project, there is nothing like this in existence anywhere else in Ireland or Britain and very few around the world that have the same scope and co-ordination over a full national territory. "The school curriculum is undergoing major change at the moment," he says. "It is moving from focusing on subjects to focusing on skills. The use of technology is now being included as a core competence for all students."

The managed learning environment, which is provided to the C2K program by leading IT products and services supplier HP, is a Web based tool that allows students to access educational software programs that are held on a central database in Belfast administered by HP. Teachers can also create course related content that can be viewed online and students can work on the content in groups, either locally or via the Internet with students throughout Northern Ireland.

The first beneficiaries of the C2K program were primary schools who went live with the system in 2001. Reaction to date has been overwhelmingly positive, according to Stewart. "The digital learning environment allows access to a broad and rich range of educational resources for the classroom," according to Stewart. "At the moment there are 200 digital resources online and the primary school teachers are delighted with the range of content available. It is helping to stimulate interest among students in a wide range of topics."

The digital learning environment is provided as a managed service to C2K by HP. It operates from a data centre in Belfast to which participating schools have fast Internet access. HP looks after all the security and maintenance requirements and ensures that only authorized users—i.e. students and teachers—have access to the content and to the messaging features so that students are protected from harmful content.

I am the director for Education & Health Care business for HP in EMEA and am particularly enthusiastic about the prospects for the EICC which will open in February. Its purpose is twofold. In the first instance it will be a centre of excellence where we can showcase what we are doing with C2K to visitors from around the globe. We can show them how we can assist with technology in education using the C2K program as a reference point. More far-reaching, however, will be the research work that will take place there on how best to use ICT in education in the future. HP is investing $1m initially in the centre and will work with Northern Ireland education on embedding ICT further into the education experience and enhancing the IT related skills of future generations of students.

Education is an area of great interest for the European Commission which is formulating long-term policy that will focus on Life Long Learning (LLL). ICT is a major factor in its deliberations.

Many countries around Europe have followed EU directives on equipping schools with computers but very few have worked out exactly what to do with those computers once they have been installed. The result is that people have spent millions on hardware but have not improved the standards of education and attainment at all. To change that the centre will conduct research into how best to use ICT to present course content and also to produce appropriate metrics for measuring the level of attainment of students and teachers. Eventually, we hope to generate a 'cluster effect' with other leading ICT companies participating in the research operation.

We know that any kid who does not have basic ICT skills ends up working for the minimum wage, if they get employment at all. We want to put processes in place to ensure that all children have the opportunity to acquire the education and technical skills they will need in the marketplace of the future.[12]

The C2K solution has been implemented whole or in part in Sardinia, Sweden, Gabon, Bulgaria, Saudi Arabia, Jordan, and France. Other corporate partners are now working with us in the Centre: Intel, CISCO and Microsoft.

8.8 Notes

1 Authors in order of the section they contributed. The chapter was compiled and edited by Waugh.
2 This chapter was compiled, edited and introduced by Barbara Waugh.
3 This section was written by Russel C. Jones.
4 This section was written by Lueny Morell.
5 This section was written by Bess Stephens.
6 For Additional Information, see: http://www.hp.com ;
http://www.hp.com/hpinfo/globalcitizenship/ ;
http://grants.hp.com/ .
7 This section was written by Didier Philippe.

8 International Labor Organisation's World Employment Report 2005-05
http://www.ilo.org/public/english/employment/strat/download/wr04c5en.pdf

9 This section was written by Iulia Nechifor.
10 This section was written by Edit Schlaffer.
11 This section was written by Clifford Harris.
12International Labor Organisation's World Employment Report 2005-05
http://www.ilo.org/public/english/employment/strat/download/wr04c5en.pdf

9. WOMEN & ICT: EDUCATION AND EMPLOYMENT ISSUES AND OPPORTUNITIES IN DEVELOPING COUNTRIES

Claudia Morrell, *Center for Women and Information Technology*[1]
Barbara Waugh, *Hewlett Packard Company*
Reem Obeidat, *Dubai Women's College*
Nancy Hafkin, *United Nations Economic Commission for Africa*
Chat Garcia *Ramilo, Association for Progressive Communications*
Margarita Salas, *Bellanet LAC*
Meredith Anderson, *Louisiana State University*
Héla Nafti, Tunisian *Alliance of Female Teachers (UNFT)*

Technology enables globalization. We hear that soon, anyone, anywhere can access information and communicate knowledge and resources. But who is 'anyone?' Where is 'anywhere?' Technology holds the promise of overcoming, or the threat of ever widening the massive gender divide. The talks presented here represent a few of the voices from the edge of this new "flat world" working tirelessly to ensure that technology-enabled globalization fulfills its promise and that no woman or girl – indeed no one – is left to struggle in isolation on the wrong side of an abyss.

Our workshop was opened by Nancy Hafkin, Director, Knowledge Working, and former coordinator of the United Nations African Information Society Initiative. Hafkin presented an overview of significant barriers to IT access faced globally by girls and women. This gender divide impresses upon us the necessity for the education of girls generally, as the sine qua non to STEM (Science, Technology, Engineering, Mathematics) education in the early years and technology education further down the pipeline; and urges access to appropriate non-formal as well as formal education for girls and women.

Claudia Morrell, Executive Director for the Center for Women and I.T., and organizer of the June 2005 international conference on women and ICTs, where many of us met for the first time some months before Tunis, gave an overview of multi-stakeholder responses to the issues outlined by Hafkin, and proposed major strategies for the change agenda, including those sponsored by her own Center. Chat Garcia Ramilo, director of the Women's Networking Support Programme of the Association for Progressive Communications (APC WNSP), then elaborated on barriers outlined by Hafkin and Morrell, and stressed the urgency of gender and locally appropriate access and applications. Speakers then provided more focused perspectives from specific countries that illuminate nuances to the issues and discussed already effective responses to them.

Margarita Salas, Program Officer for Bellanet LAC, explored the barriers to equal access and benefits from IT careers for women in Costa Rica, and proposed strategies for overcoming them. Meredith Anderson, a doctoral candidate in sociology at Louisiana State University, presented research on the changing impact of the Internet on constraints affecting women in Kerala, India, pursuing scientific careers. She concluded with a "circumvention" hypothesis that speaks to the promise of IT for women: new information and communication technologies are used to circumvent the prevailing social structure of patrifocality that restricts interactional opportunities owing to concerns for female purity and control over domestic labor.

Hela Nafti, a representative of the Women of Tunisia Association leading the education initiatives, provided a brief history of education in Tunisia from independence to the present, in which project-based, learner-centric pedagogy prevails, girls participate in equal or greater numbers than boys, and young children learn foreign languages and connect to their peers around the world through systematic deployment of computers and internet connectivity. Reem Obeidat, UNESCO Chair, Communication Technology & Journalism for Women, and Dubai Women's College, concludes the session elaborating on some of the issues for women in the Gulf States, with a focus on women in media.

One can be easily overwhelmed by the immensity of the challenges that need to be overcome to provide simple access to women and girls around the world. Some of these challenges are unique to the developing world, but most can be found in varying degrees around the globe. These presentations highlight both the challenges and opportunities that technology, and particularly ICTs, can provide. The final question is whether ICT will serve as a vehicle for positive change for women or create new barriers in their full participation and leadership in the Information Age. The globalization of technology does not provide a clear solution to this complex question, but it does allow more women and men to work collaboratively in finding that answer.

9.1   Issues in Women, ICT and Education: the work to be done[2]

There are two main interrelations between women, ICT, and education[3]:

- The enrollment and participation of girls in scientific and technological (S&T) education at all levels
- The use of ICT to improve access to and quality of non-formal and formal education, including literacy, for women and girls.

Women and girls are poorly placed to benefit from the information and knowledge economy, from a variety of angles: they have less access to scientific and technical education specifically and less access to education in general. They have less access to skills training and development which will enable them to gain information technology (IT) employment; and when they do work in the IT sector, they work at the lower, lesser-paid levels.

These initial disadvantages have prevented women and girls from benefiting equally from the opportunities that ICTs can bring; yet conversely, ICTs also offer many opportunities for women and girls to gain the education and technical skills required for them to participate equally in the IT economy. Here we see both the threat and the promise of technology-enabled globalization.

As Hafkin and Taggart (2001) argue, "The single most important factor in improving the ability of girls and women in developing countries to take full advantage of the opportunities offered by information technology is more education, at all levels from literacy through scientific and technological education.

One of the most significant aspects of these interrelations is that the gender gap widens as we move up the educational ladder. The percentage of girls and women in S&T decreases steadily as one moves up the educational structure, beginning with the primary level. This steady attrition of girls and women throughout the formal S&T system from primary education to S&T decision-making has been referred to as the 'leaky pipeline.' While globally there are more girls now in secondary and tertiary education, few are found in S&T subjects, especially physics, engineering, and computer science.

The leaks are found at every stage of the process resulting from a series of barriers to girls and women and can be categorized in four categories:

1) *Cultural and attitudinal barriers*, such as perceptions about the role and status of women, emerge across countries, despite widely different circumstances. In some societies these barriers are almost insuperable for women. At the pre-primary and primary level, these include parents' choices to invest in boys' education at the expense of girls, who are required to help with domestic chores at home for all or part of the school day. Girls who do go to primary school often are not given the opportunity to attend at secondary and tertiary levels. Preconceptions that women's responsibilities confine them to the home, and expectations that married women will not work outside the home also contribute to restrict girls' access to education.

2) *Situational barriers*. These include lack of family commitment, lack of partner support, and living in rural or isolated areas. Cost of education, especially higher education, is a major barrier when women do not have independent control of their resources and because they tend to earn less than men to begin with. In many cultures male partners tend to be unsupportive of women's higher education, particularly in non-traditional spheres, which are considered to be unsuitable for women. It is often difficult for women to travel to attend school for reasons of time, cost of transportation, safety, and perceptions of the appropriateness of traveling on their own.

3) *Qualification barriers*. Lack of formal math and sciences education or experience in computer programming skills is often perceived of as a barrier, both by admissions departments and by the students and teachers. Evidence suggests that lack of previous training in these subjects is less of a barrier than expected: in the Philippines the success of poorly-educated and low-income women in the Cisco Networking Academy Program and the achievements of young women without computer backgrounds in the Carnegie Mellon University computer science program demonstrate that women can master the basics of these disciplines quickly and apply them to a higher-level course of training or education. Women and girls do not always have the chance to enter tertiary and even secondary education. Low levels of general education are major barriers to their advancement to other levels of education in many countries.

4) *Finally, institutional barriers block women's access to S&T education*. These include the lack of female teachers and the assumptions of male teachers; inflexible admissions, selection and entry requirements which do not take into account women's varying educational backgrounds, approaches and abilities; and heavy attendance requirements for practical skills and laboratory work which are more difficult for women to meet in view of their family responsibilities. Women also do not tend to participate as fully in workplace networks, or "communities of practice."

As a result of these barriers, a series of "disjunctions" or mismatches occur between requirements of educational programs and the situation and experiences of women. These disjunctions apply generally to women's participation in education, but particularly to technological education, and occur between:

- maintenance and achievement of formal entry requirements, and overall level of educational attainment among women;
- domestication of women's labor and their educational/career aspirations;

- educational fees and women's financial dependence and lower incomes;
- traditional curricula and women's experience and approach to knowledge;
- instrumental pedagogies and women's preferred learning modes.

Within the classroom, gender differences that appear include boys dominating computers physically (pushing girls out) and girls using them for academic research and to obtain information unavailable to them more than boys. Girls in West Africa said recently that one of the advantages of ICTs were that "we are no longer dependent on boys. We are capable of solving our own problems."

In the areas of higher and vocational education, distance education through ICTs provides a great opportunity for women. Much more research needs to be done, but evidence to date indicates that distance education provides women with a means to overcome many obstacles to higher and vocational education. For example, flexibility of access time allows women to undertake their studies at convenient times for them and allows women to juggle study with family responsibilities. When distance learning is facilitated using ICTs, studies have shown that women enthusiastically and successfully take advantage of e-learning opportunities.

Overall, regarding women, ICT, and education, the work to be done falls into two main categories: the promotion of girls' education, especially in science and technology and the promotion of appropriate, accessible non-formal and formal education using ICTs from which women and girls may profit. All concerned about an equitable Information Society and capacity building in developing countries will want to pursue these goals. Unquestionably, ICTs represent an opportunity to ensure equal access to quality education. Nevertheless, equal access for girls and women to quality learning involves recognizing gender-differentiated needs, concerns and situations.

9.2 Gender, ICTs, and Education: Preparing for WSIS[4]

In the past decade increasing focus has been directed towards the gender component of the digital divide. As has often been pointed out, "women and girls enjoy... less access to information technology than men and boys. This can be true of rich and poor countries alike."[5] Specifically, in 1995, the United Nations Commission on Science and Technology for Development (UNCSTD) established a Gender Working Group to address the significant gender differences in access to and control and benefits of technological developments. In 2002 the United Nations Division for the Advancement of

Women (DAW), the International Telecommunication Union (ITU) and the UN ICT (Information and Communication Technology) Task Force Secretariat developed and disseminated a Report that led to the establishment of the WSIS Gender Caucus.[6] And in 2003, the Commission on the Status of Women, during its 47th session, developed Agreed Conclusions that were consistent with and in support of the DAW report, and urged WSIS participants to integrate gender perspectives in every facet of the Summit".[7] After some debate, the WSIS body in Geneva stated in the Declaration of Principles that "we affirm that development of ICTs provides enormous opportunities for women, who should be an integral part of, and key actors, in the Information Society. We are committed to ensuring that the Information Society enables women's empowerment and their full participation on the basis on equality in all spheres of society and in all decision-making processes. To this end, we should mainstream a gender equality perspective and use ICTs as a tool...."[8]

Five months prior to WSIS 2005, the First International Symposium on Women and Information and Communication Technology was held in Baltimore, Maryland to build collaboration and further solidify support for a unified gender message for the Tunis WSIS event. This symposium successfully gathered 238 stakeholders from all over the world to explore concrete and actionable ways to increase girls' and women's participation and leadership within all areas of ICT to address the following four areas:

- Girls' and women's increased access to ICT globally;
- Girls' and women's improved ICT literacy and usability skills;
- Women's full participation in the development and design of ICT hardware, software and content to ensure women's equitable participation in the Information Society; and
- Women's increasing presence and leadership in all aspects of ICT, including policy and decision making, regulation, program development, and the workforce.

A primary point of intervention in creating movement towards these goals was a focus on education. Millennium Development Goal 3 targets the elimination of gender disparity in primary and secondary education preferably by 2005 and at all levels of education by 2015. According to a study by Hafkin and Taggert, a critical factor for ensuring that girls and women benefit from and participate in the new knowledge society is education.[9] Yet, "women and girls are poorly placed to benefit from the knowledge society because they have less access to scientific and technical education specifically, and to education in general."[10]

To date, numerous efforts have developed to increase girls' and women's participation and leadership in ICTs.[11] The reported outcomes have been good but the combined effect of all these efforts is either unknown due to a lack of data gathering related to gender or very small due to the limited scope of each individual project. The symposium in Baltimore suggested a much broader, sweeping approach to change by creating greater collaboration among organizations. These coordinated efforts, identified prior to and developed and reported after the symposium would address the following five areas[12]:

1. *Policy and Action* – Legislative, regulatory and administrative policies that must be adopted at the international, national, and local levels as well as in the workplace to ensure access to ICT for women and girls. Action will be needed to make sure legislation is passed, and once passed, goes beyond rhetoric and translates into action on the ground.

2. *Research and Collaboration* – Research needs to be directed at identifying effective practices and programs for the use of ICT to benefit women and girls. It also needs to include women, which means academic scholarships, internships, and promotion of women faculty in ICT fields, as well as inclusion of women and other stakeholders in research design, implementation and analysis. We also need to understand better the systems for effective learning and training for women and girls.

3. *Dissemination and Communication* – Effective practices must be communicated broadly to allow for locally appropriate duplication and scaling up of success. This will require the collaboration of governments, international bodies, associations and organizations to develop methods of data collection and to monitor progress towards goals.

4. *Resource Development* – Creating the infrastructure necessary to increase access for women and girls to education and other economic, social, and political uses through ICT will require the collaboration of organizations and governments. The goal is to better identify and allocate limited resources to those areas most likely to benefit all, including girls and women.

5. *Context and Culture* – Female representation and participation in the education system as well as in the Information Society are shaped by cultural influences from the media, parents, peers, teachers, co-workers, and others. In many ways this is the most pervasive and most difficult barrier to overcome, but it must *be a central consideration in order to for all other area to be effective.*

Toward this end several strategies were outlined in the Baltimore meeting as first steps in setting the stage for full-implementation in five years. These strategies were reported to the UN ICT Taskforce[13]:

- Ensure engineer access to decision-making levels in order to communicate the aforementioned messages. This could be done by setting up a dialogue with the main public and private actors in the ICT domain, possibly at a pre-conference level.
- Lobby official delegations in order to raise awareness at national levels. It is necessary to set up a long-term dialogue where wishes/demands are discussed. The aim is to engage national administrations to support envisaged action plans to further women's participation in ICT.
- Engage women and men at executive levels to act as ambassadors for the efforts and communicate gender-related information both during and after the Summit.
- Lobby the industry by helping its leaders recognize that any action relating to gender and ICT in the developing countries would assure them an early entry into emerging markets as well as a more robust workforce.
- Emphasize common threads and work on schemes by understanding the different cultures involved, encouraging world-wide mentoring systems, finding ways to measure success, involving all stake holders, sharing any progress made with interested parties, and defining projects based on differing needs.

Finally, as with any initiative, leadership is critical for change to happen; therefore, we must ensure that women are at the decision table on all policy efforts to advance the participation and leadership of women in all areas, including ICTs.

9.3   Women, Literacy and ICTs: an Overview[14]

Nancy Hafkin and Claudia Morell have already outlined the barriers to women's and girls' full participation in the benefits of ICT. I would like to elaborate on the barriers and stress the urgency of gender and locally appropriate access and applications of ICT for women and girls.

Women's Status in Education

Two-thirds of the world's 870 million illiterate people are women, and the world's lowest literacy rates among women are found in thirteen African countries. In some African countries, literacy is less than 30 percent in local languages. Women face challenges in pursuing education at all ages due to lack of time to attend classes, family and domestic responsibilities, and socio-cultural practices that rate girls' education lower than boys. While the gender gap in primary and secondary school enrolment has begun to narrow in recent years, girls still represent 60 percent of the 100 million school age children in the developing world who grow up without access to basic education. Sub-Saharan Africa, southern Asia and the Arab States are home to 95 percent of these out-of-school children. In 35 countries around the world – 18 of them in sub-Saharan Africa, the rest in Asia and the Arab States - girls' net enrolment at secondary level is at least 6 percentage points lower than that of boys. In Central and Eastern Europe, there is less concern with girls' enrolment in primary and secondary school. Rather, the concern is with limited access to higher education due to prohibitive costs and with training for IT occupations.

Why is ICT Education Important for Women?

Literacy, language, computer skills and information literacy are critical skills for drawing some benefit from ICTs for development initiatives. Women and girls are less likely to have these requisite skills and therefore more likely to be excluded from local initiatives. Given the dominance of English on the Internet (though that is slowly eroding), women and girls are also less likely to know the international languages used on the Internet. The predominance of women in rural areas in developing country contexts means that they are also less likely than men to access computers, which are concentrated in urban settings. Information literacy is essentially the ability to evaluate different sets of information against each other, and apply the information to real-life contexts. The isolation and limited exposure of women in developing countries means that women are less likely than men to have these skills. While software is being developed and used in ICT projects targeted at illiterate women, these initiatives are pilot projects that occur few and far between, and are relatively expensive to implement.[15]

Content and Language

In the twenty-first century, most of the world's population remains in Internet silence, while the rich and powerful, most of them men, predominate in the new medium. Those excluded range from women, to non-English speaking nations, national, religious and ideological minorities, the poor in poor countries as well as the poor in wealthy countries, and the majority of the world's children. Individuals with access to the Internet are able to access information and meet with people they would otherwise not know.

The dominance of Western men, largely located in the Northern developed countries, as users of, designers of, decision-makers about, and content producers for the Internet also raises questions about what kind of content will prevail on the Internet. Furthermore, their dominance raises the questions, what will be the cultural biases of this knowledge, and how will women be portrayed in cyberspaces generally, including the Internet, video games, and virtual reality.

One of the reasons given by women to explain their low attendance at telecentres in Africa is language and content that does not 'speak to them,' noting in this sense the 'mode of address' rather than a lack of proficiency in a foreign language. For a great number of women, however, lack of proficiency in international languages is a major problem, even for educated women in Eastern Europe, Latin America and Francophone Africa, excluding them or limiting the benefits they are able to draw from using ICTs. The majority of poor women in the world do not speak the languages that dominate the Internet – English, French, German, Japanese, and Chinese.

Women's viewpoints, knowledge, experiences and concerns are inadequately reflected on the Internet, while gender stereotypes predominate. These concerns around content relate both to issues of sexism and the portrayal of women in media generally, as well as to the need for women to systematize and develop their own perspectives and knowledge, and to ensure that they are reflected in these spaces.

To facilitate more women's access and relevant use of ICTs, there needs to be massive investment of time and other resources into content development at the local level, based on local information needs. The relevance of ICT initiatives also falls short where they focus on "plugging in" women and other marginalized groups into existing global information flow, without any attention to local knowledge systems and content. This flawed approach reinforces marginalized groups as consumers of the Internet and information, and concomitantly neglects the local knowledge that may be of more relevance to women and other marginalized groups. There should therefore be greater attention paid to recognizing women and the poor as information producers, and providing relevant training in collecting, packaging and disseminating local knowledge, based on an understanding of local information needs, and that of women specifically. Such information may well be more useful for local communities in meeting their everyday challenges than "foreign" information available on the Internet.

ICT Literacy and Education Initiatives for Women

Education is an area where both developed and developing countries are applying a combination of traditional and new ICT, adapting the use of computers and the Internet, radio and television and satellites, among others, in formal and informal learning, open and distance education and in establishing e-learning centers - to support education and training of women and girls.

Initiatives that focus on educating women in poor communities and teaching them computer literacy have demonstrated the value of ICT for women. A study of nine projects with a specific focus on women and youth in South Asia showed that ICT use is valued for providing a different model of teaching and learning which is practical, functional and hands-on. New ICT also allow the process and content of education to be determined by learner preferences and priorities, thus opening up possibilities for designing and providing education in forms that are locally relevant.

Radios can play a critical role for pre-literate and rural women. A project developed in Ghana which uses radio to develop functional literacy as well as to provide information in local languages on a wide range of topics. The topics include HIV/AIDS, teenage pregnancy, nutrition, community empowerment, income generating activities, food preservation, animal husbandry, child labor, and energy-saving. Radio is also used to support literacy teaching with more detailed information that could not be provided in the classroom. Although faced with problems, such as poor radio infrastructure and inadequate airtime to offer literacy in 15 languages, it was found that the use of radio strengthened the coverage of the functional and development themes of the literacy programme, changing people's attitudes towards family planning and it contributed to the establishment of income-generating ventures.[16]

In many developing countries, computers are being introduced in schools as a tool to support the learning process. Research has shown that classrooms are not free from gender bias and therefore gender-sensitive planning of ICT interventions is a precondition to ensure equal access and effective use by girl students of computers in the classroom environment.

World Links, an organization that promotes international tele-collaboration among secondary school teachers and students in developing countries, commissioned a gender assessment study in 2001. The research focused on male and female students in four African countries: Senegal, Mauritania, Uganda and Ghana. The evaluation found that despite efforts to make the programme gender-sensitive, gender inequalities in access persisted. In some schools in Uganda and Ghana, girls do not enjoy equitable access to the computer labs. High student-to-computer ratios and first-come-first serve policies do not favor girls who are typically heavily outnumbered by boys at the secondary level. Girls have earlier curfew hours and domestic responsibilities that limit their access time. Proposed measures to correct this gender bias included encouraging schools to develop "fair use" policies in computer labs, conducting gender sensitivity sessions and advocating for reducing after-school duties of girls to give them more time.[17]

9.4   A Focus on Women in Costa Rica & ICTs[18]

Women as Professionals in IT in Costa Rica: Where We Stand and Why It's Important

Among the poor of the world, women are the poorest: we perform a large amount of unpaid, unaccounted for work. Employment and remuneration are the main source of gender inequality in Costa Rica. The rate of open unemployment in Costa Rica is higher for women (8.2% vs. 5.8% for men), as is the rate of underemployment (7% vs. 4.6% for men). Likewise, the percentage of poor families with female heads of households has grown by 10 per cent in nine years.[19] That is to say, poor Costa Rican families headed by women are ever increasing, which further intensifies the feminization of poverty in the country.

Costa Rica is directing a growing quantity of resources toward transforming information technology, to spearhead the economic development of the country. Already ICTs are generating more than $2 billion dollars annually for Costa Rica, and the industry is one of the fastest growing in the country. Yet, women continue to constitute a minority in the IT professional sector and their participation seems to be decreasing.

According to information provided by CONARE[20], the country has been successful in integrating a significant number of women at the university level and, in some cases, forming a wide majority among graduates. For the year of 2003, of the degrees conferred in the public and private university system, 60% were achieved by women. However, a closer look at the technology related fields presents a very different picture. The presence of a minority of women specifically in the area of information technology can be seen in all state and private universities. Even in institutions in which women form a wide majority at the general level, they constitute a minority in the particular area of technology. For the year of 2003, of the degrees conferred in the public and private university system in the IT field, only 22% were achieved by females.

In terms of professional careers in information technology, a special query of the National Multi-purpose Households Survey, undertaken on a yearly basis by the National Institute of Statistics and Censuses (INEC), also shows lower figures— even a downward trend—regarding women's participation as professionals in this sector. For the years of 2002, 2003 and 2004 the percentages of women employed in IT in Costa Rica are 13%, 11%

and 10%. Finally, regarding the private sector, according to the Costa Rican Chamber of Information and Communication Technologies (CAMTIC), of the total number of businesses registered with the chamber, only 7% of owners and/or managers are women.

Traditionally, the relationship between women and technology has been one of fear and distance. Since technology belongs to the public realm, it has been out of women's reach for many years. It's easy to foresee that if, as women, we don't build our capacity or gain access to the resources that are so highly valued in the Information Society, the feminization of poverty and the exclusion of women from important areas of decision-making will grow deeper. Beyond merely using ICTs, women must gain access to them professionally so that we can occupy positions of greater added value and build capacity in order to transform technologies to meet our own needs.

Since Costa Rica considers IT to be an important opportunity for development, the continued gender imbalance within the sector creates unfavorable conditions for women's socio-economic future. It's very important to examine the level of inclusion of women as professionals in the information technology sector, as well as the strategies that can be adopted to overcome the current gap and allow Costa Rican women to become full participants in the economic development of our country, as active citizens in decision–making, and in defining policies and concrete initiatives in the area of science and technology so that this key sector can also respond to women's needs and priorities.

Local Stakeholders' Vision and Strategies to Overcome the Gender Gap

Every issue's key stakeholders usually include those organizations or institutions— be they public or private—that have a very strong say in the area of interest. In order to influence such a group it's very important to know and understand how they see the subject. This research[21] interviewed stakeholders on the topic of women and IT, from four different sectors: academia, government, civil society and private enterprises.

Based on the perception of the stakeholders interviewed as well as the in-depth interviews from the case studies, the main reasons to explain the digital gender gap in Costa Rica are related to the reinforcement of traditionally stereotyped gender roles in the formal education system; the male-based approach to technology that undermines those aspects of information technology that are more socially related; and the lack of specific policies to address the issue.

The local stakeholders pointed out several strategies they considered would be most effective in bridging the digital gender gap in the professional sector. We've grouped them in the following six categories:

a) *Early Contact*: for example, provide girls the opportunity to use equipment and programs to create a closeness and familiarity with technology; develop summer camps for girls to promote science; improve vocational assistance and guidance; carry out science and technology promotional programs with a gender perspective as well as review how gender roles are promoted in schools.

b) *Pedagogical Changes*: work in partnerships integrating technology and the empowerment of women from a pedagogical perspective; create specific methodologies that take into account that not all people move easily from concrete processes to abstract ones and provide non-sexist conditions in educational environments.

c) *Turning the Focus Around*: humanize technology and give it an emotional aspect; create software, right from the start, for women as well as men; market the various development possibilities within the IT sector emphasizing how access to technology can transform peoples' lives and place young women in the media as role models related to technology.

d) *Affirmative Action*: establish equity guidelines for the private sector and IT quotas in the public university educational system; provide state-promoted ICT training in workplaces where women are employed; reformulate science and technology curricula so they attract both sexes; identify the processes of women's knowledge-building; provide grants for technology-specific educational programs; conduct campaigns in high schools to promote the integration of women in the technology sector; foster union and support among women and conduct specific studies on women and technology.

e) *Social Pressure*: Pressure the government to commit to universal access regarding ICTs and the Internet; make use of the pressure from financial sources to establish political relationships and allies and relaunch the Law of Social Equality, the various conventions, and specifically the Beijing Platform.

f) *State Commitment*: take into account the way women will use the technology, as well as more cooperative uses of it, collective creation, development of areas of interest to women, and ways of approaching the end users; create the economic conditions necessary for women's participation; incorporate the gender issue in the guidelines from the National Council on ICTs and develop coordinated public policies in order to break away from stereotypical roles.

Finally, it seems that the topic of information technology occupies very little space in the women's movement agenda, as well as in the institutions and organizations that fight for gender equity. This is crucial since gender equity is a key aspect of sustainable development and the stakeholders interviewed agree that digital gaps may further broaden the existing gender gap, hence undermining sustainable development. It is important that institutions and organizations that promote gender equity and/or sustainable development incorporate the equitable access of women to information technology professions in their strategic objectives, because this issue is not only about technology, but also development and well-being.

9.5   Gender Stratification and e-Science: Can the Internet Circumvent Patrifocality?[22]

Our work addresses the manner in which the Internet affects the constraints on women pursuing scientific careers in Kerala, India and how this impact has changed over the past decade. We examined 90 face-to-face interviews conducted between 2003 and 2004 with professional scientists in both university and government sectors in Thiruvananthapuram, Kerala, to determine the degree to which recent improvements in Internet connectivity in Kerala have differentially affected the careers of women scientists in terms of educational and research localism, the two main constraints previously identified as restricting to their professional networks.

E-science technologies have often been identified as a means through which to better Third World science and promote development by decreasing the cost and increasing the efficiency of both international and local communication, improving access to information and facilitating international collaboration. On the basis of data collected in 1994, when Internet connections were still very rare in India, Campion and Shrum attributed the lower levels of productivity exhibited by Indian women scientists to higher degrees of career localism and limited access to social rather than material resources.[23] Overall, the networks of male scientists were found to have broader range than those of their female counterparts, leading the authors to suggest that more international opportunities for women should be made available.

Kerala has long attracted the attention of development scholars due to its curious pattern of development – high social development on a weak economic base – as well as the matrilineal organization of the Nair caste. Unlike many other parts of India, the education of girls is encouraged, often more than the education of boys. The social structure, however, is undoubtedly patrifocal. According to Gupta and Sharma (2002), patrifocality differs from patriarchy in that it does not necessarily imply all-around male dominance, but is characterized by subordination of individual interests to that of the family, gender differentiated family roles and authority structures, and an ideology of 'appropriate' female behavior that emphasizes chastity, modesty, and obedience. Within this context, women are prohibited from having prolonged contact with unrelated men, engaging in travel without a proper male escort, exercising authority in household decisions, or maintaining a residence separate from their families. Gender inequity in educational, travel, and work opportunities results in lower access to social capital and embedded network resources.

Although we did not find the Indian women in our sample to be comparatively disadvantaged in terms of level of education, the location of higher education served as a good indicator of the degree of gender stratification that currently exists in Kerala. The analysis of the location of higher education suggests that Indian female scientists were constrained from acquiring their higher degrees from universities outside of Kerala. Many female respondents echoed similar sentiments in regard to limited mobility and the choice to pursue higher studies. The vast majority completed all of their degrees in the state of Kerala. Women simply did not make independent decisions to go abroad for studies—educational decisions were inextricably linked to the decisions of other family members.

The second constraint on social capital identified by Campion and Shrum is the gender difference in work related travel. In the previous study, nearly half the women sampled had no experience at all in a foreign country. Our qualitative interviews ten years yielded little evidence of change: a slight majority of respondents reported at least one visit to the developed world for the purpose of research or training. We did find evidence, however, of increased consciousness among female respondents of the professional importance of travel.

If ICTs are enabling the circumvention of patrifocality, the relative disadvantage of women in education and travel should be diminished to the degree that the Internet serves as a functional substitute for face-to-face contact. Previously, Campion and Shrum (2004) found evidence that evidence that (a) women scientists had larger local networks than men in Kerala; and (b) male scientists had more extensive contacts in India, not including Kerala. Our recent interviews revealed the possibility of change. In comparison with male scientists, women mentioned far fewer contacts within their departments and within India. Instead, they were far more likely to describe their associations with various international scientists. Many female respondents claimed that the Internet was responsible for the cultivation of their international ties. Several mentioned submitting papers to international journals or conferences about which they received information online. Also common were accounts of publishing papers in online journals and subsequently receiving email correspondence from interested readers.

This evidence leads us to propose a "circumvention" hypothesis concerning technological change. New information and communication technologies are used to circumvent the prevailing social structure of patrifocality that restricts interact ional opportunities owing to concerns for female purity and control over domestic labor. Women were found to possess a virtually unchanged degree of educational localism although they expressed a heightened awareness of international professional contacts. Women clearly *discussed* foreign linkages more than their male counterparts and may be engaging in more short-term travel abroad. We cannot establish with this analysis that women have more international professional contacts than men—but it may be equally significant if they *value* their international contacts more than men.

9.6 Women, Education and ICT in Tunisia— Understanding the Issues[24]

The Tunisian Education System: Background and Context

Tunisia became independent in 1956 and very quickly decided to put education at the forefront of its concerns. As a result, in 1958, the first major reform in education laid the foundations of a national educational system open to all Tunisians, regardless of sex, race or religion. Through this reform, quantitative education was achieved and teachers were trained. Later, in 1991, a second reform in education was undertaken and was even more focused on the future. Indeed, it established compulsory and free schooling and a new structure in secondary education. However, Tunisian education needed more ambitious goals for the future generations and in 2002, a huge, comprehensive reform was undertaken with one main objective: quality education for all, girls and boys equally, and for today's learners and tomorrow's citizens of Tunisia and the world.

In the 1960s, full access to education for all children became a reality in primary education. Today, gender parity in education is de facto with recent data indicating that the number of girls has exceeded that of boys at the secondary and university levels. Critical to achieving this goal was the need to train highly-qualified teachers and to build schools in all parts of the country, even in the most remote areas. Today, school enrolment among six-year olds is 99% with no gender disparity. Enrollment for 6-16 year olds is 90% and 12-16 year olds is 75%.

Requirements of the New Reform

Tunisians understand that education has to meet high quality standards to be competitive in a fast changing world. A national discussion, which began in 1995, led to the search and review of new learning strategies, updated learning tools and methodologies. It became obvious that Tunisia needed to update traditional teaching methods and to adopt more contemporary models of learning in new schools. These practical, methodological, entrepreneurial, and behavioral changes would help students adapt new skills and become good citizens. A decision was reached to focus first on the learner who is thus placed the core of the learning process. The mission of the school is now to ensure quality education and to prepare young people for an active life. To do so, more focus has been put on competencies to be acquired by learners who become more autonomous and more involved in the learning process. New learning streams in secondary education have been created to better prepare students for university education and the labor market. The emphasis has been put on the mastery of new technologies and the promotion of arts and culture. Finally, as the role of teachers is highly important, new standards for professionalism have been set.

Strategies for Innovation

To achieve this ambitious New Reform, equally ambitious strategies were adopted. First, students must learn at least two foreign languages; English is taught as a foreign language in secondary education and beginning in 2005, it is taught in the last year of primary education. In addition, all students are taught basic ICT use, which has meant equipping all schools with computers labs and access to Internet. In 2005 all secondary schools were fully connected and in 2006, provisions have been made to connect primary schools to Internet. ICT education is both a separate subject of study and is also integrated as part of all subjects to ensure basic technology literacy for all Tunisians.

As an English inspector, I have trained teachers in developing project-based learning in their classes as an effective tool that fully engages learners. As a member of iEARN (International Education and Resource Network: www.iearn.org) the country has access to a large number of projects of educational benefit to young people around the world. This network brings young people from various countries, cultures, and religions together to develop writing skills and critical thinking while also learning to value other cultures and diversity through meaningful projects and with the assistance of their teachers. This online environment has helped thousands of educators and millions of learners across the globe develop ICT skills but also mutual understanding and a great openness, a great sense of peace and friendship. Our shared ideal is weaving a better planet for the future generations.

Our role as educators is not always easy. It is always difficult to change our own and other teachers' traditions and habits. We resist innovations and changes. Our road is still long and hard, but I strongly believe that what we are building today will certainly become tomorrow's skilled generations of both young women and young men.

9.7 ICT: the Critical Connection for Professional Women in the Middle East — with reference to media[25]

The often complicated and misunderstood Arab World has many paradoxes. In this region, which geographically lies in Asia and Africa, are some of the poorest countries in the world and some the richest. The variation in the ICT knowledge in the region is as vast as the diversity and cultural richness of the 22 nations that comprise the Arab World. The UNDP Arab development report, The State of Knowledge in Arab Countries, proved that knowledge dissemination activities are weak and knowledge production is poor, barriers to knowledge dissemination include an absence of a strategic vision and poor socialization, education, mass media and translation.

The three primary obstacles restraining development in the Arab world are the shortage of: freedom, knowledge and women's empowerment. It is these three deficits, they argue, that hold the frustrated Arabs back from reaching their potential. Lack of freedom and knowledge has a very heavy impact on women's participation in the development in the region. Their participation in political and economic life is the lowest in the world.

In technology, women are much below men in using ICT in the region. The literacy rate is also very low for women. Even though women's literacy rates have tripled in the past 30 years, one in every two Arab women still can neither read nor write. Their participation in their countries' political and economic life is the lowest in the world

The young, university-educated, affluent, urban-based and English-speaking Internet user is also overwhelmingly male. According to the UNDP report 2003, only 6% of Internet users in the Arab States are women.

The digital society, including access, training, scientific and technical employment and women's participation in the knowledge economy imposes many barriers. If women are not active participants and contributors to the shaping of the knowledge society, they stand to lose any gains they have made in the last 20 years. Training constraints for women include cost and social practices, which in effect give men priority for computer use, training, education, and technical advancement. Cultural inhibitions that preclude women's interaction with men in public and, in some areas, preclude women's travel outside the home are also factors restricting women's access to training.

For many years, women's involvement in media work in the Gulf region and the rest of the Arab World has been an issue of debate at local and regional forums. The lack of gender awareness, moreover, is reflected in the belief, prominent among journalists and media practitioners, that general provisions against libel and defamation are sufficient to protect men and women. At the same time, the situation of the male-dominated media setting has also been critically noted. In recent years, however, the expansion of professional and college-level educational media programs in the region has opened up new opportunities for bringing about demographic changes within the region's media landscape, particularly with the rising female enrollment rates within these programs.

Yet, despite this emerging reality, the situation remains rather grim, not only in terms of the volume of female input into media work, but also in terms of the quality of their contributions compared to their male counterparts. Research has shown that while more women are attending media study programs at colleges and universities, very few of them choose media work as their permanent career. A whole host of problems arise against Arab, especially Gulf Arab, women's involvement in media work.

In this regard, it was noted that mere women presence in media organizations, though a significant step in affecting more balance in the existing biased media scene, was not the ultimate goal sought in this drive for women integration into media work. Women need to enjoy more professional mobility privileges within media organizations to take up top management positions as decision makers.

Although there is a notable increase in women's presence in media organizations in the Arab World particularly on television and radio, women continue to have limited participation and access to decision-making in the communications industry and in governing bodies that influence media policy. Further, women are still unable to shape programme content and ensure coverage of women's priority issues and concerns. Negative and stereotyped representations of women in the media continue while the projection of the cultural diversity and varying realities of women's lives remains absent. Media codes of conduct at national levels have not been effective in ensuring positive portrayals of women in the media all over the Arab World. On the other hand, gender coding operates as many women media practitioners still tend to be assigned to "soft" issues such as culture, arts and lifestyle while men are assigned to "more important" issues like politics and the economy

The UNESCO Chair for Communication Technology for Women in the GCC, which was established late in 2003, was a real call for raising public awareness of women as significant components in the media workforce, as well as for modifying existing legal frameworks and social attitudes towards women opting for media careers. Its call for empowering women media practitioners to achieve leadership positions has been the most significant outcome to date.

As the Communication implications are having the most profound effect on society these days, the Chair was heavily involved in the promotion of the ICT as a serious tool for empowerment for women in the media in the region to help overcome the long, irregular hours, highly demanding, mixed gender environment which often includes travel. These are the biggest barriers to women's participation in the media in the region. Part of the mission also included calling on media organizations in the GCC states to launch large-scale training programs to enhance women's use of IT in media work and to enable them to cope with accelerating developments in information and communications technologies in a manner conducive to improving media work practices for women.

In addition, the Chair worked heavily in calling on educational, cultural and media organizations in the GCC region to create greater awareness among media decision makers of the huge potential of information technologies as empowerment tools for women, calling on media organizations to emphasize the human and social aspects of information technology in media work and highlighting the centrality of creative women in realizing the goals of IT systems.

It is only through continued training and support from the UNESCO Chair in the region that the role of women in media will continue to grow. In the few short years that the chair has been in existence it has been shown that numerous women in the region have benefited from the training workshops and programs which are currently on-going.

9.8 Notes

1 Authors in order of the section they contributed. The chapter was compiled and edited by Morrell and Waugh.

2 This section was written by Nancy Hafkin, Ph.D., Director, Knowledge Working; Former Coordinator, African Information Society Initiative, United National Economic Commission for Africa

3 Hafkin, N. & Taggert, N. (2001). Gender, information technology, and developing countries: An analytic study. Washington , D.C: Academy for Educational Development.

4 This section was written by Claudia Morrell, Executive Director, Center for Women and Information Technology.

5 Kofi, Annan, (2003). United Nations Secretary-General. *Statement to the World Summit on the Information Society.* Geneva, 10 December 2003.

6 United Nations Division for the Advancement of Women Department of Economic and Social Affairs. *Information and Communication Technologies and their Impact on and Use as an Instrument for the Advancement and Empowerment of Women.* Report of the Expert Group Meeting, 2002. Retrieved January 7, 2006.
http://www.un.org/womenwatch/daw/egm/ict2002/reports/EGMFinalReport.pdf .

7 United Nations Forty-seventh Session of the Commission on the Status of Women. Participation and Access of Women to the Media, and Information and Communications Technologies and Their Impact on and Use as an Instrument for the Advancement and Empowerment of Women. Agreed Conclusions 2003. Retrieved January 7, 2006.
http://www.un.org/womenwatch/daw/csw/47sess.htm#conclusions .
http://www.itu.int/wsis/docs/geneva/official/dop.html .

8 World Summit on the Information Society. *Declaration of Principles: Building the Information Society: a Global Challenge in the New Millennium.* Document WSIS-03/GENEVA/DOC/4-E. 2003. Retrieved January 7, 2006.
http://www.itu.int/wsis/docs/geneva/official/dop.html .

9 Hafkin, N. & Taggert, N. *Gender, information technology, and developing countries: An analytic study.* Washington, D.C.: Academy for Educational Development.

10 Huyer, S & Westholm, G. *Toolkit on Gender Indicators in Engineering, Science and Technology.* UNESCO and the Gender Advisory Board. UNCSTD. Paris. 2005.

11 Morrell, C. &Huyer, S. Engendering ICTs for Education. *Harnessing the Potential of ICT for Education: A Multistakeholder Approach.* United Nations ICT Task Force Series 9. 2005.

12 Ibid.

13 Ibid.

14 This section was written by Chat Garcia Ramilo, Director of the Women's Networking Support Program of the Association for Progressive Communications.

15 Hafkin, N. *Gender Issues in ICT Policy in Developing Countries: An overview.* UNDAW Expert Group Meeting on Information and Communication Technologies and Their Impact on and Use as an Instrument for the Advancement and Empowerment of Women. Seoul, Korea. Nov 2002.

16 Siaciwena, R. Ed. *Case Studies of Non-formal Education by Distance and Open Learning.* The Commonwealth of Learning. Department for International Development. UK. 2000.

17 Gurumurthy, A. *Gender and ICTs, Overview Report, Bridge.* ICT in Education, e-ASEAN Taskforce and UNDP-APDIP, May 2003. Tinio, Victoria. September 2004 . Retrieved January 31, 2006. <http://www.bridge.ids.ac.uk/reports/CEP-ICTs-OR.pdf>.
18 This section was written by Margarita Salas.
19 "Tenth State of the Nation Report on Sustainable Human Development." State of the Nation Program. San José, Costa Rica. 2004.
20 CONARE. Higher Education Planning Office. *Statistics on diplomas issued.* 2001–2003.
21 Salas, M. *Women as Professionals in the Costa Rican Information Technology Sector Exploring the Relationship between Sustainable Development and Gender Gaps in the Information Society.* Retrieved January 31, 2006. http://www.iisd.org/pdf/2005/networks_dev_connection_costa_rica.pdf .
22 This section was written by Meredith Anderson.
23 P.Campion and W. Shrum, "Gender and Science in Development: Women Scientists in Ghana, Kenya, and India", *Science, Technology & Human Values.* 29. 2004: 459-485
24 This section was written by Héla Nafti, President of the Tunisian Alliance of Female Teachers (UNFT).
25 This section was written by Reem Obeidat, UNESCO Chair, Communication Technology & Journalism for Women, Dubai Women's College.

10. PROMISE AND PRACTICE OF OPEN ACCESS TO *E*-SCIENCE

Paul Wouters, *The Royal Netherlands Academy of Arts and Sciences*[1]
Christine Hine, *University of Surrey*
Kirsten A. Foot, *University of Washington*
Steven M. Schneider, *SUNY Institute of Technology*
Subbiah Arunachalam, *M S Swaminathan Research Foundation*
Raed Sharif, *Syracuse University*

10.1 Introduction

Open access is a key issue in the development of the information society. It may also shape the extent to which the generation of new scientific and scholarly research itself can be tuned to the future needs of developed and developing countries. Much of the promise of *e*-science is based on an implicit notion that open access will accelerate scientific and technological development and will increase the number of people and institutions that can tap into these shared resources. However, this begs the question of what open access actually signifies: access to what for whom? This chapter will take up this key question and look into what open access to *e*-science and *e*-research will mean, and how novel regimes of open access may affect the dynamics of knowledge creation and dissemination at the international level.

The following issues are, we think, particularly crucial in the shaping of information access in *e*-science:

-   open access to what? – how does open access to scientific information affect what *e*-researchers actually produce?
-   problems of data sharing: what are the prospects of access to and sharing of scientific and scholarly data, and what does large-scale data sharing mean for information infrastructures and knowledge practices?
-   open access and scientific accountability: should open access citation indexes be built and if so how?
-   disciplinary differences in *e*-research: how do scientific and scholarly fields differ in their capacity for open access practices and infrastructures?

- open access for whom? – which legitimate boundaries to open
  access to scholarly research are recognised and who decides upon its
  conditions?
- how open are collaboratories? – will global collaboratories promote
  open access or are they simply the new form of elitist invisible
  colleges?
- open access to scientific methodologies: how can open source
  repositories of scientific and scholarly methods and techniques be
  built?

Discussing all these questions is firmly beyond the scope of this chapter. We will focus on particular aspects by the presentation of a variety of research projects that each in their own way bring particular perspectives that are often not included in the debate on open access. Christine Hine (University of Surrey) asks us to pay attention to the tension between high level calls for open access, the development of open access technologies, and the practice of research on the ground. On the basis of a thorough study of the practice in the field of systematics in biology, she shows that a practice of open access will always be highly specific to the local context. Therefore, one should not put ones cards on a particular configuration or technology of open access. Hine pleads for agnosticism regarding the forms open access should take. Kirsten Foot (University of Washington) and Steve Schneider (SUNY) point to a growing digital divide in the area of Web archiving. Since the development of the information society produces increasing amounts of information that is born digitally, the issue of who preserves what is rather crucial. Foot and Schneider show that there is a growing need for systematic preservation of digital information resources to document the historical development of information-based societies. Not only have few countries already developed a digital preservation strategy, there are indications that the North-South divide is reproducing in this area, with important and problematic implications for the legacy and cultural heritage of the information society. A concern with the information society in the South is also key in Subbiah Arunachalam's Information Village project, which aims to bring truly twoway information and communication technologies to the villages in India. A different take on a comparable problem is taken by Raed Shariff (Syracuse University) who proposes a conceptual schema to understand the practice of open access for scientific communities in South America. The goal of his model is to compare the common obstacles facing scientific communities in different types of countries, and develop recommendations to overcome these barriers. Paul Wouters (Virtual Knowledge Studio for the Humanities and Social Sciences) discusses the paradox that the very idea of open access poses to the practice of knowledge creation. Because this practice is strongly fragmented, and the universal nature of knowledge is not a given property but the result of translation work, the development of scientific knowledge recreates ever new boundaries and barriers to open access. At the same time, the ongoing specialization in science calls for more open access regimes and mechanisms. The tension will never be solved, but does seem to be driving the debate about open access.

10.2 The Politics and Practice of Accessibility in Systematics[2]

This paper focuses on a case study exploring moves within the biological discipline of systematics to make the tools and the products of research accessible online to the wider community. I will be exploring the way in which one scientific community has experienced and explored the visions offered by digital technologies for open access. I will be arguing that high level calls for open access do indeed resonate with many areas of practice, and provide fruitful ways for practitioners to understand their work and extend it in new directions. On the ground, however, open access to scientific information turns out to be highly specific to the situations in which it is developed. It has become inevitable in many fields of science that digital solutions to the sharing of information will be developed, thanks to the prevailing cultural current that places hopes and expectations in these technologies. Specific solutions, however, are often carefully crafted for their context and in the process may explore other technologies and forms of interaction. It appears to be important, on this basis, to continue to hold discussions on the appropriate technologies for particular information ecologies, and to remain agnostic about the forms in which information should be communicated.

The community on which I focus is systematics, the branch of biology concerned with the classification and naming of organisms and with exploring the relationships between them. The practice of systematics is largely focused around collections of specimens, and the location of these collections is shaped by the legacy of the discipline in a colonial past. Alongside this enduring geographic imbalance a new awareness of the practical and political significance of taxonomic information has recently emerged. At the Rio Earth Summit in 1992 the Convention on Biological Diversity was signed, committing its signatories to share access to taxonomic expertise (http://www.biodiv.org). The complex political geography of systematics was noted, and processes of data repatriation (latterly more often termed data sharing) were proposed to address the prevailing inequalities. It is thus becoming routine for systematics institutions to make their collections databases openly available via the Internet. In contrast with many scientific disciplines which are experimenting with closed e-science communities, systematics has been positioned by a consciousness of the political dimensions of exclusion to opt for open data sharing practices.

The prevailing expectations that digital resources will be developed, both as specifically manifested in the Convention on Biological Diversity and the national responses to it, and as a broader cultural current, mean that detailed research on who will use digital resources and how has been largely sidelined. There is little requirement, in this climate, to justify an innovation by reference to an identified group of users actually calling for it, to run carefully evaluated pilot projects demonstrating enhanced access and the meeting of needs, or to conduct usability studies and detailed requirements analysis. The requirement for a digital resource is taken to be self-evident. Users, and the practices to make use meaningful are expected to emerge once the resource is in place rather than preceding and informing resources development. This "if we build it they will come" expectation is built into the current political climate which systematics faces, such that institutions cannot afford not to develop and promote these resources.

In the face of this pressure to develop digital infrastructures for data sharing in systematics, a wide diversity of solutions have arisen. Many are carefully crafted in the face of specific circumstances, developing appropriate technologies and social relations for the task at hand. Often, digital technologies will be only part of an array of solutions, with the mobility of contributors, work across the provider/user divide and sharing of information and perspectives as important as developing an end product. Some solutions for "data sharing" will be digital, whilst others may be hybrid forms (such as a capacity to produce an alternative form of hard copy identification aid from a digital resource) and others may bypass the digital altogether. Digital solutions catch the headlines in contemporary systematics, but a diverse array of work on heterogeneous solutions goes on under the surface.

Systematics represents a community within which it has come to be understood that data and resources must be shared. They are trying to find appropriate and feasible ways to make that happen, in the face of concerted pressure from policy makers and funders to deploy the digital technologies which are seen as efficient, effective and symbolically potent. Systematics is an already hard-pressed community which has seen its practitioners ageing and its funding base dwindling. It is also a thoroughly reflexive community: there are well established traditions of talking on a disciplinary level about the status of taxonomic work, and about appropriate directions for development. Systematics has thus been able to find its own sense and its own opportunity in the grand initiatives. Grand visions are made meaningful through the crafted solutions that populate them and through the ability of practitioners to interpret their activities through those visions. Whilst users may be sidelined in the policy talk that makes digital solutions inevitable, they come back in as systematists try to make sense of their work on a daily basis.

There are some messages here for an open access movement that places belief in the ability of digital solutions to realise access to information. The experience of systematics suggests that too great a focus on the movement, and too much emphasis on the ability of particular technologies to realise a desired effect can be counter productive. A belief in the inevitability of digital solutions can sideline consideration of potential users and transform it into a simple belief that they will come. From this perspective open access looks like a low cost technical fix to issues of inequality, and of course nothing is that simple. However, we can expect that within the "open access movement" a wide diversity of initiatives may proliferate, and these will make sense to those most directly involved in a variety of ways which cross and blur the distinction between providers and users of information. There will be a need to remain open to non-digital solutions, and to respect the capacity of practitioners to craft their own appropriate technologies, even whilst we celebrate the ability of grand visions of open access to inspire, stimulate and offer a way of making sense of diverse experience.

10.3 Preserving Open Access through Web Archiving[3]

Information resources are increasingly not only "born digitally" but "die digitally" as well. Many resources that are posted on the public Web have great value across the international information society-- as long as they remain accessible on the Web. However, current estimates of the average lifespan of a Web page range from 44 days to 100 days (SAP AG, 2004; Rein, 2004). There is a growing need for systematic identification, evaluation and preservation of many digital information resources to document the historical development of information-based societies as well as to provide the public, along with scholars, journalists and other social, business and political analysts, the primary digital materials necessary for many kinds of retrospective analyses. However, few countries have developed a strategy for preserving digital information resources. Web objects that inscribe many kinds of knowledge, cultural identities, social movements, and collective memories would gain value over time if properly preserved and catalogued, but most disappear as Web files are re-written and technology platforms change. Furthermore, the few large-scale, systematic Web archiving efforts underway are concentrated in the EU, the US, and Australia, led in most cases by national libraries with a mandate to preserve Web objects deemed to have national value. While laudable, this suggests a disproportionate level of loss of Web objects produced in developing countries.

Our interest in Web archiving focuses on archiving as a scholarly activity. We are concerned about the unevenness of current Web archiving for scholarly purposes, and particularly the lack of archiving of Web objects produced in the global South. We want to explore what it would take to develop an environment of what could be considered equitable archiving. In this presentation we provided an overview of the Web archiving process, identified legal and ethical issues in Web archiving which need to be addressed by the open access movement, and suggested that open access values should inform the development of digital preservation strategies.

There are several reasons why scholars are interested in Web archiving, and will be increasingly interested in the future. Web archives, when built with scholarship in mind, enable retrospective and developmental analyses of many kinds of social, cultural, and political phenomena that are enacted on the Web. These kinds of analyses are foundational to systematic social research on any topic; employing them in Internet studies allows researchers to move beyond investigations of the present. Although some types of research questions about the Web and society can be answered without Web archives, other questions can only be investigated via Web archives. For instance, questions about how relations between various kinds of actors take shape and evolve on the Web are best answered by examining how the Web artifacts these actors produce over time. Similarly, some approaches to research that might be characterized as having an "open architecture," such as grounded theory development, are enriched by access to Web archives. Archiving creates opportunities for social researchers to develop perspectives of the Web via an emergent approach; remaining open to phenomenon that emerge through the observation process, and having the opportunity to "go back in time" to trace the Web practices of various actors. Even if a particular study can be conducted based on the "live" Web, an archive of the Web objects employed in the study allows for replication of that study, and more robust evaluation of findings across studies-- thus enhancing the reliability of Web research.

Researchers who decide to archive will find challenges as well as opportunities. Technical challenges include the substantial hardware, software, and operational capacity that may be required to produce an archive, depending on the scale of the project, and the desired post-project life of the archive. Legally, copyright laws in many countries present challenges to archiving activities, even when engaged in for scholarly purposes. In the U.S., the fair use doctrine needs to be re-thought in view of Web objects. The research review boards at academic institutions need to be made aware of the scholarly value of Web archives, and new policies must be developed that support legal and ethical Web archiving for scholarship.

One ethical consideration that is largely overlooked in discussions of Web archiving is the specter of information imperialism-- that is, the ways in which current Web archiving activities replicate historical patterns in economic and political relations of privilege and dependency. By examining, in a global context, who archives Web objects, which Web objects are archived, and who has access to Web archives, we see clear indicators of a north-south divide. The Internet Archive, a non-profit organization in San Francisco, is the largest Web archive-builder in the world. National libraries and research universities in wealthy countries produce a growing number of Web archives, focused mainly on sites deemed to be of national interest or of scholarly value—most of which are produced in other wealthy countries. Some government bodies engage in Web archiving beyond what their national libraries build. Other than large, well-funded libraries, few nongovernmental organizations, whether public or private, are actively archiving Web objects. There is little evidence of Web archiving activity by any kind of organization in Asian, African, or South American countries— and relatively few Web objects produced in these countries are preserved in Web archives elsewhere. A global look at access to Web archives brings the disparity into sharper focus. Due to funding considerations and copyright concerns, access to most Web archives is highly controlled, and restricted to "members" of the archiving organization or institution. Few Web archives are actually freely available on the public Web. Some institutions in the global north host Web archives that include substantial amounts of Web material produced in the global south, but, through access policies, render them out of reach to citizens from southern countries who do not share membership privileges that might allow remote, Web-based access, and cannot afford to travel to the hosting institutions.

We propose that a concept of equitable archiving be considered in future discussions of Web archiving strategies and priorities. This concept should include ways of ensuring that sites from various cultures are archived, as Britz and Lor (2004) have argued. They offer a moral justification for transnational Web archiving; we suggest that attention must also be paid to developing a moral justification for free, Web-based access to Web archives that have already been built. Specifically, we advocate a three-prong approach: 1) developing broad collection policies to include Web materials produced in a range of countries, northern and southern; 2) funding cross-national Web archiving and archive-based scholarly activity; and 3) building global awareness of and sensitivity to the need to prospectively identify Web materials for preservation. As individual scholars, we can advance Web archiving by collaborating with libraries, museums, and traditional archives, and building partnerships with these institutions into the research grant applications we write. Imagine the potential benefits that would accrue over time if we all, as social researchers who study anything on the Web, would create archives of the objects we study, deposit those archives in an institutional repository, and insist on rapid indexing and free, Web-based, open access as the condition of our contributions.

10.4 The Information Village Research Project[4]

Access to knowledge through unhindered flow of relevant information can not only create a level playing field for researchers (lab-to-lab) in the developing world and thus hasten advances in knowledge but also can help the rural poor overcome poverty. What is more, as pointed out by Bruce Alberts and as shown by the Information Village Research Project of MSSRF, we can bring these two widely different communities to engage in a two-way communication (land-to-lab and lab-to-land)thus facilitating rural needs driving the research agenda. In a sense, the new information and communication technologies, especially the Internet and the World Wide Web, can not only help democratise the flow of information as they lend themselves readily to the public commons approach but can also help us realise the 'social functions of science' ás desired by John Bernal. Besides, such a culture of information has other benefits as was demonstrated recently following the tsunami tragedy in Asia; wherever information flow was better, relief operations could be carried out more effectively than in other areas.

10.5 Scientific Communities' Access to Public Domain Information in Latin America: A Comparative Study[5]

The critical role of science and technology in the future well-being of a country's citizens and how well the country can compete in the global market place has been continuously emphasized in the huge body of development literature produced during the last 3 decades. Nevertheless, scientific communities in developing countries still face different kinds of problems and obstacles that slow down, if not hinder, their development and potential impact and influence on their communities. Unlike research communities in developed countries who enjoy high levels of governmental and non-governmental support, advanced infrastructure, and access to public domain information, scientific communities in developing countries still struggle to get the basic requirements to conduct their research. The lack of sound government policies to promote and develop scientific research, coupled with the poor technical infrastructure and the inaccessibility of public domain information, are among the most critical obstacles that currently face the scientific communities in developing countries. With the current insufficient level of attention and interest at a national and international level to solve these problems, these obstacles are expected to remain at least for the next five to ten years.

This presentation focuses on the scientific communities' access to public domain information in Latin American countries. The paper provides a conceptual framework to study the current situation of scientific communities' access to public domain information, to identify the current main obstacles and best practices, if any, and, based on other developed countries experiences and lessons learned, to propose a set of suggestions and recommendations to handle these obstacles. Based on different development indicators (e.g., Human Development Index, literacy rate, political stability), Latin America's countries will be divided into 3 categories: least developed countries, developing countries and developed countries. Within this special categorization of Latin America's countries, one country will be selected from each category to be studied. The logic behind this categorization is to compare the common obstacles facing scientific communities in each category and more importantly, to try to customize suggestions and recommendations based on the situation in each category.

10.6 Open Access to What for Whom?[6]

Open access to scientific information is a key element in thinking about the information society. It is also a banner of social movements theories and practices, which attempt to break the shackles of present information monopolies, be they private companies or governmental bureaucracies. The World Wide Web and the Internet are usually seen as catalysts to construct new forms of public voice and to open up the available pool of data and information. The open access movement is also based on the assumption that more consumption of information, data, or knowledge will lead to a better society. This may be formulated in terms of less economic imbalance or inequality, accelerated innovation and welfare production, and improved public services in areas as otherwise diverse as health care, education, and environmental management. In short, open access is a rallying cry for a diverse collection of actors.

Moreover, open access seems to be an uncontroversial "good thing": who indeed could be opposed to open access to information? However, if one looks more closely into the matter, different actors mean different things if they refer to open access. Differences focus on: "access to what?", "access for whom?", and "access under which conditions?". Commercial publishers tend to think quite differently about these issues than, say, an average scientific group in India or South America. There is even more to it: open access is itself the product of a professional group with particular perspectives and interests: the scholars in the fields of information and library science and information economics. The way we think about open access is usually based on a set of assumptions about information and research practices that are not always as critically examined as they deserve. In other words, because open access is itself a social and political construct, although surely a valuable one, it is best to not take it for granted but open it up for scrutiny. One could say, of course, that this should not be a concern for those who strive for open access. However, why should we leave a critical examination of what open access means only to the opponents of open access? The section by Christine Hine in this chapter nicely shows how a close look at the practices of researchers and information workers can add to our knowledge of open access.

At a more general level, we think that three intellectual strategies are important to analyze open access. The first is to take resistance to open access seriously. This entails an attitude which is not primarily normative in its reading of counterarguments to the pleas of the open access movement. The second strategy is more philosophical: the analysis of the assumptions about science as a public good that underly particular open access arguments, technologies and configurations. The third strategy, on which this chapter mainly relies, is the analysis of real-world impacts and practices of open access, such as the use of the Web and Web services to promote and realize open access. This includes a critical discussion of the role of ICT in the shaping of access to scientific information. After all, the Web is not always as open as its protagonists hope or claim it to be. In addition, we address the concept of openness itself, noting that open systems require adherence to particular sets of communicative, organizational, and technological knowledges. ICT in this sense may actually be employed to foreground already powerful actors, thereby both maintaining present inequalities in resources and restricting access to new users.

This is not only a matter of technology. For example, with respect to data sharing, scientific researchers may have rational reasons to refuse to share their data (Beaulieu 2003). Data sharing may create new problems in the distribution of resources among research groups. The privacy of research subjects may be compromised by forms of open access that were not foreseen at the time of the research. Researchers may be scooped on the basis of their own data. This risk may be larger for smaller laboratories than for big research institutes. An open access regime may therefore be more advantageous to already powerful scientific actors, instead of leveling the playing field. And we should not forget that preparing scientific data for access to other researchers involves a lot of work for which researchers are usually not rewarded. No wonder that the goal of access to (raw) scientific data is and will remain a controversial issue in the years to come (Wouters & Schröder 2003). At the same time, enabling large-scale access to scientific data will only become more pressing due to the increasing role of these data in society (Arzberger et al. 2004).

Analysis of these types of controversies is necessary to better understand what open access may mean for different audiences and actor groups. It is also instrumental to tackle an interesting paradox that the very goal of open access poses to scientific and information practices, a paradox that becomes visible when we follow the second intellectual strategy mentioned above: immanent critique. Open access is based on the idea that in principle anyone could make use of scientific knowledge and data if only they had (physical) access to it. Knowledge is seen as a universal phenomenon. However, we know that the creation of scientific knowledge is embedded in very local contexts. Knowledge is part of a disciplinary matrix and only within this matrix, made up of scholarly paradigms and theoretical and methodological frameworks, does a particular knowledge claim make sense. Diffusion of knowledge is never simply diffusion, it is first and foremost translation. The universal nature of scientific knowledge is not a given property but the result of this translation work by researchers, scholars, teachers, journalists and other knowledge processors. In our discussion of open access, this means that knowledge creation is an act of segmentation and boundary creation. As a result, most scientific journals are inaccessible by definition: one needs to be an expert in a particular field to be able to understand most of them. The process of specialization in the scientific profession is strongly related to this. Knowledge grows by specialization and splitting, a process which recurrently creates new boundaries and barriers to open access.

At the same time, the increasing specialization calls for even more open access to sustain the translation process of this specialized knowledge to other domains, both inside and outside of the whole of the sciences. This leads to an inevitable paradox: open access needs to be sustained by open architectures and technologies that are themselves based on standardization and norms made universal. But in order for open access to be meaningful access to meaningful knowledge, it must be access to a very fragmented patchwork of knowledge claims and knowledge practices. This, it seems to us, is not an afterthought but is part of the very idea of open access itself. The paradox drives the dynamics of open access practices and technologies. What this means for standards for open access policies can only be explored by more empirical research of a large variety of scientific and technical work.

10.7 References

Peter Arzberger, Peter Schroeder, Anne Beaulieu, Geof Bowker, Kathleen Casey, Leif Laaksonen, David Moorman, Paul Uhlir, and Paul Wouters (2004), "An International Framework to Promote Access to Data", *Science*, Vol 303, Issue 5665, 1777-1778, 19 March 2004, DOI: 10.1126/science.1095958, http://www.sciencemag.org/cgi/content/summary/303/5665/1777

Beaulieu, A. (2003) "Research woes and new data flows", in *Promise and practice in data sharing*, Paul Wouters and Peter Schröder (eds.) Book series: Paul Wouters and Peter Schröder (eds.), The Public Domain of Digital Research Data, NIWI-KNAW, Amsterdam

Britz, Johannes J., and Lor, Peter, 2004. "Moral Perspective on South-North Web Archiving," *Journal of Information Science*, December, V. 30, N. 6, pp. 540-549.

Rein, Lisa, Interview with Brewster Kahle, Internet Archive, published by O'Reilly Open P2P, 01.22.2004, http://www.openp2p.com/pub/a/p2p/2004/01/22/kahle.html. Accessed May 19, 2005.

SAP AG, Interview with Neil Beagrie, British Library, published by SAP INFO Online, 02.08.2004, http://www.sapinfo.net/index.php4?ACTION=noframe&url=http://www.sapinfo.net/publi c/en/index.php4/article/Article-3089140c577c931a92/en/articleStatisti . Accessed May 19, 2005.

Paul Wouters and Peter Schröder (eds.) (2003), *Promise and practice in data sharing* In: Book series: Paul Wouters and Peter Schröder (eds.) *The Public Domain of Digital Research Data*, NIWI-KNAW, Amsterdam, ISBN 90 6472 184 x, 96 pp.

10.8 Notes

1 Authors in order of the section they contributed. The chapter was compiled and edited by Paul Wouters.

2 This section was written by Christine Hine, Department of Sociology, University of Surrey, UK (c.hine@surrey.ac.uk). A longer version of this paper is available at http://www.soc.surrey.ac.uk/pdfs/hinewsis.pdf

3 This section was written by Kirsten A. Foot and Steven M. Schneider. Kirsten Foot: Department of Communication, University of Washington (kfoot@u.washington.edu); Steve Schneider: Department of Social Sciences and Humanities, SUNY Institute of Technology (steve@sunyit.edu).

4 This section was written by Subbiah Arunachalam, M S Swaminathan Research Foundation, Chennai, India (subbiah.arunachalam@gmail.com)

5 This section was written by Raed Sharif, School of Information Studies, Syracuse University (rmalshar@syr.edu).

6 This section was written by Paul Wouters, The Virtual Knowledge Studio for the Humanities and Social Sciences, The Royal Netherlands Academy of Arts and Sciences (paul.wouters@vks.knaw.nl). He would like to thank Anne Beaulieu, Matt Ratto and Katie Vann for their contributions to the presentation at the conference in Tunis.

11. GAINING AND SUSTAINING ACCESS TO SCIENCE FINDINGS

Carol Priestley, *International Network for the Availability of Scientific Publications*[1]
Margaret Ngwira, *University of Malawi*
Dina El Halaby, *Global Development Network, Giza*
Maurice Long, *BMJ Publishing Group, London*
Augustin Gaschignard, *Scientific and Technical Information System, Accra*
Emilija Banionyte, *Vilnius Pedagogical Library, Vilnius*
Patricia Campion, *Tennessee Technological University*

11.1 How PERI Enhances Access to Science Information in Developing Countries[2]

Despite the massive growth in Internet connectivity and many discussions on the need to bridge digital divides, numerous higher education institutions in developing and transitional countries lacked access to up-to-date journals, databases, and other information resources. They were also challenged in their ability to communicate the results of their own research to local and global audiences.

To address these issues, in 1999 INASP joined several African university libraries and researchers in a pilot project to test the logistics of providing access to up-to-date international scholarly information and knowledge, to enable developing country research to be published, accessed and disseminated locally, and to provide appropriate training to achieve these ends. This pilot evolved into the 'Programme for the Enhancement of Research Information' (PERI) that aims to strengthen research capacities in developing and transitional countries by reinforcing local efforts to produce, disseminate and gain access to scholarly information and knowledge.

Focusing on experiences in Malawi since 2001, the speakers briefly introduce PERI's main components: delivering research and scholarly information; disseminating national research; enhancing ICT skills; and strengthening local publishing. PERI – and other initiatives – prove that providing access is but the first step towards information self-sufficiency. There are new challenges to be faced, including the effective optimization and management of available bandwidth, the ability to utilize the wealth of information through enhancing skills in selection and evaluation, and finding ways to work effectively in networks and consortia.

11.2 How GDNET Supports Social Science Researchers in Developing Countries[3]

GDNet (www.gdnet.org) is one of the core activities of the Global Development Network (GDN). The Global Development Network, a worldwide association of research and policy institutes, promotes the generation, sharing, and application to policy of multidisciplinary knowledge for the purpose of development. GDNet is the vehicle through which GDN promotes the communication of research produced in developing and transition countries to stimulate its application to policy.

GDNet provides a series of services aimed at supporting Southern researchers in producing research. It facilitates free access for developing country researchers to key services normally only available through paid subscriptions such as journals and funding opportunities. It also presents researchers with a venue to disseminate their work and make it freely available to the local as well as global research community.

GDNet has pursued two different strategies to facilitate access to online services. One is by applying strict acceptance procedures and hence performing initial controls at the global level to ensure that researchers accessing the service are based in a developing country and, therefore, are eligible to receive the service. Services offered through this strategy include access to funding opportunities from the Community of Science database and access to journal articles through Project MUSE. The other strategy is providing access to services at the regional level through the Regional Network Partners. Researchers in CIS and MENA regions have free access to online journals offered by JSTOR.

GDNet also provides librarians with a document delivery service through the British Library of Development Studies (BLDS). Based at the UK Institute of Development Studies, BDLS holds Europe's largest research collection on economic and social change in developing countries.

On the dissemination front, the Knowledge Base represents the backbone of GDNet, bringing together valuable national and regional social science knowledge that up to now has been very difficult to find. The Knowledge Base is made up of three interlinked directories of researchers, research papers, and research institutes based in developing and transition countries. The Knowledge Base currently boasts almost 10,000 documents, 3,000 organizations and 4,500 researchers. GDNet seeks out, selects, and repackages research generated in developing and transition countries to present relevant local knowledge in a clear, concise, and user-friendly format, to researchers as well as policymakers. GDNet also offers hosting services for documents that are not available online.

11.3 How HINARI Enables Health Researchers to Gain Access to Health and Biomedical Literature[4]

HINARI (Health InterNetwork Access to Research Initiative) resulted from a request by the World Health Organization (WHO) to leading healthcare and biomedical research publishers to provide online access to their current and back journals for researchers in the developing world. The publishers agreed to work with the WHO and other partners to make this possible, and the program was initiated in January 2002. More than 70 international publishers now offer full text access to more than 3,000 leading peer reviewed journals.

Library collections in very many countries have deteriorated badly in the last 20 years. Even though access to the World Wide Web is still expensive and intermittent in some of the poorest countries, the situation is improving, and programs like HINARI can leapfrog the print-and-distribute model to provide access to vast amounts of current and historic research literature. From the beginning, HINARI has been aimed to fulfill the needs of researchers and clinicians, rather than front line healthcare workers. In 69 of the poorest countries, researchers in qualifying institutions access the journal collection entirely free. In some of the lower middle income countries, an annual fee of $1,000 is collected. The publishers return all revenue to the WHO for use in training and outreach programs.

In general, HINARI is working very well. Almost 2 million PDF documents have been downloaded in the last year, and more publishers and more institutions are continuing to join this cooperative program. At the recent Partners' Meeting held at the National Academy of Sciences in Washington (21 June 2005), it was agreed to link HINARI to the Millennium Development Goals. An evaluation program is under way. Results are due to be presented to the partners in June 2006, to determine the shape of the program from 1 January 2007 onwards.

In October 2003, HINARI's sister program, AGORA (Access to Global Online Research in Agriculture), sponsored by the Food and Agriculture Organization (FAO) was launched, and the two programs run in tandem, sharing much common infrastructure, reflecting the symbiotic relationship between health, nutrition and agriculture.

11.4 How SIST Supports the Development of Information and Communication Systems for Education and Research Institutions in Africa[5]

SIST (Scientific and Technical Information System) is a cooperation project from the French Ministry of Foreign Affairs financed by 3 million euros over 3 years starting in January 2004. At present, 12 countries participate: Algeria, Benin, Burkina-Faso, Burundi, Cameroon, Côte d'Ivoire, Ghana, Madagascar, Mali, Nigeria, Senegal, and Tunisia. This project mainly aims at the following: promoting research in Africa by encouraging and developing the exchange, production and dissemination of both scientific and technological information; promoting science and technology by helping African researchers to develop their own analytical abilities in key research areas; and putting African Science at the service of sustainable development by enhancing regional research development on the priorities defined by the countries.

The presentation introduces the project and its main achievements: a scientific and technical information system installed in the twelve countries; training programs on SIST as well as in editing electronic publications; and putting in place thematic research networks.

11.5 How eIFL Supports the Wide Availability of Electronic Information in Developing Country Libraries[6]

eIFL.net is an umbrella organization of library consortia in 50 developing and transition countries. eIFL.net negotiates, supports, motivates, and advocates for the wide availability of quality electronic information by library users from education, research, professional communities, governmental organizations, and civil society.

The five main programs of eIFL.net are the negotiation of licenses with publishers, the strengthening and support of library consortia, support of open access and development of institutional repositories, advocacy for fair intellectual property rights and open source software consultancy. The primary goal of eIFL.net is to facilitate access to a wide array of academic electronic resources at affordable prices and fair conditions by actively involving library consortia from member countries in the pursuit of the objectives. In doing so, the eIFL.net Foundation aims to contribute to closing the digital gap as far as the advance of information society is concerned in developing countries.

eIFL.net's efforts have so far yielded quite fruitful results as to creating sound library consortia, empowering them with effective bargaining powers vis-à-vis the providers, and keeping participating countries updated with cutting edge trends and latest news as to information and technology services. The upcoming agenda foresees the deepening in all worklines and further collaboration with like-minded initiatives.

11.6 Pre-Internet Professional Networks of African and Keralan Scientists[7]

Information technology, and particularly the Internet, are generally seen as tools that scientists in less developed countries (hereafter, LDCs) can use to break an assumed isolation. Before the worldwide dissemination of these technologies, scholars in developed countries (DCs) usually viewed their colleagues in Africa, Asia, and Latin America as isolated from the international scientific community, and from others in their own local scientific environment, because of the lack of technological and financial resources of the research systems in which they worked. From the perspective of developed countries, this isolation was considered a problem. Few considered LDC scientists to be an active part of the global scientific community. But exactly how isolated were these scientists in the early days of the Internet, when they relied mostly on more traditional means of communication?

Most of the studies of LDC scientists' professional networks were based on bibliometric methods, examining records of publications and citations. However, such methods present limitations. First, they tend to over-represent researchers working in universities, where academic publications influence promotion, compared to those working in other public and private research centers. Second, they under-represent LDC scientists, because LDC journals are poorly represented in international databases. Finally, bibliometric searches do not reflect informal professional networks that do not directly lead to publication.

In order to correct for these limitations, and to test the hypothesis that the level of development of a research system would influence the structure of scientists' professional networks, a survey of 293 individuals involved in research on agriculture, environment, or natural resources topics was conducted in Ghana, Kenya, and the Indian state of Kerala in 1994.[8] These three locations were selected to represent high (Kerala), medium (Kenya) and low (Ghana) levels of development of a research system in LDCs. The scientists included in the sample were identified through bibliometric searches, followed up by personal nomination by the individual in charge of each department or unit that the team visited. As a result, approximately half of the final sample would come from internationally visible researchers, and the other half from invisible ones. In addition, the sample sought to represent various organizational sectors: universities, government laboratories, and nongovernmental organizations (NGOs), as well as international research centers (IRCs) in Kenya. It included a total of 157 organizations.[9] The survey instrument included questions on the respondent's professional network, research activities, supervisory responsibilities, professional memberships and activities, self-reported productivity, attitudes on agricultural and environmental issues, and the needs of their research system. Some background questions addressed demographics, education, and access to technology. The questionnaire was administered in face-to-face interviews by an international team, including one representative of each location.

At the time of the survey, 58% of the respondents reported having access to a computer and a printer (Shrum 1996). In many facilities, however, researchers had to share the equipment with others, limiting their available time at a computer. For email, the overall proportion of respondents who reported access fell dramatically to 9%, with sharp differences by organizational sector, and some by country. While 80% of the respondents working in IRCs had email, in all other organizations, the proportion never went above 15%, i.e., less than one in six respondents at each organizations had access to email. The distribution of access to email did not reflect the overall level of development of the local research system. Even though Kerala had the most developed research system, Kenya, where the IRCs were located, had the greater access to email (18% of all respondents), followed by Kerala (6%) and Ghana (3%). With such low levels of reported access to information technology, this survey gives us information on the state of LDC researchers' professional networks before the advent of the Internet.

In the survey, respondents were asked to name the individuals outside their own organization with whom they were in contact, and whom they considered "the most important for their own work." The 281 respondents who gave usable answers to this question reported a total of 1321 professional relations in 590 different organizations, for an average of 4.7 contacts per respondent.[10] Considering this result, LCD scientists in the sample can hardly be called isolated. Moreover, an analysis of the average number of contacts by location shows that level of development is not associated with more professional ties. Keralites reported a significantly lower number of ties than Kenyans and Ghanaians, with an average of 3.90, compared to 5.10 and 5.14 respectively. Also contrary to expectations, university respondents reported the lowest average (4.00 contacts).

Respondents in NGO had the highest average (6.25 contacts), followed by IRCs (5.25) and NRIs (4.61). Even though university respondents reported less ties than respondents in other sectors, a plurality of contacts took place with universities (44% of all reported ties), followed by NRIs (29%).

Further analysis addressed the diversity of the respondents' population of relationships by organizational sector and location. The majority of contacts occured within the researcher's local research system (same location or same organizational sector), but the difference in proportion between internal and external contacts varied by sector. University and NGO respondents were more likely to have contacts within their own sector than NRI and IRC respondents, regardless of their location. NRI and IRC respondents reported more ties to universities than university respondents themselves, showing that researchers in research centers saw universities as a resource. NGO respondents in Africa were more likely to rely on other NGOs as resources, but Keralan NGOs had more ties with universities and NRIs.

We were also interested in looking at the geographical distribution of external contacts, which represent over a third (34.6%) of all reported contacts: Did they take place mostly with countries that are considered the core of the global scientific community (Europe, North America), or were South-South links taking precedence? Overall, external contacts primarily involved European countries, and very few contacts were with Asian countries.[11] However, significant differences existed between locations. Kenyan and Ghanaian respondents had most of their external contacts with DCs, while Keralites had few contacts outside of India. African researchers had very few links to LDCs, contrary to Keralans, when India is taken as an external location. Because education is often seen as a primary source of professional contacts for scientists, we checked whether the location of education impacted the location of contacts. Education abroad doubled the number of contacts with DCs for the whole sample, but a sectoral analysis showed that while it did increase the number of contacts with DCs for respondents in NRIs or NGOs, it did not impact the networks of university respondents.

More importantly, we found that the association between the number of contacts in LDCs and DCs was negative in all locations, and all sectors except NGOs: Researchers with more ties to DCs had less ties to their local research community. A regression model was used to examine possible correlates of network size, distinguishing between internal ties and ties to DCs. As expected, different factors correlated with these two types of ties. Controlling for a variety of factors (sector, professional background, visibility, access to electronic resources), African respondents still had more DC and internal contacts than Keralites. Having a graduate education, professional contacts with NRIs, and being visible in international bibliographic databases were all linked to a higher number of contacts with DCs. This return on education and international visibility, however, was not detected in the least developed research system (Ghana). Visibility negatively affected the number of internal contacts, as did the supervision of postdoctoral students, who may require time-consuming supervision. NGOs also had significantly more internal contacts than other sectors. Other factors did not correlate significantly with the number of internal ties.

Overall, the results of this study indicate that at the onset of the dissemination of information technology, scientists in LDCs were already not isolated, and that contrary to expectations, the level of development of a research system did not necessarily correlate with the size of researchers' professional networks. Given that a high number of external ties tends to be linked to fewer local ties, the LDC scientific community may be seen as divided between those with an internal orientation, and those with an external orientation, the latter being more visible in the global research community. Contacts with DCs will conceivably be most affected by greater use of information technology. With the existing trade-off between internal and external contacts, one unintended consequence of the dissemination of the Internet in LDCs may be a further disconnect of LDC scientists from their local research environment, as they become more integrated in the global scientific community. The normative approach from DCs suggests that stronger global ties are beneficial for individual scientists, but does not consider the repercussions for LDC research systems. Current research investigating the impact of information technologies on professional networks will discover whether these technologies split LDC research communities between scientists implementing a locally-set research agenda, and those following the research priorities of developed countries, or build bridges between all scientists.

11.7 References

Shrum, Wesley. 1996. *Research Capacity for Sustainable Development: Report on a Field Study in Ghana, Kenya and Kerala (India)*. The Hague, Netherlands: RAWOO.

Shrum, Wesley, and Patricia Campion. 2000. "Are Scientists in Developing Countries Isolated?" *Science, Technology and Society* 5:1-34.

11.8 Notes

1 Authors in order of the section they contributed. The chapter was compiled and edited by Benson and Bijker.

2 Presented by Carol Priestley and Margaret Ngwira

3 Presented by by Dina El Halaby.

4 Presented by Maurice Long.

5 Presented by Augustin Gaschignard.

6 Presented by Emilija Banionyte.

7 The following section is written by Patricia Campion, Dept. of Sociology and Political Science, Tennessee Technological University, and is
a summary of Shrum and Campion (2000).

8 This study was backed up by the Dutch Ministry for Development Cooperation through RAWOO (Advisory Council for Scientific Research in Development Problems), and with the assistance of ISNAR (International Service for National Agricultural Research)

9 The distribution of respondents is as follows: 53 national research institutes, 48 academic departments, 31 NGOs, and 5 IRCs, which only existed in Kenya.

10 Full details on the analytical procedures used can be found in Shrum and Campion (2000).

11 For Keralan respondents, professional ties in other states of India were considered external.

12. PUBLISHING AND DISSEMINATING SCIENCE FINDINGS

Steven Rudgard, *FAO, Rome*[1]
Enrica Porcari, *CGIAR, Rome*
Noha Adley, *Bibliotheca Alexandrina, Alexandria*
Leslie Chan, *University of Toronto, Toronto*
Michael Jensen, *National Academies, Washington, DC*

12.1 The FAO Vision and Strategy to Enhance the AGRIS Model for Access and Exchange of Information on Agricultural Science and Technology[2]

AGRIS became operational in 1975 as an international initiative aiming to build a common information system for science and technology in agriculture and related subjects, based on a collaborative network of institutions. A database of almost 3 million bibliographic records has been accumulated over 30 years. An analysis of the AGRIS network in 2000 revealed some major constraints, such as limitations in the capacities of the member institutions, inaccessibility of the full text of documents, the incompleteness of the coverage of literature, and the emergence of several independent systems.

A new strategy was developed for the AGRIS network in 2002 to address these constraints, which emphasized greater decentralization and diversification of the network, a strengthened role in capacity building, a focus on full text, and a continually improving set of public domain web-enabled tools and methodologies. A recent expert consultation has endorsed the principles of the new strategy, and has emphasized the need for a strong policy and advocacy platform coupled with the closer alignment of AGRIS with other open access publishing initiatives. The consultation also advocated wider adoption of the network's information exchange standards, public domain applications, and tools that use those standards, supported by the collaborative approach to strengthening institutional capacities and

training of individuals launched in 2003 through the Information
Management Resource Kit (IMARK).

12.2 Improving Access to Global Public Information Goods: CGIAR's Approach[3]

The Information and Communications Technology and Knowledge
Management (ICT-KM) Program of the CGIAR is working towards a
CGIAR system without boundaries, an internationally distributed, unified
and open knowledge "organization." It is one of a number of initiatives
trying to transform the way the CGIAR works, in this case incorporating
new ICT and KM practices to preserve, produce, and improve access to the
agricultural global public goods needed by the poor in developing countries.

The Program is managed by the CGIAR Office of the Chief Information
Officer (CIO). The CIO, Enrica Porcari, will provide an overview of the
Program to date, covering its origins, components, results, and principal
lessons learned so far. She will present plans for the future concerning
efforts to maximize the utilization of information Global Public Goods.
Areas where there are significant opportunities for collaboration in these
efforts will be flagged.

12.3 The Activities of Bibliotheca Alexandrina in Supporting Open Access[4]

The Bibliotheca Alexandrina (BA), the New Library of Alexandria, is
dedicated to recapture the spirit of the original library from ancient times.
BA aspires to fill a number of roles: to be the world's window on Egypt; to
become Egypt's window on the world; to serve as a leading institution of the
digital age; and to lead as a center for learning, tolerance, dialogue, and
understanding. The ultimate goal of the BA is to provide "Universal Access
of All Human Knowledge at All Times for All People."

We believe our goals are possible since existing obstacles are mostly
administrative and technical obstacles which may be overcome. Our
optimism stems from the potential of creating entities working through a
cooperative framework offering accessibility, sharing and exchanging
knowledge, and a competitive framework offering comparative advantage.
BA has embarked into several activities aiming at documentation,
preservation, and dissemination of information resources. This presentation
provides an overview of BA's infrastructure and initiatives taken to bridge

the digital gap and to improve the access to information in Egypt and the region.

12.4 Open Access to the Results of Research: Lessons from Bioline International[5]

Bioline International (BI, www.bioline.org.br) is a South/North (Brazil, Canada) non-profit partnership dedicated to supporting the online distribution of journal publications from developing countries that are largely ³invisible² to the international scientific community. In recent years, more and more publishers understand the great value of open access as a way to incorporate local research into the mainstream knowledge base. Already, over 40 peer-reviewed journals are collaborating with BI and, since the start of their partnership, statistics show that document downloading has increased by ten-fold for many publications. In addition, one of the journals on the system reports substantial increases in submission rates and a three-fold increase in citation impact over a three year period. Several publishers also report that the numbers of international authors submitting manuscripts to their journals have been steadily increasing, indicating that researchers now recognize and value the increased visibility and impact offered by open access.

In addition to presenting the usage pattern of publications on BI and the impact of OA, this presentation provides an overview of BI¹s technical infrastructure, workflow, and the use of open source software and open standards to improve the access and visibility of published research from developing countries. BI does not charge for the document conversion/distribution services, but the methodology of formatting from existing technologies is gradually transferred to the publishers to increase their technical capability and develop a sustainable and independent service for the future.

12.5 Opening Up Access to Developing Countries: Activities of the US National Academies[6]

The U.S. National Academies (National Academy of Sciences, Institute of Medicine, National Academy of Engineering, and National Research Council) produces 200 reports a year on issues of science, engineering, and medicine, which it publishes through the National Academies Press. It makes every report freely available online in multiple formats, and has undertaken innovations to make our online publications maximally useful to people worldwide. The Press site receives more than 1,000,000 visitors a month to our online resource of 3500+ publications (www.nap.edu), and provides them with research tools, discovery tools, skimming mechanisms, and key-term repurposing -- the latter two particularly useful for world researchers for whom English is not their first language. We enable completely free access to high-quality PDFs to browsers located in developing countries, while charging researchers in the wealthy countries. Michael Jensen will overview the impact that "open access" publishing has had on the Press's two key drivers, maximal dissemination and fiscal sustainability; what patterns have become clear over its last decade of online publishing; and the site tools available to maximize online utility of its reports.

12.6 Notes

1 Authors in order of the section they contributed. The chapter was compiled and edited by Benson.
2 Presented by Stephen Rudgard
3 Presented by Enrica Porcari.
4 Presented by Noha Adly.
5 Presented by Leslie Chan.
6 Presented by Michael Jensen.

13. INFORMATION ACCESS AND ISSUES OF BANDWIDTH

Mike Jensen[1]
Martin Belcher, *International Network for the Availability of Scientific Publications*
Pauline Ngimwa, *African Virtual University*

13.1 The ICT Bandwidth Challenge in African Universities[2]

There are two striking facts about African universities and bandwidth. The first is that the average university in Africa has the same aggregate bandwidth as a single home user in North America or Europe. The second is that the average African university pays 50 or 100 times more for this bandwidth than its counterparts in Europe or North America. Cross Atlantic fiber for research and education networks is now being obtained for $1/mbps/month, while African institutions must pay over $5,000/mbps/month or more for the same bandwidth to connect to their counterparts in developed countries.

Prevented from full participation in the global online research community, African scholars face huge obstacles in keeping up with the latest developments in their fields, let alone making original contributions. To move forward on the bandwidth issue, collective action is now emerging on the part of African universities. But few countries in Africa have formed a national research and education network (NREN) to negotiate for better prices. There are some exceptions in Africa — South Africa, Egypt, Morocco - and about a dozen other NRENs in Africa are emerging. But they are faced with technical and policy barriers, limiting incentives to network, especially where national fiber backbones are not yet in place.

Nevertheless, by taking advantage of economies of scale, consortia of African universities are beginning to look at a variety of options to significantly reduce the cost of bandwidth for its member institutions. The presentation will give an overview and examples of some of these initiatives including the African Virtual University (AVU), the African Tertiary Institution Connectivity Survey (ATICS), the Partnership for Higher

Education's University bandwidth consortium; the IDRC's Promoting African Research & Education Networking (PAREN); the Agence Universitaire Francophonie (AUF) network of francophone institutions; and the African Association of Universities (AAU).

13.2 The Importance of Bandwidth Management and Optimization in Research and Education Institutions[3]

Many universities and research institutions in the South are faced with major obstacles in their use of networked information resources. The price of bandwidth is disproportionately high and it is costly and difficult to improve international network connectivity. Effective management and optimization of bandwidth is widely recognized as being the easiest way in which institutions can improve their access to networked information resources and yet this is rarely the case. There is an urgent demand for institutional development in the areas of bandwidth management and optimization. Practical actions and advise for senior and executive management, ICT managers and implementation staff in such institutions will be presented. Along with a review of resources and capacity development activities that are available to support institutions in this area.

13.3 The AVU Bandwidth Initiative and Access to Information[4]

The African Virtual University has adopted a learning architecture that establishes the framework for the program development model, instructional design model, pedagogical model, delivery model, and technology model. Within this framework, the learner is considered as an independent learner who takes control of the learning process while the lecturer takes the role of facilitator. To achieve this high level of autonomy, the learner should have all the learning support at his/her disposal and in particular access to information resources. The role of the library support thus takes a central place in the learning process. Further, the learning architecture is premised on the principle of "just in time" learning. This recognizes the various learning opportunities from different sources being available to the learner whenever he/she needs, wherever he or she may be and however he/she is able to access them effectively. The learning architecture therefore advocates for appropriateness and flexibility in the way technology is used to support these programs taking into consideration the diverse technological contexts across the African continent.

Along with the development of digital libraries there has been a proliferation of other Open Education Resources (OERs) which are often in digital formats. This presents the AVU with the opportunity to exploit the potential the OERs have on the development of Open, Distance and eLearning (ODeL) programs and indeed participate in their creation, organization, dissemination and use to the benefit of African Higher education. With this approach in mind, it becomes clear that the AVU has been very keen on the influence bandwidth has on the success of the usefulness of these OER. The sheer variety and richness possible in the design and development of OERs requires adequate internet connectivity if they are to be utilized effectively.

This presentation shares the AVU's experience in making these resources easily accessible to its partner institutions in the most cost-effective way. The first lesson we have learned is that there is currently inadequate bandwidth to support access to these digital resources. This is supported by a number of studies that have been carried out in the course of the last three years. The studies further show the negative impact these low bandwidth levels have had on the overall access, utilization and usefulness of these digital resources to the learner and faculty in African universities.

A discussion about how the AVU is investing in alternative creative solutions in response to these access problems is presented. This includes a project to expand bandwidth through VSAT deployment in the partner institutions at an affordable cost by aggregating demand. In addition to this, the paper discusses how local servers are being used to store and make available digital content that would otherwise require huge bandwidth if they were to be made available online, thus making it possible to easily access targeted sets of resources in ways that are both pedagogically effective and cost-effective.

13.4 Notes

1 Authors in order of the section they contributed. The chapter was compiled and edited by Benson.
2 Presented by Mike Jensen independent consultant
3 Presented by Martin Belcher.
4 Presented by Pauline Ngimwa.

14. GLOBAL INTERNET RESEARCH

William H. Dutton, *Oxford Internet Institute*[1]
Rick B. Duque, *World Science Project*
Jeremy Hunsinger, *Center for Digital Discourse and Culture*

14.1 Introduction

Research on the social impacts of Internet technologies has garnered much attention and in some cases controversy over the past decade. Early studies sounded the alarm that the Internet was creating a nation of "net-nerds", accelerating the decline of social involvement in modern society. Others claimed that it may be exasperating the digital divide and thus increasing global economic inequality. Studies looking at its impact on research capacity are recent and more difficult to assess, since the Internet's rise maps the explosion of western science and engineering over the last quarter century. The issue of the 'egg or the chicken' come to mind when determining which one drove which first. There is consensus though that the Internet has provided substantial support to cross-national collaborations in the west by reducing the problems associated with shared work over distances. It is also argued that digital archives and online publishing have facilitated, as they have accelerated, scientific productivity and communication. Recent studies have ventured outside the west, where the Internet was born and continues to be innovated, to the developing world and the newly democratized eastern European nations. Outside the west, methodological issues of causality become more manageable just as perhaps sampling and measurement become more contested. To illustrate some of these issues and give an overview of recent findings, this session review highlights global Internet research being conducted at the Oxford Internet Institute,[2] the World Science Project at Louisiana State University, and the Center for Digital Discourse and Culture at Virginia Tech University.

14.2 The Social Dynamics of the Internet: The Oxford Internet Surveys and the World Internet Project [3]

Survey research is a valuable method of investigating underlying patterns and trends across a large population, for example to investigate the underlying factors shaping outcomes of important socio-technical phenomena such as the rapid and widespread growth in the use of the Internet and related information and communication technologies (ICTs). This paper illustrates significant insights into these social dynamics obtained from two ongoing surveys of Internet use, the Oxford Internet Surveys (OxIS) and the World Wide Internet Project (WIP).

OxIS studies of the use and non-use of the Internet have been undertaken in 2003 and 2005[4], entailing face-to-face interviews with a national random probability sample of over 2000 people aged 14 years and older in Britain (excluding Northern Ireland). The WIP was founded in the US in 1999 by the USC Annenberg School Center for the Digital Future (formerly the UCLA Center for Communication Policy) and its growing membership currently covers over twenty partners in countries and regions across the world.[5] In each member country, WIP researchers (such as OxIS in Britain) conduct sample surveys of Internet use, including questions common to all members as well as ones unique to each country's own survey.

Such surveys of the social implications of Internet use have been feasible only since the late 1990s, by when the global network and related ICTs had become available to a sufficiently large and diverse proportion of the general public for meaningful data on its actual use and impact to be gathered. This paper highlights four key factors in the social dynamics of Internet use revealed in analyses of OxIS and WIP data: reconfiguring access[6]; reinforcing socioeconomic divides; digital choices and divides in patterns of use; and how cybertrust illustrates why policy making could be assisted by understanding the Internet as an 'experience technology'.

Reconfiguring Access

OxIS and WIP findings generally undermine overly simplistic and deterministic accounts of the Internet's impacts on everyday life, which have been typified by Utopian visions that see nothing but good coming from the spread of the technology versus dystopian nightmares of the technology reinforcing oppressive regimes. Instead, the surveys highlight complex patterns of use and impact shaped by individual motivations and choices within the constraints of available social and economic resources. Rather than systematically leading to predetermined impacts on social activities, this shows that the Internet can enable its users to reinforce or transform existing patterns of information and communication behaviour by 'reconfiguring access' in the ways people get information, what and who they know and stay in touch with, what services and products they consume and when and where they acquire and consume them.

For instance, the Internet is reconfiguring how people get access to information. OxIS 2005 found that at least about a quarter of its respondents would first look for information on the Internet in a number of diverse areas (e.g. 44% to plan a journey or holiday; 34% to find out about a book they had heard about; and 24% to learn about local schools). The Internet is also reconfiguring what information people gain access to. For instance, about 20% access newspapers or news services online that they do not read in print forms. It also creates new sources of information, as many respondents say they actively provide information online (e.g. 18% posted pictures/photos; 16% engaged in online discussion forums; 14% had a website; and 5% kept a blog). And reconfiguration moves beyond information, to reconfiguring how people communicate, and whom they know. About 20% of respondents had met people or made friends online. WIP findings indicate variation between countries in how far such online friendships lead to a personal meeting, indicating the significance of social contexts in shaping outcomes (e.g. in urban China an average of 7.7 friends met online are never met in person, compared with 2.6 in the USA and only 1.1 in Japan; the equivalent figures for online friends met in person are closer: 2.0 in China, 0.8 in USA and 0.6 in Japan). However, surveys in each nation show that people meet new friends online and that these online meetings lead some people to meet in real life.

Reinforcing Socioeconomic Divides through Digital Divides

The degree to which access to the Internet reinforces socioeconomic divides has become one of the central issues around Internet diffusion. The main digital divide has generally been perceived to be between those with and without access to the Internet (e.g. according to WIP circa 2003, Internet access was available to over 60% of the population in the USA, Sweden and Korea but to less than 25% in Taiwan and Hungary). OxIS data indicates only a 3% increase between 2003 and 2005 in Internet use in Britain to about 60%, matched by a 3% fall to 32% of non-users and a 2% rise to 8% in lapsed users; suggesting that diffusion has reached a plateau. Growth is principally coming in broadband access (up to 59% from 19% of Internet users in 2003). Cyber-optimists have argued that differences will diminish and even disappear as the Internet disperses more widely. Cyber-pessimists pose a darker unfolding in which non-users or limited users are likely to be those who are already disadvantaged economically and socially, such as low income groups.

WIP and OxIS figures show widespread increases in the availability of the Internet and related ICTs, thereby opening at least potential access to more and more people around the world. However, social research has highlighted the persistence of divides, as in the plateau in diffusion within Britain, and the degree that existing divides are related to socioeconomic status, such as measures of occupation, income, and education. WIP and OxIS have therefore examined the influences of such wider socioeconomic variables. For instance, across the world the highest economic quartile generally makes far greater use of the Internet than the lowest quartile (e.g. with lower:higher quartile ratios among those using the Internet of 49%:93% in Sweden; 24:81 in Britain; 28:63 in Germany; 22:55 in Singapore; and 2:24 in Hungary).

Digital Choices and Divides in Patterns of Internet Use

Both cyber-optimists and cyber-pessimists assume that all people would benefit from the Internet, and that the prime reasons for not going online are a lack of access to the technology itself or to adequate technical skills and/or financial resources. Yet, some people may also make a 'digital choice' not to use the Internet even if they have the access and resources to do so if they do not see how such use would be of benefit in their lives. This does not represent the kind of social problem indicated by the 'digital divides' concept.

For example, there are wide variations in use of the Internet by different age groups that cannot be explained by geographical or economic barriers central to concerns over the digital divide. For instance, in households with access to the Internet there can still be a divide by age in Internet use, with older people often deciding not to use the Internet for a variety of reasons (e.g. according to OxIS, in 2005 about two-thirds of over 65s in Britain are 'not at all' or 'not very' interested in the Internet compared to just 7% among 14-17 year olds and 21% among thus aged 18-34). Although OxIS has also found increases in use among the over 55s between 2003 and 2005, significant differences remain in uses and perceptions of the Internet at different life stages. In WIP surveys circa 2003, 80% and over of 16-24 year olds were using the Internet in the USA, Korea, Japan and Britain, but use among 55-64 year olds were more typically below 40%, with wide variations within countries (e.g. 95% in the younger groups and only 12% for the older group in Korea, with equivalent figures of 70%:12% in Spain and 66%:9% in Italy).

OxIS 2005 results indicate the older group is catching up in Internet use, but also provide evidence of the ways different groups with access to the technology make different digital choices about what to do online. For example: people under 24 tend to do multiple tasks in an online session (multitask) much more frequently than those over 45; significantly more users over 65 would first look for information about a Member of Parliament in a book or directory rather than first turning to the Internet; and use of the Internet for entertainment drops steeply as the age profile increases.

Other significant factors in making digital choices identified by OxIS include gender (e.g. males being significantly higher entertainment users than females) and income and self-rated Internet expertise (e.g. with the wealthiest and most expert being the most active groups in using the Internet in information-related activities). The wide range of uses investigated by OxIS also indicates how, once users have access, they make numerous different choices about what to do online. The most frequent uses (over 75% of users in 2005) were, in ascending order: making travel plans; looking up facts; surfing/browsing; getting product information; and checking email. Gambling, religious sites and investment stocks and funds (at 10% or under) were the least popular among the uses about which questions were asked.

What Cybertrust Reveals about the Internet as an Experience Technology

'Cybertrust' in the Internet and related ICTs could be critical to shaping a person's decision to go online and what they do when they are there. In turn, users' experiences on the Internet might raise or lower their level of 'cybertrust'. The OxIS survey reveals wide variations in cybertrust between individuals in Britain. Few exhibit a blind faith in the Internet and all that it offers, but most people are reasonably confident, if guarded, in the information and people they are able to access over the Internet. However, the general continuing growth patterns in Internet use, as shown in WIP and OxIS surveys, suggests there is sufficient trust to support the technology's continued diffusion, despite a general awareness of the risks entailed in exposure to unwanted mail, viruses and other potential hazards. At the same time, OxIS research shows that Internet users in Britain are not more trusting in the Internet simply because they are more trusting of all institutions (e.g. users are no more confident in other media than are either non-users or past users).

One of the most significant new understandings gained from OxIS is the degree to which the Internet is an 'experience technology', with uses and perceptions greatly influenced by actual online experiences. This interpretation arose in our study of cybertrust. Those exposed to the Internet tend to gain more trust in the technology, with even past users ('Internet dropouts') having more confidence in the Internet than non-users who have no experience with it, as reflected in WIP findings that more experienced users make more online purchases. Most predispositions to cybertrust that are associated with social and demographic characteristics tend to be mitigated over time and can be accounted for by the lessons learned from experience online. However, individuals with more formal education also tend to be somewhat more skeptical of the information and people accessible on the Internet, but also somewhat less concerned over the risks entailed with Internet use.

Conclusion: Understanding the Dynamics Shaping Digital Choices

The OxIS and WIP surveys outlined here provide some strong indicators of the main factors shaping the reasons why access to an appropriate ICT infrastructure does not necessarily mean Internet use will be taken up, even by some with meaningful access to the technology. It also helps to map the complex mix of socioeconomic factors influencing the digital choices made by people once they have become Internet users, particularly the important influence of actual use in building confidence and motivation for further uses. Policy makers could therefore usefully focus on influencing digital choices as well as closing digital divides.

This would require understanding and addressing the challenges involved in encouraging resistant groups to choose whether or not to go online, including prioritizing the capabilities and services most likely to motivate people to use the Internet, given the Internet's experience technology characteristics. However, as exposure to the Internet (like education, the other key factor in boosting cybertrust) is skewed towards higher socioeconomic groups, these strategies should take account of the need to avoid reinforcing socioeconomic and digital divides.

14.3 Internet Golpe in Chile[7]

This is a study of the relationship between scientific communication and productivity in Chilean science, focusing on the role of Internet adoption and use. The World Science Project's prior work in Africa has identified a "collaboration paradox" in the developing world: in resource-poor contexts, the high costs of collaboration may be greater than their benefits in terms of output.[8] While the Internet has been promoted as a technology that will change this relationship, our recent findings in Africa contradict this notion. However, it is not known whether this results from conditions peculiar to sub-Saharan Africa or is true more generally. In this paper, we present results from a recent research trip to Chile to conduct a video-graphic study of the scientific community there and the role the Internet may or may not be playing. The study is framed by a 1964 US Defense Department funded study, Project Camelot, an ambitious sociological investigation conceived to study the entire Chilean society to measure the capacity of people for revolution. This project failed to get authorization from the Chilean government, did not acquire solid collaborative links with local scholars and was subsequently terminated. Many charge, though, "results were achieved by other means" including CIA sponsored dissertations and peace corp volunteers. Given the socio-political upheaval that occurred in Chile less than a decade later, the scholarly world recognized the sensitive nature of projects from abroad conducting social research within less developed regions.[9] Our experience studying the Chilean scientific community is informed by the legacy of both Project Camelot and the Chilean dictatorship that followed.

Chile is an interesting case, since for most of its history it has had strong contact with the north. One local scholar punctuated, "Everything in Chile comes from abroad". Its scientific community, though like many in the developing world, has been characterized as being isolated and having low productivity. The 1973 military overthrow, often referred to by locals as simply "El Golpe", may have exasperated these limitations. This may be due to the following factors: resource deficiencies in the years following the Golpe; loss of international collaboration, resulting from the world's displeasure over the military takeover; whole disciplines and research programs that posed a threat to the new regime removed from University rosters; and the partial Diaspora of its scientific community who were either forced into exile or left for better funding opportunities and prestige in the exterior. The Internet is a development project from abroad, much like democracy and neo-liberalism, which many hope will elevate the Chilean scientific community as it continues to reconstruct since the end of the Pinochet dictatorship in 1989. Because Chile is a regional leader in economic performance and Internet access and use, it is assumed that this cyber-optimistic relationship will hold true. The World Science Project empirically investigates whether or not this assumption holds. The following reviews our video-graphic study's sample, methodology, analysis and preliminary findings.

In the Field with Digital Video: Preliminary Findings

The project collaborated with three Chilean scholars located at the Universidad de Los Lagos in Puerto Montt, the Universidad de Concepcion, and the Universidad Catolica in Santiago. These scholars were instrumental in scheduling 28 digital video interviews with university researchers in three regions during June 2004. The subjects represented both natural and social sciences and included six female researchers. Their ages ranged from mid twenties to early seventies. The oldest had received his professional degree in the late 1950's. The youngest was completing his professional degree at the time of the interview. The videotaped interviews were semi structured and focused on four major areas of a respondent's career: (1) professional antecedents, (2) present projects, (3) managing professional networks, and (4) their Internet history and practice.

The preliminary analysis of the video interviews have distinguished three key thematic categories: <u>Career Paths</u>: the legacy of dictatorship on professional careers and the importance of training abroad; <u>Science Practices and Institutional Pressures</u>: the obstacles of transnational collaborations and the impact of needing to publish in ISI high impact journals; and the <u>Internet in Professional Lives</u>: in managing professional networks, its benefits to research practices and outcomes, and its use in teaching.

Career Paths

A major theme in many of the interviews revolved around the legacy of dictatorship. Some scholars had been displaced as a result of the 1973 Golpe. They found their departments or institutes closed for an indeterminate time and either were demoted or fired. [10] One researcher was imprisoned for up to eight months by the military junta. Others were exiled or emigrated to research centers and universities abroad in other Latin American nations, the United States, the UK and Canada. Some who stayed reinvented themselves in the private sector. One actually became a beef speculator for many years, before returning to academia in his later life. For those who found opportunities abroad, their career paths took a dramatic turn. Many pursued advanced degrees and found work in universities abroad or in multi-lateral organizations like the United Nations. For the ones who joined the UN, the work took them as far as Africa and as close to home as Central America. They mentioned that their training (for example in public administration or marine biology) in the developing context prepared them well for a career in the multi-lateral development sector. When asked if these unique opportunities in academic and career advancement abroad made up for the tragedy of leaving their homelands, no one offered an affirmative answer.

They appreciated the experiences, but could not say if it was for the better or not.

The researchers I interviewed by definition did eventually find their way back to Chile to continue their careers. All had kept up contact with colleagues and family in Chile while abroad. All would make short visits to measure the situation in the country. A couple returned during the dictatorship, but then left after not being able to find steady work. But it was not until after the 1989 national plebiscite ending 17 years of dictatorship that they considered moving back for good. On return, many found the research sector had dramatically changed. Using existing contacts, most of the subjects found positions in various departments. Many reported that their international experience was a formidable calling card. Now privatized, the quickly expanding Chilean research sector provided ready employment as well.

The importance of training abroad is highlighted by the experiences of those who emigrated after the 1973 Golpe, but it is just as important in understanding the Chilean context for those who were trained over the last two decades. Chile has traditionally offered few doctoral degree programs.[11] As a result, the road to academic advancement is often through institutions abroad. With very little exception, most of the researchers I interviewed sought additional training in universities located in other Latin American nations, Europe, Canada and the United States. The importance of these experiences is both professional and intellectual. Professionally, training abroad raises career profiles on return to Chile. Intellectually, training abroad increases the exposure to literature and techniques that are in limited supply locally. As one scholar mentioned, "After my first degree, I had learned about all I was going to learn in this area locally. If I wanted to increase my understanding of my discipline, I needed to go abroad."

Most also mentioned the financial limitations of advanced training. Although the recently trained scholars have enjoyed new local sources for funding, traditional sources were exclusively found abroad. Though most sought funds in the exterior, a few were supported by the Pinochet administration through Presidential Scholarships. Having completed a doctoral degree in Spain during the 1980s, one female subject eagerly admitted, "I am a Pinochet baby". For many, though, the resources available abroad do not always cover all expenses. Some maintained their salaries at their home universities throughout their study in the exterior. Those who did stay on salary say that it was the institutional obligation, which motivated their return. But even those who did not have legal obligations say it was the moral obligation to return and help build local capacity. Also, some mentioned that family consideration brought them home, even though in many instances career opportunities abroad were much more lucrative.

Science Practices and Institutional Pressures

Another recurring theme was the importance of projects with collaborators abroad. This was especially emphasized in the natural sciences since their orientation tended to focus on global relevance. The ability to share expertise and in some instances materials and funding makes these collaborations very attractive. Chile has enjoyed much attention from research institutes in the exterior especially in environmental sciences and astronomy. Institutes from Europe (Italy, Belgium, and Germany) have originated local bases with in which many Chilean researchers have found training and career advancement. The 1973 Golpe severely reduced this kind of international collaboration. The end of dictatorship though marked the return of global partners in research. Recently, the main obstacle of transnational collaboration is the Chilean funding structure. Some researchers complained that its restrictive nature, basing funding on results, makes sharing monetary resources with collaborators in the exterior complicated. The experimental spirit of Chilean funding though, indicates that in the near future these kinds of limitations may be ironed out.

On an individual basis, the institutional requirement of publishing in ISI high impact journals for career advancement was a major pre-occupation. Many complained that there were few local or Latin American journals on this list. While others argued most of these kinds of journals are published in English only. This brought up two issues. One was the relevance of publishing in English, when local colleagues cannot read your work due to either limited subscription resources or lack of English proficiency. The other was the pressure away from local orientations of research to those that were "trendy" in the exterior. One social scientist admitted though that this ISI requirement at his university is flexible for some disciplines that are at a disadvantage such as the social sciences. Another poignantly reminded me that for the past decade he and his colleagues were so busy reconstructing their department after 20 years absence that conducting original research and publishing was simply not a priority in the last decade. Now that institutional structures have somewhat recovered, this researcher suggested that he can focus on intellectual advancement in the form of attending conferences, grant proposal writing and submitting papers for publication.

The Internet in Professional Lives

All the researchers I interviewed had personal computers in their offices. All had had some experience with computers in their training and either had first used the Internet while studying abroad, or had adopted its use quickly after the technology had arrived within the Chilean research community en mass, about 1995.[12] All had access to the Internet with a fast connection. All spoke of the importance of the technology in their work, especially in identifying and retrieving up-to-date information in their field. One researcher admitted, "You do not exist unless you are on the Internet." Another exclaimed, "Extraordinary... truly extraordinary!" A few of the older scholars regretted that they did not have access to this technology 30 years earlier. One researcher even mentioned that during the tumultuous 1970s in Latin America he and other colleagues had much of their work (life's work) confiscated during the military take over of university campuses. The Internet, he mused, would have been helpful in backing up documents.

While the access, streamlining, and duplication of information attributes of the Internet are important to account for, what I was most interested in understanding was how the professional networks of this group of researchers were being shaped. Although one scholar mentioned that after the 1973 Golpe, email would have facilitating maintaining contact with exiled colleagues, it was unclear whether the Internet was resulting in something different from before. Most relevant to my study was whether contemporary Internet use diverted networks outward toward the exterior. The quantitative phase of the study hopes to address this issue directly, but my digital video interviews were helpful in identifying the context of how this process might unfold. For example, my first interview with a Marine Zoologist suggested the functional equivalence nature of research and Internet technologies. Back in the 1960's, this researcher managed his professional networks "the old fashion way" with pencil, paper, typewriter and postal stamps. Instead of the digital archives, he had volumes of abstracts in his field catalogued at his university library, which listed the major scholars abroad. He routinely wrote to these scholars asking specific questions about their research and inquired about opportunities to collaborate with them. To his initial surprise, these world renown scholars answered back and soon he was invited to go abroad to continue his education and share with his global discipline the work he was doing in Chile.

When the Internet was introduced, this veteran scholar simply translated to digital the same kinds of information searches and communications networking he had done in the pre-digital era. He admitted, "It is a wonderful tool that makes the duration between contacts shorter and information instantaneous", but he also cautioned about the overwhelming amount of irrelevant information on the net. He added that as a result of the Internet, the journal submission process has been saturated and that the craft of writing and drawing (a once important requirement in his field) were slowly fading in the digital age. Although early in his career, he had made substantial contacts in the exterior, this scholar returned to Chile in the mid-

1970s and never went abroad again. Some of the contacts he had made came to visit and engage him in collaboration. But over time, his main contacts became local. In this case, this scholar was successful searching abroad for contacts before the Internet. The nature of his field and the local limitations demanded it. But after the Internet, his main digital objective was information searches. This leads me to consider that whether the Internet magnifies the networking process in the present might also be a function of particular fields and the local resource limitations researchers encounter today.

For the younger researchers who had studied abroad, Internet communication allowed them to maintain contact with key people and maintain access to the archive resources they enjoyed in the exterior. One scholar admitted that he frequently relied upon a colleague in the exterior to email him journals articles he could not acquire locally for lack of institutional resources. Another added that the ability to "google" a researcher and his website and either contact them directly or download posted works, was an exceptional advantage of this technology. Both these examples from the developing world also reveal that very often the Internet is being used to circumvent international intellectual property rights.

The Internet's positive impact on research practices was also highlighted in the conduct of professional lives and as a tool for research. Many echoed the obvious benefits mentioned above, the Internet's ability to circumvent local archives limitations and global knowledge access restrictions. In addition, they mentioned how convenient it was to share information with fellow scholars, register for conferences (local and international), submit journal articles electronically, and even the ability to contribute to ones field as a reviewer for a foreign journal. The latter case highlighted a latent consequence of acquiring a digital presence. One scholar said that he had been approached digitally by a foreign editor he had never personally met. The scholar imagined his mentor abroad may have suggested his name, or the editor may have read a publication of his and thought him an able candidate to be a reviewer. The Internet, in effect, had elevated this scholar to a global status without his former knowledge.

One of the interview subjects had even employed the Internet as a methodology. An exiled scholar during the Pinochet years, he became interested in immigration patterns of professionals. When he returned to Chile in the early 1990's, he was interested in learning what had happened to other professional like himself after the 1973 Golpe. He admitted that the chance of getting funding to travel all over the world to interview exiled professionals, within the Chilean funding environment of the mid 1990s, was remote. His field, sociology, was just reintroducing itself as a discipline.

National research funds were limited even for high profile disciplines, let alone his. So he "had to turn to the Internet." At first, he searched online list-serves of Chilean professionals abroad. He joined chat groups and documented these interchanges. He exposed himself to a few chat rooms as a researcher and was able to conduct at-length digital interviews about the experiences of these professional in the exterior. From these interviews and with collaboration from his university's computer science department, he was able to construct a general online questionnaire; and from the list-serves of professionals he had identified earlier in the investigation, he drew his sample. Over 400 Chilean professionals in 40 different nations completed the immigration survey he made available for a one month period on line. He later experimented with chat versus email qualitative interview techniques with a sub sample from earlier studies. He concluded that chat was by far more effective in recreating the intimacy of a face-to-face interview. Eventually, he added content analysis of online newspapers and websites to his 'Internet as methodology' toolbox. He is even considering adding 'webcam' to his chat sessions to deepen the experience. He concluded that for the social scientists in a developing nation, the Internet can be extraordinary because of its affordable cost and extensive reach.

This example above illustrates the transforming potential of the Internet in addressing global science asymmetries. A researcher in the United States for example exists within a research funding environment that could have supported an immigration study of exiled professionals abroad. Yet perhaps because the United States has not experienced an exiled Diaspora like that experienced in many developing nations over the past half century, this would not be a relevant question to ask. Paradoxically, this research question is relevant in the developing context, yet the resources are rarely available. In the case above, the Internet, as a cost effective methodological tool with global reach, closed the funding gap for this particular researcher. To lend perspective to this example of successfully employing Internet technologies in research, it is helpful to acknowledge that Chile enjoys a well-developed digital network that is supported by the greater society. It also helps that the population that this scholar was investigating was made up of professionals with advanced communication and information skills that lived in developed nations with superior Internet infrastructures. The same researcher in say Burundi, for example, interested in Burundian refugees across Africa, may not enjoy the same success. Developmental context matters here.

To a lesser extent, some researchers mentioned the impacts on teaching as well. One benefit was the Internet's vast resource of material (images and texts) that augmented lecture presentations. Some also mentioned the benefits for students: to retrieve information for class projects. But this was balanced by the apprehension that this technology may facilitate plagiarism.

Generally, the Internet was of great assistance to this group of Chilean scholars. But many of them also admitted the liabilities of this technology that included too much information, relatively little Spanish language content, and the security risk of being connected. As one scholar pragmatically suggested, "The Internet magnifies the ongoing struggle between security and freedom that frames much of the world's concerns today." Another concern was too much dependence on the technology. A scholar who had worked for the majority of his professional life in the pre-Internet era mentioned, "When the net is down, the halls get filled with researchers that do not know what to do anymore." Fortunately, this occurred infrequently; yet it does foreshadow the potential risk of dependence to a technology like the Internet that is characterized by a fast paced innovative environment and generational interface glitches. Keeping up with upgrades and mutating digital threats is a major concern in resource poor regions.

Conclusion

This study of the Chilean scientific community and the Internet employed video-ethnographic methods. We were able to engage local scholars to adopt and facilitate the project in order to address some of the ethical issues mentioned in the literature. Twenty-eight researchers were video interviewed across both social and natural sciences in university departments located in three regions. Our preliminary findings highlight a variety of issues: the legacy of dictatorship on career paths, the obstacles for international collaborations, the pressure to publish in ISI high impact journals, and the impact of the Internet on professional lives and research practices. For researchers trained in the pre-digital era, the Internet functionally replaces the past technological modes used to conduct information searchers and manage networks. One key advantage for those trained in the pre and post digital eras is the Internet's ability to circumvent local resource limitations and global publication restrictions. The Internet also increases the visibility of this group of scholars as it perhaps makes them dependent on it as well. In one case though, the Internet allowed a local scholar to carry out an immigration study surveying over 400 Chilean professional expatriates across 40 different nations. This may have not been possible otherwise in a developing nation like Chile with little research funds to offer a study of this global scope. A quantitative face-top-face survey of over 300 Chilean researchers follows this video ethnography, results of which are forthcoming. We hope that our observations and conclusions further the understanding of how the Internet may shape knowledge production in the developing world. Meanwhile, our project continues to consider the ethics of our presence as guests for science in distant lands.

14.4 Internet Research: A View from the Association of Internet Researchers[13]

Internet research as represented by the association is a pluralistic and transdisciplinary endeavor. The members of the Association of Internet Researchers (AoIR), the attendees at its annual conferences and the broader community that uses its listserves and related resources combine people from a significant number of disciplines and variant scholarly traditions. Their combined efforts define one set of understanding of the field of Internet research. The particular pragmatics of negotiating the creation and building of a scholarly organization around Internet research and the organizations nascent ecologies have further shaped the development of the field.

Internet research is certainly broader than AoIR, though it is certainly international and interdisciplinary as indicated by the association's mission. The association's primary activities surround the coalescence of scholars of Internet research. To that end, there have been annual conferences, a research annual and several other related publications. The constitution of these conferences and materials has always involved a conscious effort to be inclusive of the broader communities of Internet research. However, it is not always possible to effectively recruit new communities, new disciplines and new interests who clearly have been doing Internet research. So it is clear that while this is a paper about who is doing Internet research from the AoIR perspective, it does not represent everyone that does Internet research.

The interdisciplinary nature of AoIR is easily seen from the constitution of its conferences and publications. The question is whether there is a new set of axiologies arising that allow people from these disciplines to understand the same object of research, or if not, is there evidence that it is development of the ability to interpret materials outside of a disciplinary perspective. The evidence of this transition is found in the composition of the conference papers by discipline and the inclusiveness of the annuals. The transition from interdisciplinarity to transdisciplinarity is slow, but during its time, AoIR has come to be a new location for legitimate scholarship, cross-disciplinary collaboration and has begun to build the community necessary to make transdisciplinary research possible.

It is not surprising that AoIR has majority of members from the discipline of communications, but that only has made about 1/2 of the membership at any given time. Many of the AoIR members come from interdisciplinary departments such as media studies, information studies, and related fields. Internationally, the members of AoIR have been concentrated in North America, with upwards of 50% of the conference attendees being from the United States. However, as AoIR has moved conferences from places to place in Europe and Canada, the European and United Kingdom attendance has spiked, as one would expect when the structural impediments of travel and time-costs are significantly lessened. However, even with those impediments from the very first conference, AoIR has had attendees from all five continents in attendance. With members from over 120 countries, the local and national centered notions of scholarship, scholarly production, conferences and the rules of scholarly organizations vary significantly. This cross-national construction of differences opens new realms for understanding and negotiation based upon those varied understandings.

The tendency of international audiences to be primarily national or regional in emphasis should not be forgotten when one considers the size of the scholarly community surrounding Internet research. Localized notions of Internet research are found in like the General Online Research Organization, which used to be the German Online Research. Combined with other regionalizations within the cultures of the academia, the possibility for transdisciplinary collaboration can be hindered or helped based on national and international perspectives. We have to be careful not to overemphasize our own scholarly perspective when discussing Internet research, instead it is best to prioritize well grounded research, but with an eye to its public reception to diverse audiences.

To the extent that there are differences in local, national and the international arenas that cause disciplinary differences, there are also very real differences amongst those disciplines inside and outside of their national contexts. In some national organizations, such as the American Sociological Association or the American Political Science Association, there are already multiple divisions that deal with Internet research. Some divisions deal with the technological aspects, others deal with the governance aspects, and yet still others deal with the educational aspects of Internet research. These organizational sections have their own sessions and in large organizations they might not ever talk to each others. The boundary work that these organizations have as an ongoing activity at all levels stultifies disciplinary collaboration, not to mention the effects on interdisciplinary communication.

However, in AoIR we do not foster divisions and we do not differentiate strongly on disciplinary boundaries. The organization of the conferences has tended to be theme-based, with panels relating to methodologies and panels relating to topics. This division is meant to encourage cross-disciplinary discussion about methods and topics instead of disciplinary conversation about disciplinary concerns. Whether this works or not, has yet to be seen, but we do have several interdisciplinary books coming from material presented AoIR conferences. The organizations have also helped to foster working groups and organizational subgroups around certain issues. These groups have helped found EU networks of excellence and have provided forums for other activities related toAoIR research. These groups have started to foster international interdisciplinary conversations in interesting ways and they might be the basis for further research.

One contentious issue in all conferences is the notion of 'quality'. Quality of research varies across disciplinary groups even to the point of having a single university having a research group that defines a very narrow set of methodologies as acceptable quality. The tendency toward academic specialization and methodological uniformity in disciplines creates skepticism in other arenas. To combat this, AoIR and other groups use academic peer review processes to varying degrees of success. There is yet to be found a fair balance between the labor of peer review, the specialization required to review something adequately and the number of reviews that need to be performed per individual. In short, generalist with broad backgrounds and familiarity with the audience are in significant demand for peer review, but specialists are needed to judge some of the more narrow bands of scholarship. The problems that AoIR faces in this arena are not found in more disciplinary societies that can rely on methodological specialization and disciplinary language to communicate the validity of their research. However, it is also this language and specialization that pushes most science out of the realm of public understanding. The compartmentalization of knowledge into the realm of specialization creates real problems for legitimizing disciplinary Internet research to the broader community.

Conclusion

This chapter reviewed global Internet research being conducted in institutes worldwide. The Internet is a reflexive phenomenon that is both shaping global society and research capacity as it is providing new methodological tools for understanding the Internet phenomenon itself. The Oxford Internet Institute, in conjunction with the World Internet Project at USC's Annenberg School Center for the Digital Future, represents an ambitious comparative global study of Internet access and use. Their findings suggest that we should be mindful of assuming access necessarily means use, that there are complex socio-economic factors influencing digital choices, and that building "cyber-trust" should be emphasized in policy formulations. The World Science Project at Louisiana State University maps how the Internet is shaping research capacity in developing nations over time. Where once they were considered isolated and locally irrelevant, the Internet may be potentially elevating researchers in developed nations like Chile to a global presence. Moreover, it is allowing the circumvention of local resource limitation and international intellectual property rights law. In addition, the Internet may be creating dependency upon a technology, whose innovative nature makes it difficult for communities in the south to keep pace with. Research emerging from the Center for Digital Discourse and Culture at Virginia Tech University alludes to the complexity of scientific boundary work occurring within the emerging field of Internet Research. The field has developed from an interdisciplinary to a transdisciplinary phenomenon, creating a variety of scholarly communication challenges along both methodological and organizational dimensions. Given the complexity of the issues reviewed in this session, whether the Internet is proving to be the pathway for a symmetrical global community in terms of "cyber trust", socio-economics or even research capacity has yet to be determined.

14.5 Notes

1 Authors in order of the section they contributed. The chapter was compiled and edited by Ricardo B. Duque.

2 Study done in conjunction with the World Internet Project at USC's Annenberg School Center for the Digital Future.

3 Presented by William H. Dutton, Director, Oxford Internet Institute.

4 See http://www.oii.ox.ac.uk/research/ for more on OxIS, including access to publications giving more details of the results of past survey, such as W. H. Dutton, C. di Gennaro and A. M. Hargrave (2005), *The Internet in Britain: The Oxford* Internet *Survey, May 2005*, Oxford: Oxford Internet Institute. OxIS is sponsored by AOL, BT, Ofcom and Wanadoo.

5 See http://www.worldInternetproject.net for more on WIP.

6 The concept of reconfiguring access was developed in a synthesis of research on ICTs in W. H. Dutton (1999). *Society on the Line*, Oxford: Oxford University Press and in the context of broadband Internet in W. H. Dutton, S. E. Gillett, L. W. McKnight and M. Peltu (2003), 'Broadband Internet: The Power to Reconfigure Access', *Forum Discussion Paper No. 1*, Oxford: Oxford Internet Institute (available online at www.oii.ox.ac.uk/research/publications.cfm).

7 Presented by Ricardo B. Duque, World Science Project http://worldsci.net

8 Duque, R. B., Marcus Ynalvez, R. Sooryamoorthy, Paul Mbatia, Dan-Bright Dzorgbo, and Wesley Shrum. 2005. "Collaboration Paradox: Scientific Productivity, the Internet, and Problems of Research in Developing Areas." *Social Studies of Science* 34:1-31.

9 Horowitz, Irving Louis (1967) The Rise and Fall of Project Camelot: Studies in the Relationship Between Social Science and Practical Politics, ed. Cambridge MA: The M.I.T. Press.

10 For example, the discipline of sociology ceased to exit between the years of 1973 and the early 1990s.

11 Mullin, James and Robert M. Adam, Janet E. Halliwell, and Larry P. Milligen. 2000. *Science,* Technology, *and Innovation in Chile*. Ottawa, ON, Canada: International Development Research Centre.

12 REUNA, the Chilean IT institute, connected the university system with an intranet in 1986. It was one of the first networks in Latin America to hook up to the World Wide Web in the mid 1990s.

13 Presented by Jeremy Hunsinger, Center for Digital Discourse and Culture at Virginia Tech University.

15. SCIENCE AND ICT IN CHINA

Zhiyong Liu, *National Natural Science Foundation of China, Beijing*[1]
Qiao Guo, *Beijing Institute of Technology*
Tao Xiaofeng, *Beijing University of Posts and Telecommunications*
Xu Xiaodong, *Beijing University of Posts and Telecommunications*
Zhang Ping, *Beijing University of Posts and Telecommunications*
Kai Nan, *Chinese Academy of Sciences*
Baoping Yan, *Chinese Academy of Sciences*

The session that is reported in this chapter was organized by Zhiyong Liu for the the National Natural Science Foundation of China (NSFC). The purpose of the session was to provide a forum for researchers, practitioners, and administrators in IT to exchange their information and ideas for research and development on IT. Four Chinese scientists gave presentations on the session. International colleagues participated this session. The following four abstracts included in this document introduce basic information for IT research (especially basic research) in China. In accordance with the purpose of the session, and due to the number of presentations that could be accepted in the session, the abstracts can only gave an outline of a small part of research (especially on communications and networking) on IT conducted in China. Still, from the abstracts readers can find valuable information for basic research on IT in China, as well as the policies of the states, various particular activities and research results.

15.1 The National Innovative Ability Enhanced by Information Technology[2]

The 25 years reform in China has brought about achievements that draw worldwide attention. With GDP per capita reaching US$1000, China is now among low income countries. To become moderately well-off across the board by the end of the first 20 years of the present millennium is the grand goal of the country, and the prerequisites to realize this goal are the US$ 3000 GDP per capita, a well-balanced and harmonious society and a sustainable developing economy. This 20-year period is critical and also full of opportunities, as international experiences show that the transition bracket from low-income to medium-income is both a "golden period" and a "period of conflicts". Along with the upgrade of the consumer structure, the adjustment of industrial structure and the acceleration of urbanization, the country also has to face bottleneck problems. First there are resource and environmental constraints. Second, there are social conflicts, unemployment, an increasing urban-rural disparity, and discrepancy between social and economic developments.

To address the issue, the Chinese government has arranged for experts to engage in strategic research projects, which were carried out on the basis of a huge amount of investigation data and documents both from home and abroad. Suggestions have been made which are to have a resounding effect on policy making, as the government has subsequently decided on a shift from an essential factor-driven to an innovation-driven economy. The innovations imply both those on the system and those on science and technology, the two kinds being equally important to maintain a sustainable and harmonious economic development. It is a priority task set forth by the government to get out of the resource and environmental bottleneck. For a long time China's fast economic growth has been depending on her high resource input and consumption, a traditional way of industrialization for which China has paid dearly. Now the time has come for her to opt for a more resource-economical and environmentally friendly way of industrialization. The scarcity of natural resources in China—for example her freshwater resources per capita is only one-fourth the world average—will make it difficult for the country to achieve the goal of quadrupling her GDP in the next 20 years without relying essentially on sci-tech and human resources. Hence, technological breakthroughs are needed to raise the overall standard of resource-saving, pollution abatement, and water-saving measures, which, once employed in the domain of agriculture and water treatment, would contribute greatly to building an ecologically sound society. A new theoretical and sci-tech system taking into account China's unique conditions needs to be established, and as well as strict legal system, legislature and regulations, and a more fulsome management system.

On the other hand, the domestic restructuring of production sectors, the intense international competition and the globalization of the world's economy has set higher demands on sci-tech innovations. In all this, China faces challenges as well as historical opportunities to take over the production from developed countries and hence upgrade production structure. It has become a pressing task for China to live up to its name as one of the world's manufacture centers equipped with integrated high-tech plants and informationized facilities.

With the 21st century we enter into an era of information and we should take full advantage of the information technology in dealing with problems likely to arise in self-conducted innovations, of which a national system as well as the Management Information System (NIMIS) and Coordination

Platform (NICP) should be established with the government taking the leading role and with academic institutions, enterprises and private organizations as the main participating bodies. Other corresponding systems such as Decision Supporting System (NIDSS), Distance Learning System (NIDLS), Evaluation System (NIES), etc., are also established to support the country's innovative ability.

Starting from 2005, China enters into the period of developments through self-conducted innovations. Only with systematic methods and by advanced management means can we hope to upgrade the country's overall innovative ability so as to reach the grand target of development within the 15 years left before 2020. Therefore, a timely set-up of NIMIS, NICP, NIDSS, NIDLS, and NIRMS can help to solve the major coordination problem encountered by the country in this period and guarantees a successful realization of the country's targets of innovative development.

15.2 Research on 4G Mobile Communication in China[3]

Currently, the third generation (3G) mobile communication systems have been commercialized to support certain multimedia services. But objective of the B3G/4G has already been agreed, which is to provide users after the year 2012 with the data rate up to 100 Mbps and 1Gbps in high and low mobility environments, respectively. Numerous research plans and projects towards B3G have been initiated in East Asia, European and North America countries. The B3G research in China started in 2001 in the name of Future Technologies for Universal Radio Environment (FuTURE) project, which is being supported by national 863 high-tech program since 2002. Members of FuTURE program are also members of B3G Special Work Group of CCSA.

The objective of FuTURE is to clarify the vision of future mobile communication development, to assess new trends and new technologies, to promote the research in B3G field, and to realize the sustainable development of mobile communication through international cooperation between China and the rest of the world. The working scope of FuTURE is to organize research and discussion activities of the Forum members, to provide suggestions to initiate the R&D projects as well as the standardization research, to promote international cooperation between the Chinese and oversea organizations and to report to governments and relevant organizations the viewpoints and suggestions proposed by Forum members.

The technology focus of FuTURE includes the pre-research of B3G standardization, utilization of B3G technology in Enhanced 3G (E3G), broadband wireless access technologies and spectrum allocation and requirement analysis. The FuTURE has three working groups including

Market & Service Working Group, System & Technology Working Group and Spectrum Working Group. The Market & Service Working Group focuses on the analyzing the trends of technological evolutions and social movements toward B3G and anticipating in the global B3G pre-standardization activities. The System & Technology Working Group mainly concentrates on identifying, defining and assessing new technologies, facilitating R&D activities and standardization activities and cooperating with related entities in the world, such as WWRF, NGMC and mITF. The Spectrum Working Group focuses on facilitating discussion on spectrum for new mobile access of B3G and identifying the research required to support the use of spectrum for B3G. The members of FuTURE Forum includes manufacturers, operators, and research institutions and universities.

There are two research branches in FuTURE. One is TDD (Time Division Duplex) mode and the other is FDD (Frequency Division Duplex) mode. Both of them are investigating and demonstrating advanced techniques for B3G systems to meet the application requirements around the year 2010. Both TDD and FDD have their own advantages and disadvantages and important advancements have been achieved in the research and development of B3G radio network and wireless transmission technologies.

Since the TDD branch has some special characteristics in supporting asymmetry services and multi-hop functions, we will introduce the achievement of FuTURE B3G system with the example of TDD mode.

In this paper, the FuTURE Beyond 3G TDD Systems and key techniques, such as transmission techniques and RRM strategy, including novel cellular structure, are described in section II. The construction of a demonstration system built in FuTURE TDD Special Work Group is depicted in section III, prior to our conclusions.

15.3 FuTURE Beyond 3G TDD Systems and Key Techniques[4]

A possible system structure for B3G TDD, including AP and mobile terminals (MT), was plotted and shown at the conference. Obviously, with the increasing of carrier frequency, the cell size will decrease. Considering this tendency, the radio signal of one subscriber is transmitted and received by several antenna arrays, which are connected to one AP in B3G TDD system. By this way Multiple Input Multiple Output (MIMO) is formed easily and the radio transmission design can be sketched. The distributed antenna arrays can be connected to their corresponding AP by means of coaxial line or optical fibre. There are two possible ways for AP's connecting to IP network. One is that APs are directly linked to network. By this way, control plane and data plane are separated. So the user data will not pass control domain (CD) and there is only high layer signalling transferred between AP and CD. Another is classical layered structure and AP access network by CD. In B3G TDD the former type is preferred.

Transmission Techniques of FuTURE B3G TDD

In order to satisfy the high spectral efficiency requirements and low power consumption constraints, the advanced technologies, such as Orthogonal Frequency Division Modulation (OFDM), MIMO, Space-Time Code (STC), Joint Transmission (JT), Link Adaptation (LA), should be adopted in FuTURE B3G TDD system. Moreover, the multiple access scheme and wireless frame must be flexible for various rate services and guarantee the high reliability in the harsh wireless environments.

Radio Resource Management of FuTURE B3G TDD

RRM techniques ensure high reliability and high efficiency for radio transmission. The target for RRM design is to provide the highest system capacity and data throughput through optimizing limited radio resources. The main issue is to investigate efficient Quality of Service (QoS) oriented resource allocation strategy to jointly optimize the usage of radio resources, such as time, frequency, space and power etc. Radio resource management algorithms should support various classes of traffic while guaranteeing their required QoS.

We also suggested a multiple transmitting antenna based generalized cellular architecture - Group Cell. All these spaced antenna arrays are connected with one AP while each of them is located in a traditional cell. MTs also employ several antenna elements. Group Cell is a novel cellular construction method, shown in which fits well for new advanced physical techniques such as MIMO, STC.

Constructing a Demonstration System of FuTURE B3G TDD Branch

After about three-year research, a demo system is being developed to verify the radio transmission techniques. In this system design, there are three multi-antenna arrays connected to one AP, each of which has eight antennas. This structure includes RF front-end, base-band processing unit and router. Specifically, base-band processing unit has base-band receiving and transmitting modules, MIMO receiving and transmitting modules, control and switch modules, back-plane network. The functions of MIMO transmitting module are to perform MIMO, pilot symbol insertion and OFDM modulation. While MIMO receiving module performs synchronization, OFDM demodulation, channel estimation, MIMO decode. Base-band transmitting module implements CRC, channel coding, interleaving and QAM modulation. Base-band receiving module mainly implements decoder such as Turbo, LDPC decoder. The communication processor in the base-band module carries out MAC and Link level processing. The base-band processing unit is connected to the IP network by the router.

Conclusion

In the current information society, the number of mobile subscribers increases very dynamically. At the same time, there is also an increasing demand for various services and QoS requirements. The demand for multimedia services and data services with high mobility becomes more urgent. Therefore it is necessary to investigate B3G mobile communications with higher capacity, higher spectrum efficiency and new bandwidth to satisfy the mobile communication requirements in the year 2010 and thereafter.

In China, FuTURE program provides an attractive solution for B3G mobile communication system by creating incentives related to licensing, operation and performance. Now this project has made a great achievement and it is believed that in the near future B3G system will be put into use to meet increasing demand of subscribers.

15.4 CAS e-Science and Virtual Lab[5]

The 21st century has seen the emergence of e-science as a new research environment. In the past few years, many e-Science related programmes and projects have been launched worldwide. The Chinese Academy of Sciences (CAS), the top research organization in China, has also been carrying out many initiatives in e-Science since 2002.

What is e-Science?

A new word rich with meanings, e-Science represents a new style of doing research in the information society, with the great advantage of information and communication technologies (ICTs). John Taylor, Director General of Research Councils in the UK, described e-Science as follows: "e-

Science is about global collaboration in key areas of science, and the next generation of infrastructure that will enable it; e-Science will change the dynamic of the way science is undertaken." While more and more countries pay attention to e-Science and take actions concerning it, there are quite a few definitions and statements about what e-Science means. It does not matter which explanation is better than others – a common understanding should be that research is the objective and new technologies are the methods of achieving it.

CAS is the top research organization of China, carrying out all kinds of research in the natural sciences. CAS has more than 100 institutes and about 37,000 researchers. It has made a great contribution to the country and intends to go on playing a leading role in the national development of science and technology. Since the end of the 20th century, the advancement and applications of ICT has vastly changed people's lives, as well as researchers' work. To make sure those scientists have a sound research environment with an advanced information infrastructure, CAS has invested a lot of resources and efforts in informatization construction over the past five years. Along with this progress, e-Science became an objective and an important task of the CAS Informatization Programme 2001-2005. Currently, the next five-year programme for 2006-2010 is being devised. e-Science has been chosen as the main direction in the new programme.

CAS Informatization Programme 2001-2005

The main object of the CAS Informatization Programme 2001- 2005 was to significantly improve the CAS information infrastructure, based on finding a common platform and services on which all institutes and researchers of CAS could run.4 Some key projects of the programme are the upgrade of the CAS network, the construction of a supercomputing environment, the scientific database and its applications, and a video conferencing system, among others.

CAS e-Science Initiative 2006-2010

In 2004, CAS started planning the new programme for CAS Informatization Construction under the national 11th five-year programme 2006-2010. At the almost the same time, the Chinese Government organized more than 1,000 experts to fulfill a middle and long term national plan untiil 2020 for the development of science and technology. Some experts had worked for both plans. CAS tried its best to follow and match the national plan to its own scheme for the next five years.

The ultimate goal, or the vision, of CAS Informatization is to build a digital CAS, which would be an ideal form of the academy to take in the information society. There are two major missions: one is e-Science and the other is Academia Resource Planning (ARP). ARP is a new concept borrowing from Enterprise Resource Planning (ERP). e-Science means scientific research activities in an informatized environment; ARP means administration for scientific research in an informatized environment.

In the past five years, CAS has made huge progress in informatization construction, especially in upgrading the information infrastructure and a widely accepted understanding of its significance. Applications that could really take advantage of this infrastructure and new technologies will become the focus of the next step. While e-Science represents a whole picture of the effects that informatization brings to academia, Virtual Lab, a key concept and the core component in an e-Science context, would be the most important concrete implementation facing end users, that is to say, thousands of researchers.

e-Science Virtual Lab

Virtual Lab is not a very new word; however, the 'virtual lab' we're talking about here has its own special meanings in the e- Science context. To be more clear, we also call it "e-Science Virtual Lab" if need be.

In our e-Science framework, Virtual Lab takes key positions between applications and resources. These resources could cover all aspects of research activities, including the information infrastructure, scientific equipment and facilities, and so on. Virtual Lab is the core component to make e-Science a reality as there are so many existing resources in place, but just a few could be brought into full play even now, with an advanced infrastructure ready. The last bottleneck may be the gap between products by computer experts and end users of domain scientists. According to our experience, it would take much more effort than expected to bridge this gap. Therefore, Virtual Lab is proposed to be a basic unit of research activity in the e-Science environment. Virtual Lab is the right user interface between scientists and their e-Science environment. Through Virtual Lab, all kinds of resources could be integrated into a single access point; customized and flexible services would be provided according to the specific requirements of different domains in an easier way than ever before; multidisciplinary, multi-site and multi-organization collaboration could be carried out on a routine basis.

The Virtual Lab should have seven crucial features as follows:

- Ease of use – It should be much easier to use than current systems. To some extent this is more important than functionality.
- Resource integration – Virtual Lab should provide the user with a single operating environment under which many kinds of resources, such as supercomputers, mass storage facilities, scientific databases, digital libraries, high bandwidth link, scientific equipment, etc. could be accessed in a seamless way.
- Customized service – It should provide a user with what he or she wants completely and exactly. e-Science is a comprehensive environment, but each user may need a specific workbench individually. Furthermore, users may like to choose different services at different times or at different prices. This requires not only Virtual Lab, but also the support of a service provider that can to customize the service according to the user's demand.
- Ubiquitous research – It should benefit from state-of-the-art technologies on mobile computing and related so that user could use the Virtual Lab at any time and anywhere.
- Collaborative work – It should enable a lot of scientists, who are from multiple independent institutions, from multiple sites across the world, and from different professional backgrounds, to work together on a collaborative project or a common problem.
- Scalability – It should be able to support hundreds of users from tens of institutions, but should work just as well for three or five users.
- Management – It should interact with outer management systems, such as ARP in CAS, to help improve efficiency during the whole lifetime of a research project or other research activities.

As a pilot project, the Avian Flu Comprehensive Information Platform and Foreseeing System (AFFS) have been ongoing since May 2005. Four institutes of CAS (the Institute of Microbiology, Institute of Virus, Institute of Zoology, and Computer Network Information Center) in different disciplines are taking part in this project. A collaborative workbench based on Virtual Lab has been established, dedicated to the group of scientists within this project.

The science of tomorrow

ICTs are the product of research, and they are changing the ways we research, making e-Science the science of tomorrow. CAS has carried out some key projects to improve its information infrastructure between 2001 and 2005. CAS researchers have benefited from this informatization programme over the past five years. At the time of writing, the plan for CAS e-Science in 2006-2010 is being completed. Virtual Lab will be the core component of CAS e-Science in the coming years. We believe in and look forward to the continued success of e-Science in the information society.

15.5 Basic Research on IT in China Supported by NSFC[6]

Background information for basic research in information sciences conducted in China is introduced. Research topics and considerations for fundamental research supported by the National Natural Science Foundation of China (NSFC) is emphasized in this talk.

Chinese government attaches great importance to build up and improve its ability of innovation. Basic research is one of the most important activities for innovation ability. The annual budget of NSFC, used to support basic and some applied research in China, is increasing with a large annual growth rate. Growth can be expected in the next several years. In particular, NSFC has invested more than 300 million Yuan RMB to support basic research on IT in the year of 2005 through its Directorate of Information Sciences. On the other hand, the number of applications received every year is also increasing rapidly, especially in the past five years. The success rate of proposals for ordinary projects made to the Directorate of Information Sciences is lower than 1/5 in the year of 2005. It is a challenge for Chinese scientists to choose research topics and make good proposals to attract funds. It is also a challenge for the science society to develop a strategic plan, and to recognize important research areas and topics so that the funds can be used more effectively.

China has made significant progress in information technology, but grand challenges also exist in front of Chinese society. This can be seen from at least three aspects, including extent of the use of modern information facilities, development of computing and communication technologies and systems, and the state of development of IT devices in China. NSFC has invested a large amount of funds to support basic and some applied research in information technology in China. For the past years, research is conducted extensively on a wide range of areas, especially on new generation communication systems, networked computing, security, high performance computing, advanced information processing, SOC, intelligent control and robotics, micro- and nano- technologies, and technologies for optical and opto-electronic devices. Chinese scientists have made great progress and achievements in their research, including new techniques, new systems (prototypes), national and international standards.

Since 2004, investigation has been conducted so that a strategic plan can be made for basic research on IT in China. Some important areas can be chosen as priority areas that will be supported by NSFC in the next five years. Although the final decision has not been made, around fifteen areas are, most likely, going to be selected as priority areas for IT related research.

National Natural Science Foundation of China attaches great importance to international cooperation in supporting research activities. Not only does NSFC support important international conferences held in China, international academic exchanges and other cooperation activities. NSFC also supports (in particular, currently emphasizes) substantial coordinative research. NSFC encourages Chinese scientists conduct their research with their international colleagues, and supports substantial joint research projects. NSFC believes that the joint research activities will be beneficial to every side.

15.6 Notes

1 Authors in order of the section they contributed. The chapter was compiled and edited by Zhiyong Liu.
2 Presentation by Qiao Guo.
3 Presentation by Tao Xiaofeng.
4 This work was supported by projects of NSF of China (60496312), NSF of Beijing (4042021), National 863 (2003AA12331004) and FuTURE TDD Special Work Group.
5 Presentation by Kai Nan.
6 Presentation by Zhiyong Liu.

16. ICT AND THE KERALA MODEL

Antony Palackal, *Loyola College of Social Sciences, Kerala[1]*
Aruna Sundararajan, *Global E-School*
P.H. Kurien, *IT Secretary, Government of Kerala*
Govindan Parayil, *University of Oslo*
R. Sooryamoorthy, *University of KwaZulu-Natal*
B. Paige Miller, *Louisiana State University*

The State of Kerala, in the southwestern part of India, was the only region that received a session in the whole conference. It was, indeed, well merited, given the distinctive position that the State of Kerala holds in the developmental map of the world. With a current population of 31,838,619 people[2] living in 38,863 sq. km. area, Kerala continues to be the focus of attention for the Indian and international Scholarship as a region in the developing world with a unique pattern of development. The 'Kerala Model' of development has been a much-debated topic in the academic parlance, as it appeared to be paradoxical, exhibiting a developmental trajectory with high social achievements on a weak economic base.

The State, with its unique socio-economic and demographic characteristics, has been compared with developed nations (Ramachandran, 1996; Oommen, 1992, 1999, Vol. 1 & 2). To mention a few unique features of Kerala: the State has the highest rate of literacy in the country among both men and women; the sex ratio is in favor of women, contrary to the all India patern; Kerala has the lowest birth rate and death rate in the country, the infant mortality rate is the lowest, which is comparable with that of Washington; fertility is one of the lowest rates recorded – fewer than two per couple; so is the maternal mortality rate: two for deliveries, in sharp contrast to forty-five in India; life expectancy at birth is well above the all India average; the average morbidity rate too is an all-time low.

On the other, notwithstanding the enviable progress and unique features, Kerala remains one of the poorer regions among the States in India. The bleak economic scenario of the State contradicts its achievements. The per capita income, for instance, is notably below the national average and that of many other States (George, 1993). Nevertheless, in sharp contradistinction, a high level of consumption marks the living standard of the people. In recent years, the people of Kerala have been engaged in forms of consumption that resemble the cosmopolitan cultural forms in other parts of the contemporary world. Paradoxically, the State exhibits poor economic growth but high standard of living.

With the backdrop of these paradoxical, but high priority developmental concerns, the State has been in the forefront of ICT initiatives in the country. The recently formulated IT policy acknowledged in its preamble that it 'endeavours to delineate a strategy for harnessing the opportunities and the resources offered by IT for the comprehensive social and economic development of the State.[3]' This strategy has been conceived, realising the fact that IT constitutes the primary instrument for facilitating Kerala's emergence as a leading knowledge society in the region. It also stated that 'the growth of Kerala in coming years will be increasingly driven by the knowledge and service-based sectors, where ease of information transactions will be a key determinant of success.'[4]. The policy also recognised that the State is a highly advanced society. The wide mass base that the media enjoys in the State and the penetration that communication technologies have been able to make are definite advantages in making the State of Kerala a 100% "internetised" State - very truly, an Information Society.

16.1 WSIS and The Kerala Session

ICT undoubtedly is the world's fastest growing economic activity. It is transforming resource-based economies to knowledge-based economies. Knowledge engineering is replacing pure data into information-oriented engineering at a global level. It has been widely accepted that the humanity possesses enormously powerful tools in the form of new information technologies. The digital revolution, particularly in the fields of information and communication, has extended the frontiers of the global village, with a profound impact on how the world functions and interacts. It is an undeniable fact that the recent strides in ICT have wrought fundamental changes in the way people think, behave, communicate, do business, educate the children and entertain. They have forged new ways to create knowledge, educate people and disseminate information. The information revolution penetrates all parts of our lives. It affects the way we learn, work, communicate, do business.

With increasing access to information and knowledge, it is hoped that people all over the world could be empowered to achieve their development goals and, through improved communications, help create a more just, prosperous and peaceful world. Particularly, ICTs could play a major role in the developing regions of the world. They could help connect individuals, groups, farmers and other skilled personnel in the backward and isolated areas of the world and bring them to the attention of the national and global markets. While information and communication technologies alone cannot solve the world's problems, they are critical tools in meeting these global challenges. In short, it may be well said that information technology will have a critical role in shaping the societies and politics of the 21st century.

It has been argued that the information revolution is at present one with much liberty, some fraternity but not equality. In the backdrop of the unprecedented developments in information technology, the world today is witnessing two opposite trends. On the one hand the explosive progress in science and technology that offers uncommon opportunities for health, food, water, work, energy, and literacy and above all communication and information to many. On the other, a considerable proportion of humankind living under conditions of poverty, hunger, and deprivation feel a sense of social exclusion and injustice. Kofi Annan, in the opening statement during the World Summit on the Information Society in Geneva, has said that revolutionary developments in ICT have brought new contradictions – "the so called digital divide is actually several gaps in one. It is yet to deliver the goods or even the tools to obtain them to many of those most in need". At Geneva in 2003, the world promised to achieve a host of targets by 2015 – linking, via technology, villages and communities, universities and schools, scientific and research centres, public libraries, cultural centres, local and central government departments.

Bridging the digital knowledge divide and avoiding the inequities of the past, is regarded as the most urgent need of our time. The World Summit on the Information Society in Tunis in November 2005 therefore, made a serious attempt to grapple with the contradictions and challenges of the information-technology-driven times, besides demonstrating the progress made in technology development since the 2003 Geneva Summit. It was in this context that the Summit in Tunis, a programme titled "Connect the world" by 2015 was launched. The aim of the programme is to ensure the benefits of the digital revolution reach every country and every part of each country by the year 2015, which is also a benchmark year for achieving the UN Millennium Development Goals. As part of the "Connect the World" movement, India has launched "Mission 2007" - every village a Knowledge Centre programme aiming to provide knowledge connectivity to every village of India by August 15[5], 2007.

The State of Kerala had begun early attempts to become the first IT-literate State in the country. This programme, called IT @school, which was initiated in July 2002, envisages that all the pupils in both government and aided schools in Kerala will be given compulsory education in IT from Standard VIII. There are about 1.5 million students in all the 2600 schools in Kerala. Along with this in the late 2002, Kerala launched another programme meant for the entire population. Akshaya- Bridging the Digital

Divide - as the programme is named, aims at making at least one person in every family a computer literate. The purpose of the project is to make people e-literate for the basic use of cyber fluency. Upon completion of this scheme it is expected that the number of Internet users will increase to 20 percent of the population. The Information Kerala Mission (IKM) is yet another major attempt aimed at computerizing and networking all the 1,215 local bodies of Kerala. There are also computerized centres at district headquarters called FRIENDS where people can pay their telephone bills, electricity charges, property taxes and vehicle taxes.

The Special Kerala session in the PPF conference was set in the backdrop of the ICT initiatives and the developmental imperatives of the State. In general, it sought to examine the state of the art of ICT driven developmental endeavours and the nature, dynamics and the effects of communication networks in the State. More specifically, it included deliberations,

1. Situating the ICT programmes of the State from a historical and policy perspective in the context of the distinctive developmental scenario of the State,
2. Appraising the Ashaya programme in Kerala, an initiative of government of Kerala that aims at making Kerala an IT literate State,
3. Assessing the links between the social divide and the digital divide with special reference to the Akshaya programme initiative in Kerala,[6]
4. Exploring ICTs in relation to personal communication networks by examining the factors associated with mobile phone usage in Kerala,
5. Investigating diachronically the nature and structure of knowledge production in Kerala vis-à-vis ICTs.

The session included five presentations organized in two parts. The first part of the session was a panel discussion by Aruna Sundararajan and P.H. Kurien, the two administrators who played the lead role in the development of IT sector in the State. The second part of the session was presentations by academicians on research conducted on different aspects of ICT in Kerala. It included presentations by Govindan Parayil, Centre for Technology, Innovation and Culture, University of Oslo, R. Sooryamoorthy, University of KwaZulu-Natal, South Africa, and Antony Palackal, Loyola College of Social Sciences, University of Kerala, India.

16.2 ICT for the Masses – the Kerala Experience[7]

ICTs are emerging as a powerful tool for development, and are clearly vital for the long-term growth and efficiency of a nation. However, developing countries, which arguably need ICTs the most, face formidable obstacles and challenges in widely harnessing them for the common good. These barriers are in the form of poor infrastructure, inequitable access, absence of basic skills among large sections of the populace, lack of relevant content, scarcity of resources and so on. These can often seem insurmountable in the Indian context, as they are so deep-rooted and endemic.

ICTs are still a relatively elitist, urban phenomenon in India. Their impact on the masses is yet to be widely felt. However, a range of innovative experiments is currently underway as governments and service providers increasingly deploy ICT tools to reach the rural poor. Innovations range from community networks that deliver e-governance and e-commerce to public ICT kiosks offering low-cost Internet access; form popular communication and computing devices to ICT-enabled healthcare and education.

There are a range of noteworthy examples in rural ICT dissemination from different parts of the country. Some of them include the Gyandoot community network to deliver e-governance and other services to remote, tribal pockets in Dhar District of Madhya Pradesh; the M.S. Swaminathan Foundation's 'information villages' in Pondicherry, where villagers can access expert agricultural and other relevant information electronically; the Warana project in Maharashtra where ICT has transformed a rural cooperative. Not all of these initiatives are uniform in the intensity of technology deployed and the scale of their impact. Some are more sustainable than others. However all of them illustrate innovative applications of ICTs to improve the lives of the poor in unconventional ways, often in environments unfriendly to ICT induction.

A number of these initiatives also highlight fundamental dilemmas of ICT induction. For instance, how does one go about estimating the technology needs of a populace? What level of technology induction would be deemed appropriate in a give context? What is the trade-off between ICT needs and other, more pressing, day-to-day concerns? Have ICT projects in fact delivered tangible, measurable gains to citizens, compared to costs? At the operational level, how does one tackle chronic issues such as access, content, language, etc.? These are some of the issues to be explored in the potentially high-impact ICT projects in the State of Kerala. Kerala offers an interesting framework to examine these issues, owing not merely to the State's advanced developmental attainments, in particular its high literacy levels, and consequently higher level of ICT preparedness, but also because of its pioneering and successful models of mass dissemination.

The ICT projects in Kerala cover FRIENDS, an example of a relatively simple ICT-enabled access point to government for improving service levels; The Information Kerala Mission (IKM), a pioneering e-governance project that promises to transform administration at the grassroots; and Akshaya, Kerala's pioneering ICT dissemination initiative. Each of these projects reflects a distinctive approach to ICT induction collectively. These cases highlight common dilemmas inherent in the endeavours and provide insights into how major challenges have been addressed.

FRIENDS centres are single-window IT-enabled front-end facilities were citizens can remit payments to government and public utilities and access basic public services at one point. Besides the convenience of interacting with a single agency rather than multiple departments, these centres offer other advantages such as accessibility beyond office hours and on holidays, a modern ambience in which quick courteous service is offered by a trained staff to attend to customer needs. The centres also often function as help desks. Starting with one centre in 2000, 14 such centres are today operational – one in each district headquarters – catering to about five million citizens in the State.

The Government of Kerala embarked on a radical decentralisation in the latter half of the 1990s, devolving sweeping powers and functions to local self-government institutions in the State; and entrusting these institutions with enormous responsibilities. The problems confronting local self-government institutions were manifold. Years of neglect had atrophied many legacy systems devised earlier; the staff was often corrupt and ill equipped to deal with expanded responsibilities and the elected representatives were yet to come to terms with a vastly changed scenario. IKM was conceived as a comprehensive ICT intervention to address these challenges. The project involved a complete re-engineering of all key processes followed by comprehensive automation of finance, personnel, planning, welfare and developmental functions.

The IKM project team worked closely for over three years with elected representatives, staff and community members to overhaul and rationalise procedures for ICT induction, devise appropriate decision support and management information systems for effective monitoring, design, develop modern citizen-ICT interfaces, automate workflows across departments and build ICT capacities to operate the new system. However, formidable challenges remain. IKM is a hugely ambitious venture, with all issues inherent in change management projects being of large magnitude. These include technical and logistical issues such as large-scale equipment procurement and deployment across 1,000 locations, extensive organizational restructuring and procedural reform across departments and institutions and managing transition problems and stakeholder expectations. By its very nature, IKM is a long-term undertaking. Its full impact would perhaps take years to unfold. One thing is however certain: the project is set to mark a paradigm change in grassroots governance in India.

Friends and IKM represent two unorthodox approaches to ICT induction that nevertheless promises radical change in the experience of governance of the citizen. Traditionally, back-end computerisation has been the prime focus in government, rather than the front-end. Similarly, governments have hitherto typically followed a 'trickle down' approach in inducting ICT, with higher levels being targeted first. Such trends have been reversed in these two projects. FRIENDS show that the extent of success is not determined by the intensity of technology deployed but how effectively it is leveraged to improve the overall productivity in a system. Even fairly simple technological intervention, effectively leveraged often yield dramatic results. FRIENDS also provides a rare instance of quick results in e-governance by focusing on citizen front ends, rather than waiting for the completion of back-end re-engineering which is often time-consuming and problematic.

Akshaya is Kerala's pioneering ICT dissemination initiative launched in the northern district. Conceived initially as a modest IT literacy drive covering one district, the programme subsequently evolved into a mass dissemination project aimed at universalizing ICT access and skill development in the State. The project has three components which correspond to the central issues that underlie the digital divide and constrain widespread ICT usage by the ordinary citizen – lack of access, skills and relevant content. A key distinction between Akshaya and other similar ICT projects of its kind is its integrated or holistic strategy to address the three issues of access, skill and content simultaneously. It is therefore a unique endeavour to perceptibly enhance the overall level of ICT demand through a mass-awareness building and training campaign covering the entire State.

Akshaya is one of the most ambitious ICT dissemination projects undertaken anywhere so far; because it seeks to empower an entire community across a State, including its most backward and remote segments. While FRIENDs represents the tried-and-tested approach towards using ICT for public welfare (where citizens are passive recipients of services). Akshaya seeks to use ICTs as a powerful lever for enabling the poor and the most disadvantaged to transcend traditional barriers that have stood between them and the unfettered exercise of their rights and choices for economic development, and for playing a more meaningful role in society.

16.3 Akshaya: A True Example of 'ICT for All'[8]

Like most noble ventures, it started with an inspiration. Then along the way, it was infused with character, a moral fibre. As the journey continued, it took a definite shape. And finally, it became a reality. On the 18th of November 2002, the President of India inaugurated 'Akshaya', a venture powerful enough to transform the lives of 65 lakh families in the State of Kerala.

Akshaya, an initiative of the Department of IT, Government of Kerala, aims to bridge the digital divide by disseminating e-literacy among the State citizenry and to transform the State into India's leading knowledge society. The project has three major objectives, viz. providing (1) Access to IT infrastructure including internet connectivity through setting up of ICT access points (Akshaya Centres) within 3 Kms from any household (2) IT Literacy Training to one member in every household and (3) Making available relevant content, ensuring continued usage and adding value. One Akshaya centre caters to every 1000-1500 households and is established under Private Public Partnership. As the locations of these centres are strategically planned and spatially distributed to cater to the people in all parts of the State and are connected through the internet, they will form a powerful network to guide and support the e-governance initiatives, community development interventions, e-commerce and information dissemination.

Under this project, one person in all the 65-lakh families in the State would be familiarized with the basic use of computer making it the largest rural computer-learning project worldwide. This involves setting up around 3000 broadband enabled information hubs called Akshaya e-centres across the State and training over 10,000 e-literacy instructors. Each e-centre, run by private entrepreneurs, will cater to the requirements of around 2250 families and make available the power of networking and connectivity to the common man.

The project was piloted in the district of Malappuram. For taking ICT to the masses, a total of 430 Akshaya e-centres have been set up to cover the entire 3,550 sq km and to support over 6 lakh families of the district. The Akshaya e-centers have been spatially distributed so that there is at least one within a radius of 2 kms of any household in the district. The e-centres, besides as training centres for the e-literacy, would also provide a range of value added services to the local community in its second phase. Each Kendra will be a one-room facility equipped with 5-10 computers, printers, scanners, web cam, IP phones and other peripherals and software required to carry out various ICT based services.

The Akshaya e-centres run by private entrepreneurs as a self sustaining unit will impart training to the local citizenry using a specially developed interactive CD-based tutor with Malayalam commentary. After the 15 hours training module a person would have functional knowledge of computers, would be able to send e-mails and access relevant e-content on the net.

At the end of the pilot stage, the following objectives have been met.

1. With training imparted for 600,000 individuals, at least one person in every family in Malappuram district has been made e-literate, making Malappuram the first 100% e-literate district in the country.
2. The functional knowledge enables the trainees to use the computers for common uses like sending e-mails, Internet browsing etc;
3. Establishment of 430 Akshaya e-centres within 2 km radius of any household.
4. The e-centres have been spatially distributed through out the district and each will cater to around 1000 – 1500 families.
5. Creation of around 2,400 direct employments and 12,000 indirect employments.
6. Increased PC penetration into rural areas.
7. Access to one of the largest creation of e-content in local language on all topics of relevance to the common man even in the remotest part of the district.

The wireless broadband connectivity infrastructure that has been established through project Akshaya affords several value added services to be offered through the e-centres in the district of Malappuram. Since the locations of the e-centres are strategically planned and spatially distributed to cater to the people in even the remotest part of the district, they form a powerful network to bring the full benefits of all e-governance initiatives of the Government to the common man.

The e-centres provide G2C, G2G, C2C, C2B, B2B AND G2B information interchange and dissemination and act as decentralized information access hubs for the citizen needs. Collection of utility bills and taxes now done through 'FRIENDS' centre is integrated with Akshaya e-centres thereby minimizing transaction cost and time to citizens. Electronic payment of certain utility services like telephone, water and electricity bills is now possible. The broadband enabled e-centres also enable all types of activities like e-commerce, internet telephony, IT enabled agriculture and health services, video conferencing, online grievance redressal, insurance, on-line ticketing, 2nd level computer training etc. No person in the district of Malappuram will have to undertake long bus journeys and wait at the counters to pay their utility bills. All such bills are accepted at the Akshaya e-centres. This is the first time in the country that Rural Internet Banking &

Financial Services has been made available to rural population covering an entire district.

The success of the project in the pilot district of Malappuram has prompted the Government to replicate the project in seven more districts. The roll out is currently in progress and the e-literacy phase is expected to be completed by mid 2006 and the service delivery facilities are expected to be operational by end 2006. The entire State is expected to be covered by the end of 2007. The project, when completed, will make Kerala the first e-literate State in the country and a model in development for the entire world.

16.4 Does the Social Divide Reinforce the Digital Divide?[9]

It is believed that ICTs have enormous potential for solving the problems of development. *Human Development Report 2001,* for instance, expresses the hope that advancements in ICTs and biotechnology "will lead to healthier lives, greater social freedoms, increased knowledge and more productive livelihoods" (UNDP, 2001, p.1). However, diffusion of ICTs is very limited and uneven in most parts of the developing world. For example, the number of telephone lines per 1000 people in 1999 was 27 in India compared to 682 in the U.S.; within India, this figure varied between 301.8 in Delhi and 4.8 in rural Bihar in 2003. It is important, in this context, to bridge the digital divide, and, thereby, the development gap between rich and poor regions, so the argument goes.

The digital divide is more often seen merely as a technological access problem – a problem of poor telecom infrastructure, Internet connectivity, and so on. Although investment in ICTs access is important to bridge the digital divide, there have not been many attempts to understand the digital divide as part of a larger social problem. This paper is an attempt to understand how social inequalities – between members of different class and gender – prevent the closing of the digital divide. This paper is partly based on field studies conducted in two rural locations in two South Indian states— Kerala and Andhra Pradesh. Various projects and programmes to use ICTs for enhancing developmental opportunities are going on in both states. Based on empirical evidence gathered in 2002 at Malappuram in Kerala and Kuppam in Andhra Pradesh, we sought to establish the close links between the social divide and the digital divide.

We examined the factors associated with the diffusion of ICTs in rural areas, and the potential role that ICTs can play in the development of rural areas. Our contention is that for meaningful diffusion of ICTs, policy makers must pay attention to the social dimensions of the digital divide. So we submit that ICTs can play a potent role in rural development, but only if the basic obstacles to rural prosperity are removed through radical changes – through land reforms, revitalisation of rural credit, greater state intervention in rural infrastructure, and universal primary education. Given this proposition, ICTs could be said to be powerful tools for development konly under right social and economic conditions. We argue that capabilities to use the information, particularly to convert the information into useful knowledge, depends on the social context of the users. In this context, we are of the opinion that the revolutionary potential of rural ICT centers has been blown out of proportion. For example, what is the use of information on market prices for commodities for the subsistence farmer or information about employment market for the illiterate? So the supply (diffusion) of ICTs in itself does not give an individual the capabilities. This capability depends on whether the individual has the right social conditions to make use of ICTs (information).

The area of study selected in Andhra Pradesh was the i-community project (IC) in Kuppam and the sample villages selected were Kadepalle and Venkatepalle, which had ICs within 3 miles radius in 2002. In Kerala, Akshaya project was studied and Pulippadam village in Malappuram was the sample village. 45 households each in Kuppam and Malappuram were selected using stratified sampling Based on landholding size, we sampled 113 males and 102 females and 118 males and 122 females in Kuppam and Malappuram respectively.

The following three questions were asked to understand the nature of diffusion of ICTs.

1. Have you or any of your family members heard about computers?
2. Have you or any of your family members ever heard about the IC in your locality?
3. Have you or any of your family ever made use of the services at the IC in your locality?

Findings corresponded to our assumptions about the social context of the users. Social disparities were less in Malappuram than in Kuppam. It was found that social divide and digital divide reinforce each other. In Kuppam, persons who used computers were better educated and they also belonged to relatively richer households. There were only seven households in which one or more members used a computer. Median landholding for these households was 3.04 acres (median for the whole sample was 0.71 acre). These seven households also accounted for 73% of the sample with at least high school education. More strikingly, no woman in the Kuppam sample used a computer.

In Malappuram, the situation was better for persons in poorer households largely due to higher literacy and educational opportunities. For example there were two Muslim women in the sample, aged 22 and 23, studying for PG courses, beloging to poorer households having 0.1 acre of land. Both were well-versed in using computers and were looking for jobs through the Internet

Unlike Kuppam, computers were facilitators of social and economic mobility in Malappuram.

How do we explain the difference? Kerala has a history of public action that helped to create favourable social and economic climate (land reforms, mass literacy, better public health, roads, telephones, etc.) whereas Andhra has yet to introduce any of these measures in any meaningful manner. There prevailed high social and economic inequality in Andhra compared to Kerala. Kerala has favourable conditions, but it can do far better than what it has achieved so far. Kerala lacked any clear policy guideline on harnessing ICTs for innovation, productivity growth and job creation. Andhra is ahead of Kerala in terms of IT industry promotion and infrastructure investment. If Andhra can create the same social conditions as Kerala, it can out-perform Kerala.

16.5 Mobile Telephony and the Structure of Personal Networks[10]

Mobile telephony, like any other modern means of communication and probably ahead of the arrival of the Internet and email, has earned a niche of its own. Modifying the social conception of space and time, cell phones are used not only to strengthen time and space but also to transform social relations (Fortunati, 2002: 528) and social networks of contacts. For prolific users, cellular telephony helps to maintain social networks and to commence new relationships by defining individual personal spaces (Oksman and Turtiainen, 2004: 324).

Respondents for this study were sampled from three institutions –two academic institutions and a software concern– in the capital city of Thiruvananthapuram in Kerala in late 2002. A brief summary of the findings is presented here. About one-third of the respondents have their own mobile phones showing a clear sectoral disparity between the private and public sector respondents. Nearly half (42 %) had never used a cell phone in their life, while one quarter (25%) had used it before but did not have a chance to own one. The division between the private and public respondents tends to be sharp: four per cent of the private respondents had never used a mobile phone as against 51 per cent of public respondents. As regards the duration

of ownership of mobile phones, owners are not novices but are familiar with
the technology for quite some time. About 69 per cent of the respondents
have been using it for a period of at least one year. Thirty per cent are daily
mobile users, while 28 per cent are daily email users.

Does the use of mobile phones, concurrent with access and use of ICTs
(computer, the Internet and email), complement the communication needs of
the respondents? The difference is statistically significant between the daily
mobile users and non-daily users in their computer, Internet and email uses.
More often than not, the use of the computer and the Internet varies
according to access. With more mobile daily users having a home or work
computer, the difference is quite vivid between the daily mobile phone users
and others. Significantly, daily users are more (71%) connected to the
Internet than the non-daily users (67%). Clearly, as evident in the case of
home computers, mobile telephony complements the Internet. In other
words, those who use the cell phone daily are more likely to access (or use)
the Internet. Internet connectivity—and the use of the Web and email--
support the presence of a close relationship between daily mobile use and
ICTs, complementing each other.

Are the social networks of individuals influenced and shaped by the
communication technologies they adopt, possess and use? We have found
that the difference is significant between the daily users and non-users (both
mobile and email) in the number of network ties. Daily mobile users have
more mobile phone and email networks than non-daily users. The pattern is
just opposite for face-to-face, letter and landline network ties. Similarly,
daily email users maintain more mobile phone and email networks, as also in
the diversity of the means of contact.

No significant difference between daily and non-daily users (both the
mobile phone and email) in the total network size is noted, though there are
differences in specific networks. Non-daily mobile and email users maintain
more family network ties than the daily users, while friendship and romantic
ties are more for daily mobile and email users. In the composition of work
networks, we could not find any significant variation between daily and non-
daily users. Unlike the non-daily users, the daily users, both mobile and
email, do not seem to have many local contacts, as evident from their
networks in the capital city, hometown, other town and other rural districts
in Kerala. Daily users, on the other hand, have more non-local network
contacts (outside Kerala and India). In particular, the index for external non-
local contacts is significantly higher for daily mobile and email users. The
diversity of relationship locations, too, shows noticeable differences between
daily mobile and email users. Daily mobile phone and email users tend to
develop and maintain more global contacts than their non-daily counterparts.

The empirical analysis in this study provides several striking findings: the respondents either tend to use multiple technologies to interact with others (a "technology cluster") or are oriented towards traditional face-to-face methods. For these individuals, all technologies are not equally relevant to this technology cluster, siince landline and cell phones are substitute for each other, while cell phones and email are complementary. Respondents who are technologically-oriented have a different social structure than the rest, with fewer family ties and more non-local ties. Diffusion of mobile telephony modernizes social relationships with a notable decline in kin and increase in non-kin relationships.

16.6 The Structure of Knowledge Production in Kerala[11]

This paper rests on the basic assumption that ICTs have the potential to make societies increasingly knowledge based. The seemingly universal benefits of ICTs have led some to argue that the diffusion of ICTs in developing areas will lead to the globalization of science. Most importantly, it will lead to the integration, participation, and visibility of developing world scientists in the global scientific enterprise. Scientific development in the present day world is intertwined with innovations in ICTs. ICTs, therefore, are often treated as the panacea for development. The approach of the paper is that the Internet is an essential tool in the conduct of research. As the Internet becomes a pre-requisite for research and international collaboration, it is important to understand its impact on developing scientific communities. The paper made an attempt to diachronically examine the structure of Internet use and its association with publication productivity in scientific endeavors. The study addressed two basic questions: 1) To what degree has the research community in the developing world adopted the Internet? 2) To what extent does Internet use influence research productivity?

The observations and conclusions arrived at in this paper are based on an empirical study in 2005 of 260 respondents. Face to face surveys were administered to scientists belonging to a variety of research fields such as agriculture, biological science, engineering, mathematics, information technology, chemistry, physics, and geology in government research institutes and academic institutions. All were located in or near Trivandrum, the capital of Kerala. The participants of the study therefore belonged to two organizational types, namely, governmental research sector and educational sector. However, the analysis and interpretation of the data is made in the backdrop of the findings of the similar study conducted in 1994 (Campion and Shrum, 2004) and 2000 (Ynalvez et. al, 2005) in the same organizations. The study is, thus designed to be a longitudinal one.

Internet adoption and diffusion is conceptualized in terms of four primary dimensions. The first dimension refers to the degree to which individuals define themselves as users of telecommunications technology—specifically, whether one defines oneself as an "email user." The second dimension refers to the degree to which a particular technology is present and available for use within the environment – the aspect of Internet-access within the organization. The third dimension pertains to personal experience in the use of Internet. The fourth dimension is related to the social and cultural practices that constitute Internet use — that is, the diversity of behaviors associated with the employment of contemporary email and web technology. Hence the four dimensions that the study intended to examine are the use, access, experience, and practice of Internet.

A baseline study in 1994 (Campion & Shrum 2003) had showed that only 1/10 of the scientists had access to mainframe computers and email. The use of ICT had not become common in scientific endeavors. Only 6% of the scientists reported some access to email. Hence it was observed that scientists gave very low priority to the development of both domestic and international electronic communication networks. In 2000 (Ynalvez et.al, 2005) 42% of the respondents possessed a computer in their personal office and over seven people on an average used it. The scientist used to spend on computer approximately five hours a week. On a comparative frame, it was found that government scientists had more hours of use of computer per week compared to the scientists working in the university sector (< 1hr).

In 2000, only a minority had a personal computer in their office even when it was available at work. Personal computers were not so much 'personal' as 'public'. Two thirds of both men and women reported ready access to email either at the office or home. Three quarters of scientists had their computers at home Internet connection. A large majority of the respondents described themselves as Internet users (86%; i.e. 9/10). But very few had ready access (6/10) and for most of them, the use of the Internet had not become part of everyday practice. It was observed that education was the most consistent dimension defining the digital divide, especially in terms of Internet practice and experience. Those who have acquired their highest degree from a developed area seemed to hold clear advantages in the practice and experience of Internet. They had the advantages of direct association, learning and modeling from those who use the Internet in the developing countries and may have established a network of communication partners.

Collaborations in research become more local and region specific, with fewer international associations. Men reported significantly larger international networks than women. Women, on the other hand, had more local contacts. In terms of productivity, government research institutes were found to be more productive, compared to academic institutes. In 2000, there were indications that the Internet may increase the visibility of scientists in foreign journals. It also appeared that temporal and spatial dimensions constituted workplace privacy, i.e. the issues of space and identity – that transformed Internet connectivity into a collaborative research tool, which makes science a truly global enterprise.

Our new data, collected in mid 2005, showed a dramatic increase in the use, access practice and experience of ICT related activities among the scientists of the same locations. A majority of men and women scientists tend to consider that matters have improved because of Internet. Computers with connectivity, both at the office and home, were available to nearly all respondents who participated in the study. Those who do not use computers seemed to be nil. However, among the very few non-users the majority are women, although both men and women seemed to recognize the substantial importance of the use of web and email for their scientific enterprise. But men continued to spend more time in research. Productivity, measured in terms of publications in national and international journals, seemed to have increased in general. There was a sharp increase in the productivity of men, especially in terms of publications in foreign journals. The difference in the productivity of men and women became sharper. The gender factor involved in this case of digital divide hence constituted an import aspect of the study.

The current scenario of the scientific enterprise vis-à-vis ICTs revealed that the distinction between user and practitioner is increasingly disappearing. One implication of this is that the extremes of use and nonuse that previously characterized scientists in Kerala may be disappearing, so that this particular "digital divide" is becoming non-existent or trivial. But a positive correlation between connectivity and productivity has not been established. Productivity may still be contingent on social, structural and organizational conditions rather than access and use of ICT.

Gender parity in professional activities and organizational resources seemed to prevail. However women appeared to have fewer external collaborations and professional contacts compared to men. Their publications in foreign journals also seem to have decreased since 2000. So it may be concluded that the shift in Internet based science has not yet translated into occupational benefits for women, though it may have enabled them to circumvent global isolation but organizational localism may still prevail. Transcending social capital necessitates addressing the patrifocal orientations in the professional climate in order to reduce gender inequities in the knowledge sector in Kerala.

16.7 Conclusion

Phase I of the World Summit on the Information Society, which met in Geneva in December 2003, gave shape to a shared vision and put forward a concrete plan of action to build a development-oriented, equitable and inclusive Information Society, "where everyone can create, access, utilize and share information and knowledge, enabling individuals, communities and peoples to achieve their full potential in promoting sustainable development and improving their quality of life". The second phase of the Summit in Tunis has reiterated the urgency for bridging the digital divide in all fronts so as to hasten the efforts at eradicating the social divide at a global level. The Kerala Session in the PPF Conference was a loud proclamation that ICTs are not merely tools for information and communication, but enable paradigmatic shifts in institutional and organizational networks and dynamics in the State.

Akshaya project, for instance, aims at improving governance and introducing reforms primarily to pave the way for improved delivery of essential services to citizens in terms of transaction enabled information and communication, particularly for the disadvantaged sections of the society. ICT driven initiatives of the State hold the potential to transform both governance and development delivery in a manner that can overcome structural bottlenecks in these areas. They promote greater efficiency and transparency in the planning, monitoring and delivery of development, through easier coordination, increased information sharing, and more effective outreach. Studies on the structure of knowledge production and communication and the effect of mobile telephony in communication and social network in Kerala have revealed the fact that ICTs transform the nature of communication networks, collaboration, knowledge production and productivity in Kerala.

The Special Kerala Session, more importantly, revealed the fact that ICTs are not only deeply embedded in communication and collaboration, but also social development. Within the framework of ongoing structural change in the global economy, the dynamics of technology, growth and employment are in perpetual interplay. However, the effect of ICTs in shaping spatial, temporal and social relations in Kerala cannot be denied. The State of Kerala seems to be fertile ground for the growth of ICTs, given its improved socio-economic conditions. It appears that the Government of Kerala understands the enormous potential of ICTs not only as a tool for improving governance and creating more jobs, but more significantly, as a means to enhance the standard of living of the people.

The State at various levels could further the efforts at harnessing ICTs in view of improving the standard of living through use of Information and

Communication Technology in all sectors as a tool to enhance productivity, efficiency and optimum utilization of resources. It is also recognized that application of ICT could also facilitate decentralized administration and empowerment of people. At this juncture, perhaps, what appears to be important is the creation of IT-specific infrastructure in different parts of the State. This includes removal of barriers in the regulatory environment, making it pro-active and sensitive to the needs of industry and the masses. Human Resource Development is a very critical aspect in the development of ICT. The Government needs to sense the urgency for consolidating and strengthening the core competence of the state on the human resources front to propel the development of IT industry.

Internet Connectivity is very fundamental to the success of IT led development initiatives in delivering the planned services and administering interventions in various sectors. Internet connectivity makes possible timely and effective communication between the rural population and government departments and agencies, in ways that were previously not possible. Internet connectivity plays an important role in democratic processes, too. The Rural Internet Connectivity harnessed through Akshaya Project is expected to bring about significant socio-economic changes in the State. It has also been found that Internet Connectivity also changes the structure of knowledge production and the patterns of communication of the scientific enterprises of the State. In the development front, Internet connectivity will open up many opportunities. Databases and other information sources can be accessed, providing information on distant markets, market and consumption trends, and future markets. Detailed information regarding "best practices" methods and techniques can be made available, to the great advantage of agriculture, fisheries, and cottage handicraft industries.

16.8 References

Campion, P. and W. Shrum 2004. 'Gender and Science in Developing Areas', *Science, Technology, and Human Values* 29: 459-485.

Fortunati, L. 2002. 'The Mobile Phone: Towards New Categories and Social Relations', Information, *Communication and Society* 5(4): 513-28.

George, K. K. 1993. *Limits to Kerala Model of Development: An analysis of fiscal crisis and its implications*. Thiruvananthapuram, Centre for Development Studies.

Government of Kerala, *Information Technology: Policy Document*, Thiruvananthapuram: Department of Public Relations, Government of Kerala, 2001.

Oksman, V., and J. Turtiainen 2004. 'Mobile Communication as a Social Stage', *New Media and Society* 6(3): 319-39.

Oommen, M.A. 1992. *The Kerala Economy*. New Delhi: Oxford and IBH.

Oommen, M.A. 1999. *Kerala's Development Experience Vol. 1 & 11*. ed. New Delhi: Concept Publishing.

Ramachandran, V.K. 1996. 'On Kerala's Development Achievements'. ed. *Indian Development: Selected Regional Perspectives*. J. D. A. Sen. Delhi, Oxford University Press: 205-356.

Ynalvez Marcus, Ricardo Duque, Paul Nyaga Mbatia, R. Sooryamoorhy, Antony Palackal, and Wesley Shrum. 2005. 'When Do Scientists "Adopt" the Internet? Dimensions of Connectivity of Developing Areas', *Scientometrics* 63: 39-67.

16.9 Notes

1 Authors in order of the section they contributed. The session was co-organized by Paige Miller; the chapter was compiled and edited by Shrum.

2 As per the latest *Census 2001*.

3 Government of Kerala, Information Technology: Policy Document, Thiruvananthapuram: Department of Public Relations, Government of Kerala, 2001.

4 Ibid, 2001

5 India's Independence day.

6 Editorial Note: While the presentations in the Special Kerala Session were uniformly positive in their assessment of Akshaya Project, other presenters at the meeting were relatively sceptical about its success, both in terms of usage and in terms of the business model it represents. Paraphrasing one researcher from a leading producer of computer software—"we would be very much interested in these types of kiosks—if they worked."

7 Presented by P.H. Kurien.

8 Presented by Aruna Sunderrajan.

9 Presented by Govindan Parayil.

10 Presented by R. Sooryamoorthy.

11 Presented by Antony Palackal.

17. RESEARCH PROCESS AND CONNECTIVITY IN THE INFORMATION SOCIETY

R.Sooryamoorthy, *University of KwaZulu Natal[1]*
Paul Nyaga Mbatia, *University of Nairobi*
Wayne Johnson, *Hewlett Packard*
George E. Okwach, *Kenya Sugar Research Foundation*
Daniel Schaffer, *Third World Academy of Sciences*
Carthage Smith, *International Council for Science (ICSU)*
John Dryden, *OECD*
Qiheng Hu, *Internet Society of China*
Wiebe Bijker, *University of Maastricht*
Wesley Shrum, *Louisiana State University*

One of the key objectives of the "Past, Present and Future" conference was to inject a note of realism in the run up to phase two of the World Summit on the Information Society. This might seem strange, given that the original sponsor of the event, the Society for Social Studies of Science, is an international, professional association whose members are often thought to advocate various forms of social constructivism. The conference brought together active scholars, who do research on global and national ICT issues, with policy makers, program managers, and senior organizational leaders. One of the constants throughout the three days of the meeting is not any particular theoretical, organizational, or ideological advocacy, but an overarching sense that the past, present, and future of <u>research</u> in an information society must include not only innovations in information technologies themselves, but also the ways in which these technologies interact with and are constituted by the social, political, and developmental contexts in which they are embedded. The "seamless web" of science, technology, and society was never more apparent than in the variety of presentations that follow.

The opening and closing plenary sessions were chaired by the Kenyan and South African coordinators of the World Science Project[2], while the "bookends" for the conference were two movies produced for the science and engineering events of Phase I and Phase II of WSIS. The Opening Plenary session reprised "Before the Horse," an ironic video essay on several paragraphs from the Summit documents that pertain to the globalization of science through the Internet. The final event of the conference was "After the Fact," a meditation on the continuing problems of development in the specific context of scientific institutions and Internet connectivity.[3]

The sections that follow examine crucial issues in understanding the Information Society, with a special focus on the process of research and the institutions that conduct and support it. The contributions to the plenary sessions moved from the problems of connectivity in a small research institute in sub-Saharan Africa, to the WSIS process itself in relation to the research and educational sectors so important to the Information Society. The importance of capacity building for the scientific institutions of the developing world was a focus of several keynote speakers in the opening and closing sessions, with contributions from the private sector (Hewlett Packard), international organizations (OECD, ICSU, TWAS, and the Society for Social Studies of Science), as well as national research and academic organizations. These latter institutions possess remarkable potential for the collection, analysis and dissemination of data that could be harnessed, given the right conditions. Finally, speakers at the opening and closing sessions discussed barriers of access to scientific data and information, as well as the important and continuing issue of the "scientific" digital divide.

17.1 African Research Institutions and the Problem of Connectivity?[4]

The Donor

The subject of our two part discussion today is a research institute. All of you have seen a drawing of the view from its Guest House when you visited the web site of this conference: http://worldsci.net.[5] The name and identity of the research station does not matter: it is typical of many rural research institutes in Africa. About two dozen agricultural scientists are based here, in an arid region where farmers could benefit immensely from a portfolio of research projects on a variety of issues targeted at improving productivity. By the same token, it seems very much as if the scientists who make this their home and workplace could benefit immensely from a reliable, always-on connection to the Internet.

This research institute served as a symbol for our conference, a symbol of the constraints of connectivity, of the Information Society, of Africa, of development and reagency (Shrum, 2005). Several of the key paragraphs in the Plan of Action adopted at the Geneva phase of the World Summit on the Information Society (paragraphs seven, ten, and twenty three) refer explicitly to the importance of providing a connection to the Internet for research institutes, universities, and schools. I first set eyes on the place in 1994, just after its new buildings were inaugurated. I visited again in 1999 and dreamed of seeing it fully connected, just as all universities and research institutes in Europe and the U.S. were, by then, online.

Partly inspired by this institute, we began what is now a six country project, investigating the effects of the Internet on research networks, communication, and collaboration—what some would call the globalization of science. Partly inspired by this institute, we began to work to make this connectivity happen, at least in the sub-Saharan African countries of our study. What if scientists at our institute could collaborate with scientists from abroad through email? What if they could have access to all the current agricultural research journals? What if they could just Talk Now with whomever they liked, and Have Unlimited Access to the information they needed on the web? We would help our partners build local area networks, funded by the U.S. National Science Foundation. Admittedly, by comparison with other donors—multilateral and bilateral organizations, international NGOs—we were small. But the amount of money needed was not large—a few thousand dollars could buy the hardware, the cables and connectors, a computer that could be employed as a server.

It was, to be sure, fun to have money—now try to engage some problems rather than just writing and talking about them! But there is a problem with the "wide-eyed and bushy-tailed" approach—that is, the first timers in Africa, Latin America, and Asia, who have come to "make a difference" They think doing projects is mainly about doing projects, rather than making money. Having spent enough time in the developing world, we saw what most donors and project managers see. You do not have to look very hard for it. Let us call it "leakage."[6] We decided to make a couple of commitments in the early days of our project. They are simple ones, really, but awfully hard to keep, since for most donors and NGOs spending a certain quantity of money within a given amount of time is a necessity. In this, we were lucky: our project is a research project and not a development project. The first commitment is that those from the developed world should not earn any money from the project—not even a per diem.[7] The second is that those from developing areas should not earn any more than necessary to accomplish project goals, based on local prices. There should be no leakage.

The irritating thing about sociologists—for those of you who are not sociologists—is that they will take that leakage, and make it the subject of another study.

One more commitment had particular importance for Internet connectivity in sub-Saharan Africa. We decided that our project would not pay for variable connectivity charges (e.g., monthly phone or cable bills) in the places where we worked. It was simply not sustainable. By 2001, state operated telecommunication monopolies were still charging exorbitant fees for data and connection services. At one time we calculated that the entire budget for our five year project would have been gone in one year if we had signed on with the standard monthly charges by Kenya telecom. Sometimes you just have to wait for the break up of these enterprises, but it is sometimes a long wait.

We bought sufficient hardware for the institute in 2002, and secured an agreement with a local partner to provide the installation. After a year had gone by, nothing substantial had happened. A full account of the project would involve not only technical problems such as the lack of a clear line of sight to a nearby town and a certain copper wire found to be unsuitable for carrying a signal. It would involve more robust details such as secret cabals, death threats (fortunately, of no consequence), theft (fortunately, not our equipment), installation of barbed wire surrounding a water tower that was considered (but never used) for a wireless connection point, threats of transfer to hardship posts, and an Italian named Paolo who believed the problem might be solved through a well-connected Internet café owner. Since most of these events happened before the first phase of the Summit—and given the Plan of Action that had been adopted in Geneva—it seemed a worthy goal to see whether this connectivity could be accomplished by the second, Tunis phase.

It saddens me—but now only a little—to report that if you go to the institute today, you do not have much chance to send an email, and browsing the web is not really an option. It will be on a slow, dialup connection, as before. And it will be through a phone call to town, from the office of one or two of the scientists who have funded projects. On the other hand, you can still sit on the veranda of the Guest House. And if you brought your materials with you, some very good work may be done.

The Recipient

Among the many reasons for low use of Internet by educational and research institutions in sub-Saharan Africa is inadequate appreciation of the true power and usefulness of this tool. Much of the third world countries still have very low rate of Internet connectivity, or the use of the Internet as a source or a means of exchanging information, compared to the rest of the world.

As we look back at what happened in our situation in a research centre in Katumani in Kenya, and as we observe other institutions, we see a number of factors that play part, and being responsible for this poor performance or low rate of progress. These factors can be multiplied and replayed in many parts of Africa, to varying degrees.

Low Budgetary Allocation to National Research Institutions

Dwindling government and donor funding to national research institutions means that top management must prioritize and limit funding to those areas perceived to have the potential to produce immediate and demonstrable results. Internet connectivity is rarely perceived as such. Institutions that have low capacity for revenue generation, and that rely on donations and financial goodwill, will not give priority to Internet connectivity at the expense of direct and field research.

Lack of Enthusiasm from the Scientists

Having failed to secure additional funding to support sustained Internet connectivity, we thought that we would use the power of demand to convince top management that scientists needed this facility, and that its provision would significantly increase their productivity. If we could demonstrate that an institution that is connected to the Internet is a highly productive society, then we could argue successfully for extra funds. Apart from formal awareness seminars for scientists, we constantly took advantage of our regular management meetings to urge for deeper interest in the use of Internet.

This approach, however, met with very minimal success. Quite a number of scientists had direct donor-funded projects, and were able to afford dial-up Internet connectivity for their offices. But increased interest did not happen. At one point in time,[8] Katumani had 48 research scientists (bachelors degree and above), consisting of 13 doctorates, 28 Masters, and seven bachelor degree holders. Of the 13 scientists with doctorate degrees, four were totally computer illiterate and six knew computing to varying degrees, and frequently used PCs (mainly for writing documents (word processing) or analysis of data (spreadsheet or statistical package). Of these six scientists two had maintained some email communication, using largely commercial cybercafé facilities (e.g. email with yahoo accounts). To the rest (and indeed the majority) of scientists in the centre, personal computers are nothing more than modern typewriters and large calculators.

Three scientists had desktop PCs in the offices, for their exclusive use. Of the three, only two maintained continuous Internet connectivity through a dial-up system to a Nairobi-based ISP (90 km away). We both maintained the Internet access through funds of our respective projects. Out of 48 scientists, only two had direct access to Internet connectivity in their offices. The rest were either uninterested in the Internet, or could not afford it.

Why the apathy among scientists in the use of Internet? To a very large extent, many scientists (and top managers included) in LDCs (Least Developed Countries) view the Internet merely as a part-time hobby, rather than an essential tool for day-to-day performance. A few postulates can be developed from the Katumani experience:

- We have a system in Kenya that largely does not recognize and reward information usage. There are two examples to highlight this. First, promotion is rarely based on published works, or the frequency and quality of publication. Two, postgraduate theses/dissertations still cite old literature or "grey literature" without serious reprimand by supervisors and/or examiners. The use of the Internet for bibliographic search is simply still very minimal.

- In our research institutions the emphasis is mainly on technology transfer as opposed to research for the sake of generation of new knowledge. This emphasis results from the demands by donors and governments for demonstrable impacts of the funds spent on research. It is, then, commonly assumed that technology transfer to a resource-poor subsistence farmer in a rural African setting is less demanding of Internet resources than field/lab research. This may explain the general lack of interest in Internet connectivity among many scientific researchers in LDCs.

In summary, the problem of low Internet connectivity among research scientists in Africa is complex. The provision of broadband ICT infrastructure is only one part of solution. There is need to address a host of internal factors –social, economic, political, and environmental.

17.2 Role of Science and WSIS in the Establishment of Information Society[9]

An important question to ask about the relationship between WSIS and science is: What is the role of science in the creation of information society? First, science underpins ICT developments and so shapes the information society. Through scientific activities, scientists accumulate knowledge useful to the development of ICTs. Indeed, without science, it is difficult to promote technological innovations such as ICTs. Second, scientific progress is dependent on access to information and data. Scientists with easy access to information and data are the very ones with the highest potential to innovate. Indeed, the difference in productivity and innovations between scientists from developed and developing countries is largely explained by their differentials in access to information and data. Due to high rates of access to information and data, scientists from the developed countries are more productive and innovative.

Third, WSIS presents a unique opportunity to address the knowledge divide in science. Obviously, by bringing all stakeholders together, WSIS has presented the problem of the digital divide as a global agenda for all. Fourth, to make WSIS successful in its mission, scientists need to engage with other stakeholders on information and data issues. To make good use of the strategy of sharing data scientists should not just talk among themselves; rather, they should engage with other stakeholders. Knowledge is more valuable when it is shared with others. Strategies for making WSIS more effective in the creation of Information Society include:

- Partnership with international organizations that focus on, generate, manage or analyze scientific data such as ICSU, UNESCO, CODATA, CERN, TWAS and others. What contributions can each of these stakeholders make? It is necessary to document the specific activities of each of these organizations and delineate their relevance in the WSIS process.
- Draw from past WSIS initiatives such as PrepCom1 and address the agreed upon concerns or principles.
- As proposed in March 2003, implement the defined agenda for action for science in the Information Society. The agenda has already been distributed widely and endorsed by national and international bodies.
- Draw from the several high profile science events in the Geneva Summit.

This discussion affirms that science has a critical role in the development of the Information Society. But we need an effective WSIS process to forge a strong linkage between science and IS; such a process should reduce the range of barriers that contribute to the persistent ICT-related problem of the digital divide. A recent editorial in *Science* (Iwata and Chen, 2005: 405) highlights the role of science in tackling the problem of digital divide by positing that: "Now, with the second phase of WSIS taking place in Tunis in November 2005, the scientific community needs to take lead in demonstrating how science –and universal access to scientific data, information, and knowledge– can make a critical difference in sustainable development and overcoming the "digital divide."

This is the greatest challenge of the WSIS process.

Geneva Declaration of Principles

The role of science in creating Information Society is well captured in the principles set forth in 2003 in Geneva. The principles were stated as follows:

- We recognize that science has a central role in the development of Information Society.
- We should remove barriers to equitable access to information for scientific activities and facilitate access to public domain information.
- We need to promote universal access with equal opportunities for all to scientific knowledge and the creation and dissemination of scientific information

While these are remarkable principles that reflect on the concerns to be addressed, they can only change the status quo if they are put on the ground and practised. Practically, more efforts should be directed in the identification of specific actors and their respective roles at different levels to tackle the problem of digital divide. Though the latter problem now looms large, particularly in the developing countries, to tackle it effectively requires the active participation of development actors from the developed countries. More resources must be harnessed from the North to liberate the South. How to do it and promote the development of ICT sector in the poor South is the challenge of WSIS process that targets the creation of an Information Society by 2015.

Agenda for Action: Overcoming the Problem of Digital Divide

Even with the launch of the WSIS documents in Geneva in 2003 that strongly affirmed the central role of science in developing an information society and supporting the principle of universal access with equal opportunities for all– the problem of the digital divide is still pervasive worldwide. How can it be tackled to remove barriers in the creation of an Information Society? The following courses of action are suggested (which can be challenged):

- *Provide affordable and reliable Internet connectivity for all universities and research institutes*: While this is a noble idea shared by many, the main challenge (especially in the developing countries) is to source the required resources to make things happen as suggested. Unless there are stakeholders from the rich North willing to help improve connectivity in the poor South, this course of action will not be tenable in some parts of the world.
- *Capacity building and education*: This is a very general strategy that needs to be unpackaged. For example, what aspects of capacity are lacking in the poor South and that need to be addressed? Who should build capacity? Should it be the State, private organizations, civil society or foreign experts? Past experiences have shown that

capacity building is more effective when it is spearheaded by the local actors and when it is participatory.

- *Full and open access to public data*: While this is the ideal situation, there are existing barriers especially in the poor South that inhibit the realization of the ideal. The internal barriers such as illiteracy, minimal investment in ICTs and poor connectivity should first be overcome. There are also external barriers to be tackled –such as exploitation of the developing countries by the rich North as well as operation of an ICT regulatory framework that favours the rich North.
- *Interoperability and metadata standards.*
- *Collection and preservation of digital data*: It is important to clarify the specific actors at all levels that should be charged with this responsibility.
- *Equitable access to scientific information*: As noted earlier, this is an ideal of the Information Society.
- *Promote scientific literacy*: This is doable internally and externally at different levels. However, the required resources should be identified.
- *Research on ICT use in key priority areas*: This idea is noble but the challenge in the developing countries is to raise money for research. Who should fund such research in developing countries?
- *Identify the role of scientists in decision-making in/for the Information Society*: To benefit from the proposed principles guiding the Information Society, scientists should be involved in decision making at all levels. Practically, the involvement of scientists in decision making could enhance Research & Development and ultimately, enhance scientific innovations.

Major Unresolved Issues

Despite the preparatory actions in Johannesburg (2002) and the formulation of remarkable principles in WSIS in Geneva (2003), the grand march towards the Information Society is still faced with major unresolved issues including:

- *Internet governance and freedom of the press*: The central issue here is to formulate a global functional framework to oversee Internet governance and the freedom of the press. This will entail establishment of a globally accepted authority to take charge of the Internet and freedom of press that could easily be abused.
- *Solidarity fund*: Efforts must be put to raise this fund that is required, *inter alia*, to implement the principles of WSIS.

- *Role of open-access publishing and open-source software*: Further, there is need to address the issue of using political agreements to implement e-science actions locally and internationally.

Beyond identification of these unresolved issues, we need viable means to address them. As a way forward, WSIS should establish a body (e.g., a commission) to address the general problem of implementation of its principles. Such a body should draw membership from North and South to enrich its understanding of the real barriers facing the WSIS process worldwide.

Partnership between WSIS and ICSU

How can ICSU contribute effectively to the WSIS process? Through its various units, ICSU can add value to the WSIS process by enhancing access to data among all stakeholders. More specifically, the role of selected units is as follows:

- CODATA –deals with policy and management.
- INASP –focuses on information access.
- World Data Centres and Services –these facilitate data collection, analysis and dissemination worldwide.
- Global Observing Systems and GEO.
- Global Environmental Change Programmes.

Through these outlets, ICSU promotes the generation, analysis and dissemination of scientific data required to promote, *inter alia*, the development of ICT sectors. The policies of ICSU include: (1) full and open access to scientific data, and (2) universal and equitable access to scientific publications. These policies are congruent to those of the WSIS. To enhance full and open access to scientific data, ICSU suggests the following actions:

- establishment of two way access;
- constraints must be minimized;
- establishment of stable systems for providing universal access to quality data;
- need to develop new economic models;
- involve scientists in policy development; and
- address the diverse needs of scientists in developing countries.

To accomplish all these actions:

- long-term planning and investments by all stakeholders (besides the State);
- professional data management to insure integrity of scientific findings;

- Modernization of current infrastructures and systems of data management;
- develop new infrastructures in some areas or regions;
- enhance international, interdisciplinary coordination; and
- support national and international policies.

Overall, these constitute an impressive package of actions, but unless they are implemented, these actions will not add value to the WSIS process. There is a need to specify the actors responsible for the suggested action and a time frame to indicate timings for specific actions. In line with suggestions and as the way forward the *creation of a coordinated global initiative* to undertake the following is essential:

1. Develop a long-term strategic framework.
2. Create an International Scientific Data and Information Forum (SciDIF).
3. Create a new ad hoc strategic committee to make it happen.

As a critical note, we observe that rather than create too many new bodies or initiatives, WSIS should endeavour to harness the potential of the existing bodies –say in data collection, analysis and dissemination. This would enable the WSIS process to save much-needed resources and work with fewer stakeholders. Creation of new bodies should be limited to fields that are currently underserved by the existing ones.

17.3 Open Access and Capacity Building in Science And Technology[10]

In the information age, a country's prosperity and international competitiveness basically derive from its scientific and technological strength and its innovativeness. Therefore, most developing countries consider capacity building in science and technology an urgent task and increase their investment in S&T. Increase in investments is indispensable while the formation of public policy that is facilitating the effective flow and application of information and knowledge seems more important for the elevation of ability in putting knowledge to use quickly, effectively and creatively.

There are many public policy issues of a global nature that are impacting the dissemination of information and knowledge. Among them a very important one is the issue of IPR (Intellectual Property Rights) protection. In this issue there are three factors that are often ignored:

1. IPR protection in developing countries should be a gradual process that is commensurate with the level of general development. The history of developed countries reveals that they also underwent such a transition from a time when IPR were inadequately protected to a time when they were. But

the policy evolution taken by developing countries is not understood and accepted by the developed world today. The pressure causes the protection of IPR in some developing countries to exceed the level of their development, even to exceed what is required by the WTO and is practiced in developed countries. This trend still continues to be strengthened.

2. In developed countries antitrust laws and laws protecting the rights and interests of consumers coexist with laws protecting IPR. These play a counterbalancing and restrictive role to benefit IPR users. But many developing countries do not have sound antitrust and consumer interest protection laws. At present, most knowledge products and IPR belong to developed countries or to trans-national corporations located in developed areas, so they have the prerequisites for a knowledge monopoly. This objective possibility has sometimes turned into a real knowledge monopoly in developing areas because of the lack of balancing policies.

3. In many developing countries there are no laws and regulations for sharing knowledge. This situation further increases the lack of balance between withholding and sharing knowledge.

These factors worsen knowledge sharing and capacity building in S&T. An example is the sharp and persistent elevation of the price for scientific periodicals. During the past 16 years, under an average inflation rate of 3.1 percent, the average growth of periodical subscription prices has been 9.5 percent. Since the 1990s many activities have taken place to promote the Open Access to scientific knowledge and information. The promulgation of the Berlin Declaration on Open Access to Knowledge in the Sciences and Humanities in October 2003 has been supported and signed by 55 countries and regions including China. As a new model for scholarly exchange and publication, open access policy is considerably improving the free flow of scientific information and findings, elevating the effectiveness of scientific research activities and at the same time greatly promoting the S&T capacity building.

17.4 The Role of TWAS in Developing the Information Society[11]

The Academy of Sciences for the Developing World (TWAS), formerly known as the Third World Academy of Sciences, is a merit-based science academy located in Trieste, Italy. It operates under the auspices of the United Nations Educational, Scientific and Cultural Organization (UNESCO) and receives most of its core funding from the Italian government. The Academy was created in 1983 and recently celebrated its 20th anniversary in the Great Hall of the People in Beijing, China.

TWAS largely functions like other merit-based science academies –for example, the Royal Society in the United Kingdom, the US National Academy of Sciences and the Chinese Academy of Sciences. But there are two significant differences. First, it is globally, not nationally, based. And second, it honours scientists across the developing world. Today, the Academy has more than 800 members living in 90 countries. Eighty-five percent of its members come from the developing world and 15 percent from the developed world. The latter are scientists who were born in the developing world and who now work in the developed world, or scientists from the developed world whose research focuses on issues of particular importance to the developing world.

The membership profile of TWAS is virtually the mirror image of the global profile of scientists in which 75 percent of the scientists are from the developed world and 25 percent from the developing world. These proportions are now undergoing a steady shift thanks largely to the growth of science in Brazil, China, India, and several other developing countries. In addition to serving its membership, TWAS sponsors a wide-ranging set of capacity building programmes for scientists from the developing world, including one of the world's largest South-South (developing world to developing world) fellowship programmes for doctoral and post-doctoral students. This programme, under which 250 fellowships are made available each year, is largely sponsored by the governments of Brazil, China, and India.

TWAS also provides administrative support for several other international scientific organizations that share the Academy's mandate for the promotion of science, especially in the developing world. These organizations are:

- The Third World Organization for Women in Science (TWOWS) seeks to increase the presence of women in science, especially in leadership positions. With more than 3,000 members, it is the largest organization of women scientists in the world. TWOWS held its 3rd general assembly and international conference in Bangalore, India, in November 2005.
- The Third World Network of Scientific Organizations (TWNSO), which is an institutional network of science ministries and research councils that serves as the diplomatic arm of TWAS. The purpose of TWNSO is to encourage governments to invest greater resources in science and to make science a critical tool in their economic development efforts. TWNSO currently has about 157 members.
- The Inter-Academy Panel on International Issues (IAP), which is a network of merit-based science academies from both the developed and developing world that seeks to build the capacity of its member

institutions, especially their capacity to raise the profile and influence of science academies in the corridors of their governments and international institutions. IAP currently has 92 members.

- The Inter Academy Medical Panel (IAMP), which is a network of merit-based medical academies or medical divisions within national science academies from both the developed and developing worlds, carries a similar mandate to that of IAP but focuses exclusively on medical and public-health issues. IAMP has 51 members.

The Academy's expertise in information and communication technologies (ICTs) is found among its members and the members of its affiliated organizations. Like virtually all organizations worldwide, however, TWAS has been dramatically affected by the revolutionary changes that have taken place over the past several decades, causing it to alter its strategy in light of the rapidly changing conditions in the developing world.

First, as an enabling technology, ICTs have "enabled" a number of developing countries –notably, Brazil, China and India– to make significant progress both in building the capacities of their scientific communities and in effectively pursuing science-based economic development strategies. Second, as the success of these scientifically proficient countries mounts, other developing countries have become more interested in investing in science and technology.

These trends have led TWAS: (1) to increasingly target its resources and programmatic initiatives towards the scientifically laggard among the developing countries, especially those in sub-Saharan Africa, and (2) to develop programmes, often in partnership with its affiliated organizations, TWNSO, TWOWS, IAP and IAMP, that seek to put science to work to help lay the groundwork for sustainable economic growth. These programmes take the form of describing best practices in addressing such critical societal problems as access to safe drinking water, development of renewable energies and the conservation and wise use of indigenous and medicinal plants; the issuing of statements and reports on critical global issues in which science plays a critical role (for example, HIV/AIDS in Africa and the opportunities and risks posed by genetically modified plants); and the sponsorship of workshops that help scientists develop the necessary skills to deal effectively with public officials and the public at large.

TWAS's recent effort to broaden the range of its activities parallels, to some extent, parallel policy trends in ICTs when it comes to developing countries in the following ways:

First, there is increasing discussion of targeting at least a portion of the funds invested in ICTs on nations and regions that are lagging behind so that they can be brought up to speed, enabling this global technology to become truly global. Second, there is increasing interest in encouraging developing nations that are proficient in ICTs to lend a hand to developing nations that are not. Third, there is growing recognition that focusing solely on efforts that make ICTs more readily accessible, while important, is not enoughMore attention must be paid to how this new technology can be put to use to help advance the economic and social well-being of people.

TWAS stands ready to help advance a broad-based ICT global policy and would welcome an opportunity to:

- Make available a number of its South-South fellowships to graduate and post graduate students seeking degrees and advanced training in ICTs.
- Assist in the preparation of a monograph that highlights the most successful initiatives in ICTs that address real-life problems in the developing world.
- Help in the creation of an electronic portal offering extensive information on ICT fellowship opportunities, upcoming conferences, university programmes, and job openings. This portal would serve as a one-stop site for a broad-range of information on ICTs, seeking to make the enormous amount of information that is now available more accessible.
- Support the creation of ICT centers of excellence in the least developed countries, especially in countries in sub-Saharan Africa.

17.5 The Information Society after the WSIS: The Role of OECD[12]

It is now a fact that the application of Information and Communication Technologies (ICT) globally, presents the fastest means of creating an information society. Due to barriers of access to ICT, the problem of the digital divide is prevalent within and between countries. In response to this concern, the first World Summit on Information Society (WSIS), held in Geneva in 2003, set out eleven principles to help countries of the world navigate through global and borderless cyberspace. Indeed, a Plan of Action was adopted during the summit that promised to put all the villages of the world online by 2015. In his official opening speech, the UN Secretary General found the Geneva summit as unique and noted: "where most global conferences focus on global threats, this one will consider how best to use a new global asset" (Stauffacher & Kleinwachter, 2005: vii). The Geneva summit underscored the potential of ICT in improving the lives of people worldwide; but this is achievable when people are empowered to access ICT from where they are – homes, villages, schools, and business.

The second phase of WSIS, held in Tunis from 16-18 November 2005, was a follow-up to the Geneva (2003) summit. Before the official opening of WSIS II, the World Science Project[1] (sponsored largely by the Society for Social Studies of Science and Hewlett Packard) held an official side event on Science and Technology in Tunis from 13-15 November 2005. The overarching theme of the side event (that preceded WSIS II) was *Past, Present and Future of Research in the Information Society.*

In its operations, OECD utilizes its think-tank and policy coordination system that enable it to extend its networks. Through OECD, governments of advanced economies think together on common (social and economic) challenges. Its work programme is fact-based and oriented to forward-looking policy development. Practically, OECD is engaged in:

- the development of comparable (development) indicators;
- economic and policy analyses;
- peer review and persuasion;
- recommending guidelines, non-biding soft law, conventions and codes;
- dialogue to create networks (in science and IT) with policy makers and practioners; and
- the outreach activities to create partnerships with other IGOs.

Challenges of Creating a Knowledge Economy and an Information Society

In a global world whose navigation is largely dependent on the available knowledge and information, the term development entails creating knowledge economies and information societies. This conceptualization of development lays emphasis on the role of ICT that is instrumental in the generation of knowledge through research and the sharing of information through connectivity to various ICT devices. How do countries meet the challenges of creating knowledge economies and information societies?

There are lynchpins (economic fundamentals) of the transformations entailed: globalization, Research and Development (R&D), Internet connectivity and highly skilled human power. By investing in R&D, a country should come up with innovations to facilitate, for example, economic transformation. The investment in ICT should expand Internet connectivity while training of human resource should boost human capacity in all fields. To perfect these transformations, efforts should be put to improve the quality of government policy making at strategic levels viz, regional or sub-national levels.

To facilitate the suggested transformations, OECD has found the need to formulate its ICT policy. This policy is under the jurisdiction of the OECD's Committee for Information, Computer and Communications Policy that contributes to:

- growth studies;
- globalization and structural adjustment;
- intellectual assets and value creation; and
- OECD country review.

It is imperative to note the critical role of ICT policy in the creation of knowledge economy and information society. Yet in many developing countries, ICT policy is non-existent. Where the ICT policy has been formulated, there is lukewarm support from the government making it difficult to effectively implement the policy. One of the biggest challenges in the developing countries is to strengthen ICT policy formulation and implementation. This would eventually expand connectivity, promote R&D, facilitate globalization, and expand knowledge-based and information-led development.

Internet Infrastructure: Then and Now

Over the recent past, what notable changes have taken place in the Internet sub-sector?

- Rapid *decline in the price of computing and communications* (explained by the availability of new technology and heightened competition in the market).
- As an impact of the first change, *growth of the ICT sector*. This has significantly affected businesses, government and individuals.
- As networks converge towards the Internet, we have *increased our trust* in the Internet as a source of information and reliable means of communication.

All these could be regarded as positive changes for they enable countries to overcome the challenges of creating knowledge economies and information societies. There is a critical question here: what does this mean for the "digital divide?" Globally, these positive changes within the ICT sector have not been experienced evenly. In particular, the developing countries have only experienced modest changes in their ICT sector. Practically, in these countries, 50 percent of the population lives in poverty; only a few can afford to access the Internet. Further, due to poor ICT infrastructure, only a tiny fraction of the population is connected to the Internet. This has limited the impact of ICT at all levels. These realities facing the developing countries affirm the existence of the digital divide. The latter connotes a contradictory situation where developed countries on one hand, have adequate ICT infrastructure to serve their citizens while, on the other hand, the developing countries have inadequate and underdeveloped ICT sectors. This underscores the enormous challenges facing the developing countries in their endeavours to create knowledge-based economies and information-led societies. How can the problems associated with the digital divide be addressed to evolve a global world better served by the ICT infrastructure?

The price of "always on" has dropped from $0.36 in 1997 to $0.01 in 2005. The net sales of amazon.com –a company whose sales are largely transacted through the Internet– increased tremendously from 1997 to 2004. There was also impressive growth in the contributions of ICT investment to GDP growth for developed countries like Sweden, United States and Denmark.

There are notable *social costs* of the growth of the ICT worldwide. For example, we have ample evidence of the increasing complaints of fraud. In this regard, Internet-related fraud complaints to the US Federal Trade Commission rose from 55,727 in 2001 to 205,568 in 2004. In addition, there are other social costs that include escalating attacks of the Internet that have become more sophisticated. Such attacks take the form of root compromise, user compromise, denial of service/distributed denial of service attacks, website defacement, detection of malicious logic, introduction of a virus/worm into a network, misuse of resources, spam email and fraudulent email. How are we going to deal with the social costs of the ICT growth and its impacts? To enhance the world's increasing trust and dependence on ICT, it is mandatory to invest in endeavours to overcome the human-made obstructions meant to incapacitate the sector. Admittedly, such obstructions cause havoc in developing countries where the capacity to protect the ICT sector is limited –making them the first targets of all forms of attacks. OECD could initiate networks focusing on ways of making the ICT increasingly reliable globally or strengthen existing ones that work to protect the sector from various threats and attacks.

OECD and WSIS

How can OECD contribute to the World Summit on the Information Society? To start with, we need to enhance understanding of the Information Society (IS), its measurement and analysis. Thus far, OECD has developed the capacity to measure and analyze all kinds of variables (concepts) and hence, could contribute in the operationalization and measurement of IS. Further, OECD could contribute significantly in the following:

- Collaborate on measuring ICT for development;

- Analyze the impacts of governments and other stakeholders in the promotion of ICT development;
- Team up in building confidence in the use of ICT (e.g., in the management of obstructions) – this would increase trust in ICT globally; and
- Improve access to data and information – in particular, OECD could spearhead the regulatory reforms required to bridge the digital divide; it could also facilitate access to publicly funded research data.

To tackle the identified tasks successfully, a functional partnership should evolve between OECD and WSIS representatives. Thereafter, an operational framework should be drawn specifying the specific roles, obligations and responsibilities of each party. Only then can WSIS access the wealth of information currently under the custody of OECD. On the other hand, through such a partnership, OECD can disseminate its massive data worldwide, easily and cheaply.

After the WSIS

The objectives of the WSIS (e.g., MDGs) are entirely consistent with the OECD mission; this suggests that the two organizations could easily complement each other if they forged a partnership. However, such a partnership could largely serve the interests of the developed countries given that OECD membership is limited in its memberhip to these countries. Nevertheless, there are other drawbacks facing the OECD. It does not have operations on the ground and is rarely seen to take action. We must ask how can these limitations of OECD be addressed to: (1) improve its global image; (2) contribute to the development of the ICT sector and reduce the impacts of the digital divide? These limitations require a reformulation of the OECD mission and restructuring of its operations to make it an all-inclusive organization. As well put by Kofi Annan (2005: viii): "The future of the IT industry lies not so much in the developed world, where markets are saturated, as in reaching the billions of people in the developing world who remain untouched by the information revolution."

Despite the documented limitations of OECD, the following contributions consistent with its current role:

- collection of key development indicators worldwide and analysis of the same; since the OECD is a reputable organization in data gathering and analysis; WSIS could draw from its best practices and policy;
- establish an Internet governance forum;
- establish a UN global alliance;

- facilitate integration of ICT into ODA strategies; and
- participate in other strategic follow-up mechanisms?

Overall, OECD has great potential in the development of the ICT sector worldwide. However, to tackle the persistent problem of the digital divide, it is essential to restructure the organization, review membership criteria and reformulate its mission. These measures would make it an all inclusive organization to serve the globe. Through its effective networks, OECD is able to collect accurate data worldwide required for the measurement of key development indicators. Currently, with a well developed ICT sector, the world could benefit by accessing the various data bases that OECD has developed over time. This is part of the challenge to be tackled in building the information society. As Utsumi (2005: xi) rightly says: "The digital revolution, particularly in the fields of information and communication, has extended the frontiers of global village, making a profound impact on how the world functions and interacts. Unfortunately, too many communities still remain unhooked from this phenomenon, creating a new knowledge gap."

Accordingly, certain barriers must be cleared for the world to benefit from the stock of knowledge and massive data under the custody of OECD. As part of ICT development, the WSIS should address such barriers and improve connectivity worldwide. However, as noted by Kleinwachter and Stauffacher (2005:1): "WSIS is much more than the digital divide. The information society is not a single-issue problem. The information revolution penetrates all parts of our lives. It affects the way we learn, work, communicate, do business, educate our children and entertain ourselves. The WSIS process is about how we are going to organize the globalized world of tomorrow where the Internet makes everybody neighbours, just one click away."

17.6 University Relations for Capacity Building and Economic Development[13]

There are really two important topics under this theme: first the overall subject of globalization and second, Hewlett-Packard's (HP) response through university relations.

First, let's define globalization. It is the process in which geographic distance becomes a factor of diminishing importance in establishing and maintaining cross border political and socio-cultural relations. It can be thought of as widening, intensifying, speeding up and growing worldwide interconnectedness.

Critical for developing countries in an era of globalization is capacity building. Economic development involves influencing growth and restructuring of an economy to enhance economic well-being of a community, region, state or nation and its citizens. Capacity building is a part of economic development, and in a knowledge-based economy means connecting jobs and people. Local jobs reduce the brain drain. To attract jobs into a region and secure employment, people need to develop skills, competencies and values aligning with a complete value chain that extends from basic research, to advanced development, to commercialization, and to manufacturing, marketing, distribution and sales. Capacity building develops and employs a region's knowledge and educational resources across the whole value chain to gain economic advantage in the global economy.

The World Bank identifies four pillars to a knowledge economy and education and training underpin them all. Engineering education plays a key role in capacity building. If technology and knowledge form the basis for meaningful economic development in the future (and economic studies have shown that technology change drives as much as 85 percent of per capita income growth), and if economic success in knowledge based economies depends largely on the capabilities of people credentialed in meaningful and consistent ways, then engineers are the kingpins for taking knowledge and generating output that results in sustainable growth.

Looking at engineering graduates based on the most recent data from the NRC Science and Engineering Centers Report of 2004, the number of engineers graduated around the world varies widely. China is approaching 300,000, India 200,000, and the US 59,000. Even smaller countries such as Korea graduated over 56,000 students. The China picture is particularly compelling: there are more students in colleges and universities in China (20 million) than there are in the US., Russia and Japan combined. Further, China doubled the number of science and engineering Ph.Ds from 1996 to 2001 to more than 8,000.

Korea shows similar dramatic changes based on its investment in education and research. In 1963 the total R&D investment in South Korea was $4 million dollars. In 2003, it was $16 billion dollars. The research work force grew from zero in 1963 to over 198,000 in 2003. Korean investment in science and technology development in this period grew from less than a quarter of a percent of GNP to almost 3 percent, with a profound effect on the number of jobs for its citizens. Similarly, Taiwan invested 520 million dollars in the Hsinchu Science-Based Industrial Park in 1980. The Park now employs 90,000 people and has created a large number of spin-off companies, at last count over 300.

So the question for HP is what should corporations like us do about all this? What is our contribution? Let us briefly discuss this.

As a reference, HP is a very large Fortune 11 size company with operations in 170 countries with 43 currencies and 15 languages. Worldwide there are six HP Labs operations and the company produces 11 patents per day. HP's University Relations reports into R&D which reports directly into the office of the Chairman. The HP University Relations staff of 24 people spans the globe. Our mission is to deliver talent, technology and sales opportunities to HP by fostering university relationships worldwide that integrate investments in research, recruiting, philanthropy and public advocacy. We manage an upstream knowledge transfer process by managing the whole "Knowledge Supply Chain," similar to the material supply chains we hear often discussed.

We have three major strategies: relationship development, technology programmes and external engagements.

Relationship development results in intellectual capital, HP market-technology and thought leadership. Relationship begins with traditional tactical engagements and moves over time into richer relationships until it reaches what we call 'strategic partnership,' where both partners work together to tackle world challenges beyond either the university or the company, but relevant to the business of both. We represent this development graphically with our "University Relations Partnership Continuum." Relationship development occurs through programme managers who align the strategic interests of HP stakeholders (R&D, recruiting, philanthropy, marketing, sales and research) with the particular strategic goals of each university. Currently we have relationships with between 70 and 100 universities worldwide.

Our second strategy, technology programmes, integrates HP research, philanthropy and sales programmes with university research directions. Programmes vary in maturity and scope and include the Gelato Federation to encourage research on Itanium over Linux, Digital Publishing to research new enterprise and educational applications, Tiramisu to enhance grid participation, and research programmes in security, digital entertainment and planet scale computing, nanotechnology and mobility that align with university priorities.

The third strategy is external engagement to affect policy and address challenges related to higher level education. We focus on four areas: intellectual property and government partnerships, engineering accreditation and education, the engineering/science pipeline, and learning science. Some of our engagements involve all four areas. For example, we drove the early stages of a major development in Latin America called, "Engineering for the Americas," an engineering education quality assurance and capacity building initiative. One output of the long-term engagement is the Lima Declaration, whose intent is to build local engineering capacity to create knowledge that insures the solution of local needs and opens the chance to compete for global opportunities. This HP initiative now has sponsorship by the Organization of American States, the United States Trade and Development Agency, the World Federation of Engineering Organizations (WFEO), the Western Hemisphere Initiative, and by the major education accrediting agencies in the US, Canada and Mexico and experts and volunteers from across the universities and the Americas.

To conclude, HP is a company that believes that capacity building and globalization will provide significant economic advantage for the world and will contribute to HP's global mission and sales opportunities worldwide.

17.7 Conclusion

The opening and closing plenary sessions of the PPF conference reflected a diversity of viewpoints on the WSIS initiative in relation to the globalization process and the way in which the research sector may address the developmental and technological needs of developing areas. In particular, the globalization process has transformed communication technologies and presented the world with unprecedented opportunities for the exchange of information. Countries with fully developed ICT sectors are forging ahead in the creation of an Information Society and the educational and scientific sectors have always been at the forefront of these developments. However the concern is that these same sectors in some developing countries, particularly those in sub-Saharan Africa, ICTs have yet to benefit the majority of scientists and researchers. When even the educational and research sectors themselves experience such problems, it is not hard to understand why the majority of people in developing areas have yet to benefit from connectivity and access to information. This is the biggest challenge we face today. It is hoped that improved access and connectivity will considerably improve the flow of scientific information and data.

Globalization was likened to a moving bus. Once you get onboard, you are okay and assured of reaching your destination. Most citizens in the developed countries are already in the bus. But the majority of the citizens in the developing countries are yet to board the bus. In fact, many cannot even get to the road to catch the bus.

17.8 References

Annan, Kofi. "Opening Statement Made During the World Summit of Information Society in Geneva, 10th December 2003." In *The World Summit on the Information Society: Moving From the Past into the Future,* Daniel Stauffacher and Walfgang Kleinwachter, eds, New York: United Nations Information ICT Task Force, 2005.

Iwata Shuichi, Robert S. Chen. Science and Digital Divide. *Science* 2005, 310: 405.

Kleinwachter, Wolfgangand and Stauffacher, Daniel. "Introduction." In *The World Summit on the Information Society: Moving From the Past into the Future,* Daniel Stauffacher and Walfgang Kleinwachter, eds, New York: United Nations Information ICT Task Force, 2005.

Shrum, Wesley. 2005. "Reagency of the Internet, or How I Became a Guest for Science." *Social Studies of Science* 36, 1-36.

Tharoor, Shashi. "The Millennium Development Goals, WSIS and the United Nations." In The *World Summit on the Information Society: Moving From the Past into the Future,* Daniel Stauffacher and Walfgang Kleinwachter, eds, New York: United Nations Information ICT Task Force, 2005.

Utsumi, Yoshio. "Preface." In *The World Summit on the Information Society: Moving From the Past into the Future,* Daniel Stauffacher and Walfgang Kleinwachter, eds, New York: United Nations Information ICT Task Force, 2005

17.9 Notes

1 Authors in order of the section they contributed. The chapter was compiled and edited by Shrum.

2 The Opening Plenary was chaired by Paul Mbatia, Chair of the Department of Sociology at the University of Nairobi. Dr. Mbatia has been the national coordinator of the World Science Project since 2000. The Closing Plenary was chaired by R. Sooryamoorthy of the University of KwaZulu Natal. From 2000 through 2002, Dr. Sooryamoorthy coordinated the Indian wing of the project at Loyola College of Social Sciences (Trivandrum, Kerala). Since 2003 he has led the South African branch of the project from Durban. The World Science Project is an international on-going research project that began in 1994 and is currently funded by the U.S. National Science Foundation to: (1) examine the connectivity of scientists and researchers to the ICT (such as the email and Internet), and (2) assess the impact of ICT on the productivity of scientists and researchers. Initially, the project covered three developing countries viz., Ghana, Kenya and India. Other countries that have recently been included in the project are South Africa, Chile and the Philippines. Details of the project are available at http://worldsci.net.

3 Both movies are available without charge on DVD. Please send an email request to shrum@lsu.edu or write Wesley Shrum, Dept of Sociology, Louisiana State University, Baton Rouge, Louisiana, 70803).

Before the Horse (2003) deals with the difficulties of doing development work. Internet connectivity has been a major initiative of the international aid community since the 1990s. Yet most universities and research institutes still do not have "connectivity" in the ordinary sense. Subtitled "An Essay on Paragraphs Seven, Ten, and Twenty Three of The World Summit Plan of Action," Internet connectivity is viewed as potentially useful, but subject to many of the same problems that have plagued past development initiatives in Asia and sub-Saharan Africa. Filmed in Kerala (India), Kenya, and Ghana. *Before the Horse* was screened three times at the World Summit on the Information Society, Phase I, Geneva , December 2003: (1) Role of Science in the Information Society (CERN); (2) Information Society film screening (ICT4D); (3) Engineering the Knowledge Society (International Federation for Information Processing).

Story Line: The movie is built around three sequences, questioning conventional views of connectivity. In the first part, shot in Kerala , India , the Internet is described as a life-changing event. In the second, filmed in Kenya , great expectations for a connectivity project are dashed, when it is discovered that cables are missing and some of the collaborators may be mainly after money. In the third, filmed in Ghana , a university professor explains 'how things work' in the development game.

After the Fact (2005) was made as a sequel to Before the Horse. Phase I of the World Summit on the Information Society was intended to set an agenda for action, while Phase II (Tunis , Tunisia 16-18 Nov 2005) was intended to implement and report on that agenda. But the time frame was short and the complexity of problems relating to the digital divide was immense. Filmed in Kenya and Ghana. Screened twice at the World Summit on the Information Society (Phase II, Tunis , November 2005).

Story Line: Opens with a famous slave castle in Ghana , where a young African man is heard speaking to an African American tourist: he wants to go to America. Next, a reconstructed (but absolutely true!) scene from 1994, again in Ghana. A waitress near Cape Coast sees a mysterious machine—not knowing what it is supposed to do, she may understand it better than it's user! (Cut to Nairobi in 2005 leads to a montage of dishes, telecommunications gear, and signs of the flourishing ICT market.) Back again to 2000, where two administrative officers in the Vice Chancellor's office at JKUAT describe the difficulties of dialup connectivity. In the final scene ("There was a time...") two professors at a Ghanaian university talk about the connection to the Internet that they once had, but lost.

4 This presentation was delivered in two parts. The first, representing the perspective of a funding agent and project initiator, was by Wesley Shrum, who has made annual site visits to the institute in question since the late 1990s. The second, representing the perspective of the recipient and project implementer, was by George Okwach, former director of the research institute.

5 The "Acacia Tree" that serves as a backdrop for the conference web site is an original pastel on silk drawing by Susan Arnold. Editor's note: After 2005 http://worldsci.net is no longer the direct link to the "Past, Present, and Future of Research in the Information Society." The conference archive has been moved down one level and may still be found through that website.

6 As one of our more colourful Chilean informants put it, by way of praise for a sister institution, "you don't see some resources leaking around there."

7 This does not imply they should lose money. That is, they should get their expenses paid. But they should not stay in fancy hotels.

8 At present, the staff is smaller, and the number on station at any given time may not be more than 25.

9 This section was contributed by Carthage Smith.

10 This section was contributed by Qiheng Hu.

11 This section was contributed by Daniel Schaffer.

12 This section was contributed by John Dryden.

13 This section was contributed by Wayne Johnson.

Index